Buddha
or
Bust

Buddha
or Bust

Perry Garfinkel

In Search of Truth,

Meaning, Happiness and the Man

Who Found Them All

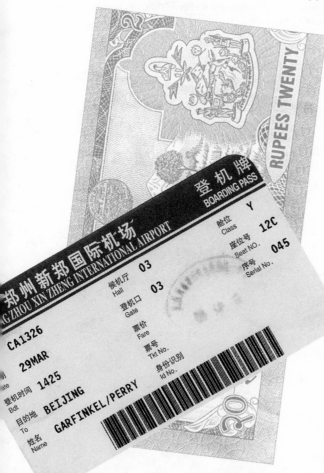

Harmony Books
New York

Published in the United States by Harmony Books, an imprint of the Crown Publishing
Group, a division of Random House, Inc., New York.
www.crownpublishing.com

Harmony Books is a registered trademark and the Harmony Books colophon is a trademark
of Random House, Inc.

Library of Congress Cataloging-in-Publication Data

Garfinkel, Perry.
Buddha or bust : in search of truth, meaning, happiness and the man who found them all /
Perry Garfinkel.—1st ed.
Includes bibliographical references and index.
1. Garfinkel, Perry.   2. Buddhism—Social aspects.   3. Religious life—Buddhism.
4. Spiritual biography.   I. Title.
BQ960.A75A3   2006
294.309—dc22   2006000585

ISBN-13: 978-1-4000-8217-9
ISBN-10: 1-4000-8217-X

Printed in the United States of America

DESIGN BY ELINA D. NUDELMAN
MAP ILLUSTRATION BY JACKIE AHER

10 9 8 7 6 5 4 3 2 1

First Edition

Lillian E. Garfinkel
  Whether you know it or not—and I suspect you don't—you are my Buddhism teacher, Mom.

Ariana Garfinkel and Ryan Romeiser
  There could never be a father who loved his daughter and son-in-law more than I love you.

Contents

Acknowledgments

I offer a deep bow of gratitude to the following people. Neither this book nor I would be quite the same without them.

Shaye Areheart, the publisher of Harmony Books, understood what I had in mind even better than I understood.

Julia Pastore, Harmony senior editor, encouraged me to probe deeper into my feelings, and to do so in a timely fashion.

Cary Wolinsky started this by having the wisdom to water a seed that had been planted many years ago.

The staff at *National Geographic* magazine: Bernard Ohanian, former associate editor, who encouraged me to develop an idea that would become an assignment; Oliver Payne, manuscripts editor, who kept asking, "How's Buddha?"; Alan Mairson, senior writer, who pushed and questioned me in the proposal stage; Heidi Schultz, researcher extraordinaire, who added significantly to my own fact collecting; Erika Lloyd, former editorial coordinator, a joy to work with; and, most of all, Peter Porteous, senior editor, who applied pressure when necessary and showed patience when required from first draft to last.

Steve McCurry, ace photographer, tolerated my picture suggestions—and yes, Steve, you can recommend a lead anytime.

Candice Furhman is the agent I'd always been looking for.

Sue and Shel Mattison kept my bills, and my head, in order and stayed tuned by e-mail around the world.

Alan Senauke, former executive director of the Buddhist Peace Fellowship (BPF) in Berkeley, was my Buddhist Deep Throat, offering direction, contacts and access to people and places I never would have figured out on my own. In gratitude, I am donating a percentage of the profits from *Buddha or Bust* to the BPF.

I also want to thank the friends who fed me ideas, encouragement and inspiration in all its forms from the beginning: Wes Nisker, Arlan Wise, Julie Berriault, Daniel Goleman, Joseph Goldstein, Jon Kabat-Zinn, John Bush, Mirabai Bush, Joely Johnson, Mark Mazer, Liz and Mike Zane, and Sheila Donnelly Theroux.

All living beings, whether they know it or not, are following this Path.

—The Buddha, White Lotus Sutra

Emancipate yourselves from mental slavery; none but ourselves can free our minds.

—Bob Marley, "Redemption Song"

An artist has got to be careful never really to arrive at a place when he thinks he's at somewhere. You always have to realize that you're constantly in a state of becoming. As long as you can stay in that realm, you'll sort of be all right.

—Bob Dylan, in Martin Scorsese's documentary
No Direction Home, Part 2, 2005

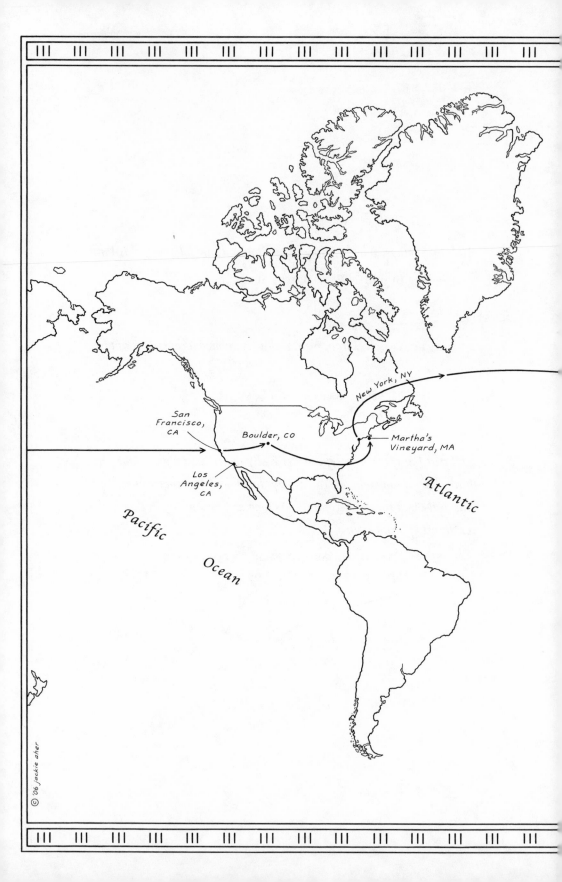

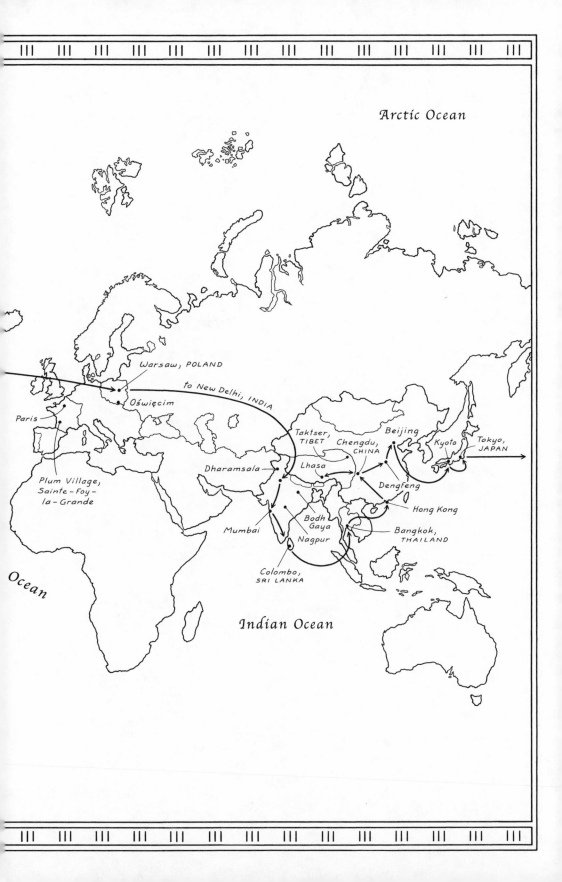

Arctic Ocean

Warsaw, POLAND

to New Delhi, INDIA

Oświęcim

Paris

Taktser,
TIBET

Beijing

Chengdu,
CHINA

Kyoto

Tokyo,
JAPAN

Dharamsala

Lhasa

Plum Village,
Sainte - Foy -
la - Grande

Dengfeng

Hong Kong

Mumbai

Bodh
Gaya

Nagpur

Bangkok,
THAILAND

Ocean

Colombo,
SRI LANKA

Indian Ocean

Buddha
or Bust

one

Buddha Rising

A 2,500-Year-Old Idea That's More Relevant Than Ever

You can't ever get everything you want. It is impossible and you will never fully succeed. Luckily, there is another option; you can learn to control your mind, to stop outside of this endless cycle of desire and aversion. You can learn not to want what you want, to recognize desires but not be controlled by them.

—THE BUDDHA

The fundamental teachings of Gautama, as it is now being made plain to us by study of original sources, is clear and simple and in the closest harmony with modern ideas. It is beyond all disputes the achievement of one of the most penetrating intelligences the world has ever known.

—H. G. WELLS, IN *Outline of History*

The man who taught me the most about Buddhism wasn't a monk with a shaved head in saffron robes. He didn't speak in Sanskrit code, and he didn't live in a Himalayan monastery. In fact, he wasn't even a Buddhist.

He was Carl Taylor, a lifelong San Franciscan who looked to be in his late 40s. At the moment he just looked cold, sitting upright in a bed rolled into the gardens off the hospice ward at Laguna Honda Hospital near San Francisco's Twin Peaks. It was a high blue-sky summer afternoon, but in this city that often means a bone-penetrating chill. Carl was dying of cancer.

I was spending a week with the Zen Hospice Project, a group of

Buddhist volunteers who assist the staff of the 24-bed hospice unit at this, one of the largest public long-term-care facilities in the United States. The project, now emulated around the world, uses two of Buddhism's central teachings—awareness of the present moment and compassion for others—as tools to help bring a degree of dignity and humanity to those in the last stages of their lives. They're not easy lessons to learn.

I sat beside Carl, helping adjust the well-worn flight jacket he used as a blanket. He wore his terminal diagnosis with resigned bravado. I tried to make small talk, but it was going terribly. What words of solace can you offer someone who doesn't have long to live and knows it?

"So what kind of work do, er, did you do?"

Long silence. Slow drag on his cigarette. An eternity passed as we watched a white tuft of cloud break the blue monotony and move across the sky.

"I don't really talk about my past."

Okay. Squirming to keep the conversation moving forward, I mentally scrolled through my list of questions. But if I couldn't ask about the past and there was no sense in asking about the future, that left only the present. And in the present, I was learning, there are no questions; there is just being. This made me feel awkward at first: Stripped of his questions, the journalist has no identity.

But Carl seemed content to have me just sit there, my company alone helping to ease some of his suffering. Once I accepted that I had nothing to do, nowhere to go and, perhaps most important, no one to be, I relaxed. Carl glanced sideways at me and smiled. We both understood I had just learned a small lesson. Together we watched another cloud go by.

That week I learned other lessons from the Buddhism 101 syllabus—lessons about the impermanence of life, about our attachment to the way we want things to be and the disappointment that comes when those things don't come to pass, about physical and mental suffering, about the value of what Buddhists call Sangha, which best translates to community. But most of all I saw how the lessons one man learned in India 2,500 years ago have been updated and adapted to the modern world.

Around the globe today there is a new Buddhism. Its philosophies and practices are being applied to augment mental- and physical-health therapies and to advance political and environmental reforms. Athletes use it to sharpen their game. Through it, corporate executives learn to handle stress better. Police arm themselves with it to defuse volatile situations. Chronic pain sufferers apply it as a coping salve. Because its teachings have such contemporary relevance, Buddhism is now experiencing a renaissance—even in countries like India, where it had nearly vanished, and China, where it had been suppressed.

Buddhism is no longer just for monks or Westerners with disposable time and income to dabble in things Eastern. Christians and Jews practice it. African Americans meditate alongside Japanese Americans. In the United States alone, the number of self-declared Buddhists jumped from 400,000 in 1990 to more than 3 million by 2001, James Coleman, a sociologist at California Polytechnic State University, writes in *The New Buddhism*. And according to a 2004 study published in the *Journal for the Scientific Study of Religion,* one in eight Americans—more than 37 million—believe that Buddhist teachings have had an important influence on their spirituality.

The Zen Hospice Project is one example of "socially engaged Buddhism," a term coined by the Buddhist monk Thich Nhat Hanh, who was exiled from Vietnam in the 1960s for his nonviolent antiwar activities. Still "engaged" at the age of 79, he traveled in his native country for three months in 2005—the 30th anniversary of the Communist Party takeover of Vietnam—spreading Buddhist teachings where he had once been a pariah.

In southern France, at his Plum Village retreat center, he regularly hosts, among other groups, Palestinians and Israelis in workshops on conflict resolution and peace negotiation. Such sessions often begin with animosity, Rev. Hanh told me, and just as often they end with embraces.

"It all starts with a spin on an old adage: 'Don't just do something, sit there,' " he said in a wisp of a voice. A rail-thin man with large ears and deep-set eyes, Rev. Hanh was sitting on the porch of his cottage overlooking verdant Bordeaux vineyards. It seemed incongruous to be talking in the heart of a region that attracts worshippers of Bacchus, not the Buddha. "With all this socially engaged work, first you must learn what the Buddha learned, to still the mind. Then you don't take action; action takes you."

Indeed, action had taken me on an expedition of epic proportions, an ambitious and at times arduous journey in search of mankind's most endangered—and elusive—prey. I circumnavigated the globe in pursuit of nothing less than truth, meaning and happiness. I tracked a man almost half a billion people today firmly believe found all three—and then some. Then I navigated this man's legacy, charting the migration and mutation over two millennia of the rather simple tactics he developed for capturing this quarry.

He has gone by many names—Tathagata, Sakyamuni, Siddhartha Gautama—but is most recognized by the form of address that honors his wisdom: the Buddha, "the awakened one."

Though his philosophy gave rise to a religion long practiced throughout Asia and, over the last century, in pockets of the West as well, my quest was not of a religious nature. Nor, I now believe after studying his life, was the Buddha's. He—like me, like you, like anyone who thinks, feels, emotes—simply wanted answers to questions that are of such a universal nature that they transcend the isms and cut to the soul of what it means to be human. Questions that plague, taunt, challenge, befuddle, frustrate, inspire and drive people on from approximately the moment they are weaned.

"Who am I?"

"Why am I here?"

"What is this whole thing called life?"

And the biggie: "How can I make it to the weekend with a little less suffering and a little more happiness?"

Truth. Meaning. Happiness.

I was questioning all three—and quickly coming to what seemed in my mind to be the very plausible conclusion that none of the three existed—when the Buddha appeared to me in the form of the juiciest assignment of my life. And none too soon.

National Geographic magazine accepted my proposal to write a major feature vaguely entitled "In the Footsteps of the Buddha." Keeping my ego in check, I learned that I got the assignment because one of the magazine's ace photographers, Steve McCurry (he shot the famous profile of the angry green-eyed Afghani girl), already had a running start with images of Buddhist monks and statues largely from throughout Asia. They advanced me a hefty expense budget, issued me a round-the-world unlimited-stops business-class plane ticket and shot me up with all variety of vaccinations while I shot myself up with typical journalist's fantasies of cover stories and *Larry King* appearances. "See you in ten weeks," they said. I parlayed that 10 into 10 more, plus a little more travel money and, eventually, the book you hold in your hand. But what I really got back was much bigger—nothing near enlightenment but a cosmic bailout for sure.

I organized the expedition with the chronology of Buddhism in mind. From the Buddha's birthplace at the border of India and Nepal, I would follow his path in India. Then I would track the teachings' passage, first to Sri Lanka, and then through both Southeast Asia and the Himalaya Mountains to China and Japan, eventually on to Europe and the Americas. In effect, I would circumambulate the globe, in the same manner that Buddhists circle sacred sites or temples three times. My angle was to report on the worldwide engaged Buddhism movement, about which I thought I knew something but which turns out to be much more widespread than I imagined. In *Engaged Buddhism in the West,* Christopher S. Queen, a Harvard lecturer on religions, defines socially engaged Buddhism quite simply: It is "the application of the dharma, or Buddhist teachings, to the resolution of social problems." Spearheaded by an international interconnected web of nonprofits and NGOs—from the Buddhist Peace Fellowship (BPF), in Berkeley, California, to the International Network of Engaged Buddhists (INEB), based in Bangkok; from the Center for Contemplative Mind in Society, in Northampton, Massachusetts, to the Greyston Foundation in Yonkers, New York; from Zen Peacemakers in Montague, Massachusetts, to Thich Nhat Hahn's Community of Mindful Living, with branches throughout the world—Buddhist practitioners were coming out of the monasteries, literally and figuratively. Establishing AIDS/HIV treatment centers in Cambodia, participating in peaceful protests against executions at San Quentin State Prison north of San Francisco, launching prison reform initiatives in India, counseling young teens at pregnancy centers in Thailand, and more, monks and lay people were actively trying to lessen suffering in the world.

And I would get to cover it all.

For even a dabbler such as I would have described myself, getting the green light on the assignment was like winning the trifecta of Buddhism. I would gain multiple levels of "merit," highly desirable chips redeemable in this lifetime or the next. My work would be what Buddhists call "right livelihood," meaning not only was my job not harming other sentient beings but also my writing subject might benefit mankind and the environment. I would get to interview some of Buddhism's leading thinkers and practitioners, meaning every day would be like auditing a course entitled "Ultimate Dharma Talks." I would get to stand in places where the Buddha stood, sit in caves where he sat, walk across rice fields where he traveled—just to visit these sites, the Buddha told his followers, was to gain merit and insight. Plus, I was getting paid to do it, I would see my byline in one of the world's most recognized magazines, and hopefully I'd be elevated to the A list of Interesting Dinner Guests on the small island where I live. Could love and enlightenment be far behind?

On a personal level, the timing was excellent. Things were falling into place. Finally. It felt as though someone had suddenly sprinkled magic dust on me, and its effect was to reverse the slippery slide my life had taken. What I didn't know at the time was that things would get even better. For a while. Then they would, well, change. And change again.

To understand the full epic-ness of this expedition, we have to go back to . . .

July 2003, the shag-carpeted floor of my mother's New Jersey living room, my back in a spasm, my mother hovering over me. Zero latitude, zero longitude of my life. It is one year since my father's death and it is just catching up how much I miss the man I spent so much time pushing away. I had come home for the unveiling, the Jewish tradition of visiting the gravesite one year after interment. I am, for all intents, homeless, temporarily living in corporate housing in the Valley, L.A.'s waiting room for has-beens, wannabes, and never-will-bes. The woman I am dating had nicknamed me Mr. Turtle; I could fit all my worldly possessions on the West Coast in my Subaru Forester, and often did. That same girlfriend, whose very L.A. lifestyle I would never to be able to afford, which she herself can't afford, has put me out after discovering some improprieties I am too embarrassed to repeat even to myself.

My so-called career is being flushed down the toilet bowl. Two ghostwriting projects I had relocated to California for have fizzled. The *New York Times,* to which I had been contributing since 1986, lately has rejected every story idea I've proposed. It's been months since my last significant writing work. I have put my life on credit cards while waiting for this Grail of a *Geographic* assignment to come through. But I am losing hope. The thought that the attempt has been an exercise in self-delusion leaves me free-falling into oblivion, not to mention literary obscurity. One of my mother's lines keeps coming back like an errant mantra: "Perry, you don't have a pot to piss in."

And now this. I am writhing on the floor, eating shag carpeting. Minutes before I had bent over in an awkward maneuver—riding a bicycle, I had stopped to lean over and pick up a turtle that was waddling across the street—and experienced what felt like a drum roll ripple down the left side of my lower back. My back completely gave out; the left side crumbled like a graham cracker and I could not stand. Somehow I got myself back to my mother's a few blocks away and now I am collapsed on the floor. The irony does not escape me that trying to save my namesake, a turtle, has caused my current predicament.

No position is comfortable. I know the feeling well. This is the third "back event" in two years that has left me so debilitated I had to lie in bed for 10 days, dosed to the legal limit on Advil, left to crawl to the bathroom because I could not stand. And did I mention the pain and *suffering*!? I immediately recognize the severity of the situation and in my mind am already canceling the flight I had booked back to L.A. for the next day, intending to give my West Coast life one more shot. I am imagining days laid up in a suspended hell realm called New Jersey, albeit a shag-carpeted hell realm.

My mother is sitting there nagging me with her shouldas. "You shoulda packed last night. You shoulda been more careful. Why do always put everything off to the last minute?" It's a fast track to her critique of my entire life, predictably ending with the "pot to piss in" punch line.

My back had snapped. Now my mind snaps. She becomes the evil enemy, and, in a Darwinian act of self preservation, I completely shut down emotionally—to her, to myself, to the reality of the desperate depths to which I have now literally fallen.

The physical reality is that I have what has been diagnosed as a degenerative disk. On top of a mild case of scoliosis, now I have developing bone spurs. My last X-ray clearly showed the first two tiers of what looks like a Chinese pagoda being built between two lumbars of my lower back. Soon it will be a place of worship; chiropractors will come from near and far to marvel at its construction. But it does not take a crafty writer ever on the lookout for a good metaphor to see the situation for what it is: a metaphor. I can't *support* myself. I have no infrastructure. My life is crumbling. I can't even stand to piss in the pot I don't have. Over the next week and a half, days lived in a fog of denial, Advil and humiliating crawls to the bathroom, the double-headed monster residing within me—the dark humorist and the eternal optimist—rears its ugly heads and intones, "There's nowhere to go from here but up."

I returned to L.A. with a commitment to my own reparations act: to repair my back and rewrite the metaphor. I went to a Santa Monica nutritionist, a former bodybuilder who convinced me first to change my diet before I try to correct my structural issues. His hallway full of signed celebrity publicity shots smiled down on me—I swear the one of Xavier Cugat actually laughed at me—and followed me as I left his office with fat-burning pills, a high-protein/low-carb daily menu and guidelines to drink as many ounces of water a day as my body weight, along with the strong recommendation not to wander too far from a toilet. Through the next weeks he would e-mail me such New Age inspirational gibberish as "P.S. Stay zoned in on the ownership of your highest level of expertise. Acknowledge that you are the essence of that experience."

But I was made privy to a more relevant mantra that would follow me around the world, like my own private Jiminy Cricket. Come close and, breaking the privacy rules of the Cult of Rehab, I will whisper it: "Core-trunk stabilization." This regime of simple floor exercises, designed to strengthen the muscles surrounding the whole pelvic region, were demonstrated by a physical therapist in Encino, one of those look-alike towns along Ventura Boulevard in the Valley. Core-trunk stabilization kept me in the vertical position for the duration of my travels and does to this day. Every time I did the exercises—on the bare floor of some very funky hotel in India, on the richly carpeted floor of the Four Seasons George V in Paris—I thought of that Encino therapist stuck in a strip mall upstairs from a Pep Boys and a Taco Bell, and I sent her lotuses of gratitude.

The Buddha must have been watching me try to take care of myself because about six weeks later a *National Geographic* editor called announcing that I got the assignment to write the piece. My first thought was not whether I could handle the logistical nightmare of setting up interviews in eight countries according to a schedule I had not yet created; of calling, e-mailing and leveraging every contact I had established over the last 30 years in this field; of reading everything I could get my hands on about the engaged Buddhism movement. No, it was "Would my back hold up schlepping luggage across airport terminals, on trains and buses, sleeping in beds of questionable structural integrity?" The resounding answer I talked myself into believing: "It can't *not!*" (I could almost hear my back sigh in relief upon receiving my business-class air ticket in the mail.) Luckily, I would have a helping hand with luggage, logistics and language in each country through the services of in-country cultural liaisons—their *Geographic* code name is "fixers"—who work with visiting writers and photographers on assignment for the publication. Implicit in that nickname is that they fix what we uncouth Westerners break—whether it's cultural mores, social faux pas, hotel minibar rules—or arrange for visas when they are impossible to get, hotel rooms when they are unavailable or access to important people otherwise indisposed. I wondered if their portfolios included fixing broken backs.

It was then that I was sprinkled with the magic dust. And just about the same time I also discovered the sound track to the movie that my life would become for the next year. You will not guess the song, I assure you. I myself would not have guessed in 10,000 lifetimes. I would have thought some Dylan song *("How does it feeeeel/ To be on your oooooown?")* But in fact it's a song called "Lose Yourself," by the rap singer Eminem, about whom I had known only that he was white, from Detroit and controversial for some antigay lyrics in one of his songs. I also knew "Lose Yourself" was the hit track from the film *8 Mile,* in which Eminem starred as a character identical to himself. I saw the film mostly out of curiosity. I walked out of the theater and went directly to a Tower Records and bought the CD.

I hate most of rap and hip-hop music. It's all so violent, so male testosterone driven, so misogynistic. "Bitch this," "motha fucka that," "my gang can beat up your gang" kind of stuff.

But this song was different. In this story of a loser rap singer who steels himself for a comeback, to redeem his honor, the lyrics reveal an insecure and vulnerable man, at the bottom of the barrel, a complete contradiction to the machismo image most rappers try to cultivate. The opening sets it off immediately from the rest of this genre: a haunting piano solos for eight measures, delicately establishing a riff that permeates the tune. Then a guitar chops off chords in double time with dangerous urgency. Eminem quietly speaks, asking what you would do if you had just one chance to achieve all your goals. Would you seize that opportunity? Or blow it?

Was he speaking directly to me, or was I suffering from an extreme case of Buddha Narcissism, in which everything that happened to, around or within earshot of me contained a tangential reference to some Buddhist ideology? Or was he speaking to everyone at the end of their rope? And the hook:

You better lose yourself in the music, the moment . . .

His tagline whispered into my ears:

You can do anything you set your mind to, man.

I played the cut throughout my workouts, while I was writing, on my evening constitutionals, idling in traffic on the 101 or the 405—and any other time I needed a dose of belief in myself. At first I listened purely for the motivation—I *can* do anything I set my mind to. But then the lyrics began to speak to me from another place. Though I highly doubt Eminem would know a bodhisattva from a bodacious babe, I detected an underlying Buddhist theme. By losing himself in the moment, that is by being present in the moment, he finds himself. If he focuses his mind, he can achieve anything. It sounded to me like the Buddhist practice of mindfulness, paying close attention to the moment.

I knew I'd let too many opportunities pass me by. I knew that my time was almost up, that a man in his 50s is on the downward-sloping side of the roller coaster and that success was my only option.

You can do anything you set your mind to, man.

Those last words, in the low tone of a man trying to sell himself to himself, became my other mantra.

I was ready to take my shot.

There were more forces at work here than my personal predicament, and the rest of the "hill-of-beans-in-this-crazy-world" monologue. It was my good fortune and timing to get this assignment when a wave of interest in Buddhism was cresting worldwide. In the last decades of the 20th century, Buddhism was booming and, I conjecture, will be booming well into the new millennium. A few facts I collected:

- In 1987, there were 429 Buddhist centers in North America. By the end of the 20th century, the number had grown 260 percent, to 1,062 centers, reports Dr. Coleman in *The New Buddhism.*

- There were about 400,000 declared Buddhists in the United States in 1990. In 2001, that number was estimated to jump to as high as 3 million, according to a study conducted by sociologist Barry Kosmin, when he was at City University of New York.

- In a 2004 study, published in the *Journal for the Scientific Study of Reli-*

gion, sociologists Wendy Cage and Robert Wuthrow found that one in eight Americans believes Buddhist teachings or practices have had an important influence on his or her spirituality.

On a more anecdotal level, the Buddha Boom is evident everywhere.

Madison Avenue, modern culture's ultimate barometer of what is hot and what is not, has embraced Buddhism and bows to its selling powers. "Zen" now appears on dozens of products, from skincare lines to an Internet company to an alarm clock. Zen Cart is a free e-commerce shopping-cart software package.

"Karma" has also been co-opted. Karma is the name for a new and widely advertised MP3 player (Zen is the brand name for a rival MP3 player). It's the name of a soap product ("Karma is not just a fragrance; it's more of a life choice," reads the promo copy). Karma Labs is the developer of adventure games for Macintosh and PC. Columbia University Computer Graphics and User Interface Lab was in development on a product to be called KARMA (acronym for Knowledge-based Augmented Reality for Maintenance Assistance), a head-mounted display system for laser printer maintenance.

None of these products has anything to do with the actual definition of karma, which is Sanskrit for "deed." In both Hinduism and Buddhism, according to the law of karma, an individual's physical and mental actions determine the consequences in his or her life, and his or her next life. In short, karma is the law of cause and effect. Each action causes a reaction.

Likewise for the word "nirvana," the Buddhist state of enlightenment, a word universally recognized and almost universally misunderstood but which nonetheless graces many a product package. Along with the requisite skin-, hair- and health-care products, Nirvana was, among other things, the name of a distributor of cannabis seeds and other marijuana products. Nirvana Golf Technologies makes golf clubs. Nirvana is the digital library division of

General Atomics, which develops high-tech systems from nuclear fission and fusion.

Then there was the seminal Seattle grunge band that called itself Nirvana. In a manner of speaking, the band's leader, Kurt Cobain, took the word literally when he took a gun to his head and blew himself away. The word most closely translates in English to "blown out," or "snuffed out," extinguished like a candle. Years after the band was formed, Cobain explained that to him the word meant "total peace after death," as reported in *Never Fade Away: The Kurt Cobain Story,* by Dave Thompson. The Buddha probably meant it as total peace *before* death. Cobain's suicide note reportedly contained this grunge twist on Buddhist wisdom: "It's better to burn out than fade away."

It was in a hotel room in Washington, D.C., watching TV the night before my last pitch meeting with the *Geographic* editors, when I saw how pervasively "nirvana" had penetrated to heartland America—whether we knew what it really meant or not. I looked up from studying my notes to see a Taco Bell commercial promoting "enchilada nirvana." There was a guy in a tie and white shirt, knees crossed, levitating in the air, virtually beaming with an enchilada-eating grin. Subliminally—hell, right there in living color—they were suggesting that ingesting a corn tortilla stuffed with cheese, chicken, rice and beans, salsa and cilantro (guacamole and sour cream optional) could produce a psychological state of personal fulfillment beyond whatever your Judeo-Christian religion of choice was serving up. The funniest (scariest?) part was that much later I found a 2003 study by New York–based Intermedia Advertising Group, which tracks TV spots for *Nation's Restaurant News,* ranking Taco Bell's Enchilada Nirvana spot for the Chicken Enchilada Bowl fourth among all TV spots in effectiveness.

In the arts world, the Buddha was hot, too. In L.A. that summer of 2003, three major museums—UCLA's Fowler Museum, the Los Angeles County Museum of Art and the Bowers Museum of Cultural Art in Santa Ana—were showcasing Buddhist exhibits and, incidentally, garnering plenty of publicity. In San Francisco, the Asian Art Museum, newly moved to the city center area, had redesigned its exhibit around the history of Buddhism. On the other coast, in New York's Chelsea district, the Rubin Museum of Art, built as a labor of love by Donald and Shelley Rubin, opened in October 2004 in the former Barneys men's department store as the first museum in the Western world dedicated to the art of the Himalayas and surrounding regions. Images of the Buddha dominate the exhibits.

Buddhism had clearly captivated the imaginations of the arts and intellectual communities. A consortium of 20 organizations and institutions in New York were participating in a series called The Buddhism Project: Art, Buddhism and Contemporary Culture, with art exhibitions, lectures, performances and other events. At the same time a sister group based in San Francisco was hosting Buddhist programs all over the greater Bay Area under the umbrella Awake: Art, Buddhism and the Dimension of Consciousness.

> *Buddhism has the characteristics of what would be expected in a cosmic religion for the future: it transcends a personal God, avoids dogmas and theology; it covers both the natural and spiritual, and it is based on a religious sense aspiring from the experience of all things, natural and spiritual, as a meaningful unity. Buddhism answers this description. If there is any religion that would cope with modern scientific needs, it would be Buddhism.*
>
> —ALBERT EINSTEIN, IN *Albert Einstein: The Human Side,* EDITED BY HELEN DUKAS AND BANESH HOFFMANN

Where things started to get really interesting for me as a longtime health and psychology writer were in the findings emerging from cutting-edge research investigating the effects of Buddhist-based meditation on the body and the mind, aka body/mind or holistic medicine.

I first knew one researcher as Jonny Kabat-Zinn in the 1970s, a regular at Dance Free, a Cambridge weekly institution where everyone flailed wildly around to rock music in a Harvard Square church hall—*without* partners—in a physical expression of the neo-Thoreauvian self-reliance everything-goes cultural movement of those times. I also knew he was an avid Zen, martial arts and yoga practitioner and had a PhD in molecular biology. When his friends heard he was going to working-class Worcester, in central Massachusetts, to set up a clinic testing his theories that these Eastern disciplines could help reduce stress and chronic pain, and even more impossibly convince a medical establishment firmly entrenched in old paradigms, they (or maybe just skeptical me) thought, good luck, Jonny.

Now 30 years later he is *the* Dr. Jon Kabat-Zinn, a household name to anyone involved with holistic and/or preventive medicine and to many outside those disciplines. He is emeritus professor of medicine at the University of Massachusetts Medical School, where he was founding executive director of the Center for Mindfulness in Medicine, Health Care, and Society, and founding director in 1979 of its world-renowned Stress Reduction Clinic. It was featured in Bill Moyers's PBS documentary *Healing and The Mind,* on NBC's *Dateline,* on WCVB's *Chronicle* and many other media. His books, such as *Full Catastrophe Living: Using the Wisdom of Your Body and Mind to Face Stress, Pain, and Illness* (Delta, 1990) and *Wherever You Go, There You Are: Mindfulness Meditation in Everyday Life* (Hyperion, 1994), are bestsellers. To those 13,000 patients who've completed an eight-week Mindfulness-Based Stress Reduction Program (MBSR), he is a Buddha-sent, though they would probably never use the Buddha's name.

MBSR has become a model throughout the world. At its core is the simple Buddhist meditation technique called *vipassana.* In an effort to help nonspiritualists adapt the practice, Jon decided early on to call it mindfulness, as opposed to *vipassana* or even meditation. At the time I thought it was a mistake, a dilution of the practice, to use that nomenclature, but once again I was proven wrong. Not only did he and his staff (he is now retired from the program) remain true to the roots of Buddhism, but also he made Buddhist mindfulness accessible for the mainstream.

Published research documents that a majority of the Stress Reduction Clinic patients report lasting decreases in both physical and psychological symptoms, as well as increased ability to relax, greater energy and enthusiasm for life, improved self-esteem and increased ability to cope more effectively with both short-term and long-term stressful situations.

Someone else I knew from those heady Cambridge days was a recent graduate of the Harvard graduate school of psychology. Now Dr. Richard Davidson is director of the Laboratory for Affective Neuroscience, Waisman Laboratory for Brain Imaging and Behavior at the University of Wisconsin, where he uses functional MRI and advanced EEG analysis to study interactions between prefrontal cortex and the amygdala in the regulation of emotion. In the *Proceedings of the National Academy of Sciences* in 2004, for example, he (and others) reported that "long-term meditators self-induce high-amplitude gamma synchrony during mental practice." To translate, he's making waves showing Buddhist meditation's effect on brain waves. Attaching electrodes to the foreheads of Tibetan Buddhist lamas while they were meditating, researchers found that the activity stimulated in several regions of their left prefrontal cotexes—an area of the brain just behind the forehead that recent research had associated with positive emotion—was especially high. That is, he proved neurologically that meditation could indeed make you happier.

Somewhere along the way Buddhism had morphed from religious movement to popular cultural phenomenon to some kind of all-purpose panacea. Like those early overzealous snake-oil salesmen, some people were looking to Buddhism to fix *whatever* ailed them. And others were looking to it as a bull market. Having problems finding your lifemate? Read *If the Buddha Dated: A Handbook for Finding Love on a Spiritual Path,* by Charlotte Kasl. Want to become a CEO? Take the "Buddha in the Boardroom" seminar offered by Lloyd Field, CEO of an organization called Performance House. Improve your parenting skills? Follow the advice in *Buddha Mom,* by Jacqueline Kramer.

Pick your Buddhist obsession. Tea ceremony, Zen archery, origami, ikebana, kung fu: all and more were offered at your local community center. There was probably some lineage-holding master nearby from whom you could also take teachings. All you had to do was Google your town plus Buddhism.

So why? Why Buddhism and why now? Whether you call it a religion or a philosophy or a "lifestyle choice," why was Buddhism gaining in popularity? In the great Jewish tradition in which I was raised, those questions in turn prompted other questions: How did this all get started? Who was the man responsible for this whole phenomenon? Who was the Buddha?

two

Welcome to the New (Axial) Age

Was the Buddha the World's First Baby Boomer?

In divining that the experience of pain was an inseparable concomitant of consciousness and will, the Buddha has shown a penetrating psychological insight. Hinduism regards man's universe as being an illusion; the Buddha, anticipating some of the schools of the modern Western psychologists by about twenty-four centuries, held that the soul is an illusion too.
—Arnold Toynbee

Your work is to discover your work and then with all your heart to give yourself to it.
—The Buddha

I am staring at a stack of the best biographies of the Buddha when I suddenly realize this expedition is impossible. Discrepancies about many facts of his life are the rule, not the exception, including even when and where he was born. Years of his life are unaccounted for. The earliest recorded evidence of him, his talks or his teachings postdate his life by 500 years. We cannot accurately chart his itinerary. We have no idea whatsoever how he may have looked, and know even less what his personality was like. Here, more or less, are the basics.

Siddhartha Gautama, who later came to be known as the Buddha, was born in about 563 BCE in the Himalayan foothills village of Lumbini in what today is Nepal, near the Indian border. The son of King Suddhodana of the powerful Shakya clan, the prince was born under such auspicious circumstances—beginning with his mother Queen Mahamaya's dream upon becoming pregnant of a large white elephant with six tusks entering her womb through her right side—that sages predicted he would become either a most powerful monarch or an enlightened man. (Siddhartha translates to "one who has accomplished his goals.") King Suddhodana hoped it would be the former and began to groom his son for that destiny, showering him with every human comfort possible as well as tutelage by the wisest men in the land. Cloistered from the riffraff of society, he passed the first three decades of his life without great circumstance. Along the way he married; his wife, Yasodhara, was a beautiful young woman of noble blood.

In the centuries after his death at the age of 80, as his reputation grew, fact intertwined with myth, and a legendary Buddha was born as well. This Buddha toddled out of his mother at birth, fully conscious, and lotuses appeared under his first seven steps. He had superhuman powers. He had the mental powers to tame wild animals simply by staring at them. He could be in two places at once. There are stories of him traveling to faraway places in one night.

Both accounts agree, however, that at the age of 29, now a father and bored with his opulence, he ventured out of his palace for the first time and encountered old age, sickness and death. So moved was he by this first brush with the painful realities of life that he left his comfortable home to search for an end to human suffering. Over a six-year period, he withstood all the deprivations of his fellow Hindu seekers—he fasted, he observed silence, he lived alone in a cave—until he realized he was no happier than before. There must be another way, he thought, a "middle way" between indulgence and asceticism. He decided to sit in meditation under one of the broad pipal trees that dotted the plains of the Ganges River until he found his answer. Over the next seven days he examined his thought processes to discover how and why man often creates his own mental suffering, how he puts himself in a state of perpetual dissatisfaction that gnaws at his very being and sabotages his ability to be happy. In effect, he conducted the world's first psychoanalysis—on himself—several thousand years before Freud. He devised an extraordinarily uncomplicated formula. Based not on faith, as in other religions, but on empirical observation, it was a succinct syllogism—four points of deductive reasoning—that he called his Four Noble Truths:

1. That there is suffering in the world, whether mental or physical.
2. That there is an origin of suffering, namely, a fundamental ignorance of the cause-and-effect relationship of all actions, called karma.
3. That by eliminating the cause, you can eliminate suffering.
4. That there is a method to eliminating the cause, and that method is called the Eightfold Path, a moral compass leading to a life of wisdom (right views, right intent), virtue (right speech, right conduct, right livelihood), and mental discipline (right effort, right mindfulness, right concentration).

Under that tree, he utilized a method of inquiry that simply required paying attention to his own mind—but *really* close attention. This method, which is the core practice of the Eightfold Path of Buddhism, is meditation. Though the technique may differ within each of the many sects of Buddhism—eyes closed or slightly open, in silence or chanting phrases, alone or in groups, facing the wall or other meditators—almost all begin by paying close attention to your own inhalation and exhalation. There is nothing mystical or otherworldly about it, no levitation, no out-of-body experience. With each in and out breath, your awareness becomes more refined, more focused. Breathing in . . . you become aware of the sensations of your body, and of your most distracting organ, your mind. Breathing out . . . you experience a release of body tension, and you struggle to bring your wandering mind back to your breath. In . . . the air tickles the tip of your nose.

Out . . . the pain in your knee subsides, the mind still meanders. In . . . "Shouldn't I be doing something more useful with this time?" Out . . . "Who's the 'I' in that last thought?" With ever more subtlety, eventually you come to understand, sometimes painfully, sometimes joyfully, what Siddhartha realized. "We are what we think," he said.

He emerged from under the shade of the tree as the Buddha, "the awakened one." (The tree is now known as the Bodhi Tree, given the species name *ficus religiosa*.) Until his death, he traveled the several-hundred-mile corridor in what are now India's Bihar and Uttar Pradesh states, sharing his insights with all who'd listen.

The Buddha did not intend his ideas to become a religion; in fact, he discouraged following any path or anyone's advice without testing it personally. His dying words, as it's told, were "Work out your own salvation; do not depend on others." Nonetheless, within several hundred years of his death, Buddhism had become a religion, and eventually one of the major religions of Asia. Today, with 379 million followers, it is the world's fourth-largest organized religion. (Christianity has 2.1 billion followers, Islam 1.3 billion, and Hinduism 870 million. Traditional Chinese religion, which is not counted as organized, has an estimated 405 million followers.) All of this from an inquiring mind that simply wanted to know:

"Who am I?"

"Why am I here?"

"How can I find happiness?"

The Buddha was not the first to ask these questions. These riddles have kept men and women awake around cave campfires and back-yard mesquite grill barbecues since approximately 800 years before the Common Era. In fact, he was among a small advance guard of thinkers who woke up from their Later Primary Civilization slumber into an era that has been dubbed the Axial Age, so named because these innovators created the axis around which concepts about life began revolving and have continued to spin right up to last night's newscast.

They included the Hebrew prophets of Palestine: Isaiah (ca. 740 BCE), Jeremiah (around 600 ca. BCE), Daniel (ca. 600 BCE) and Ezekiel (ca. 570 BCE). The Persian father of Zoroastrianism, Zoroaster, was also active during this period (about 600 BCE). Mahāvīra, the founder of Jainism, was born in 540 BCE. In China, the philosophers Confucius and Lao-tzu (6th century BCE) left their mark in Confucianism and Taoism, respectively. The West produced the Greek wise men, Socrates (ca. 469–399 BCE) and his protégé Plato (ca. 427–327 BCE), and later Aristotle (384–322 BCE), who brought us critical and rational thinking.

"The Axial Age marks the beginning of humanity as we now know it," writes Karen Armstrong, a former nun and author of several books on world religions, in *Buddha,* one of the most readable biographies I plowed through.

She made it sound like a thinking man's big bang, a burst of consciousness from 800 to 200 BCE that makes you wonder what they were putting in the drinking water back then and how we can tap it now.

"In a world that had suddenly become alien and desolate . . . ," she writes, "an increasing number had come to feel that the spiritual practices of their ancestors no longer worked for them . . . that the world was awry . . . that their experience of utter impotence in a cruel world impelled them to seek the highest goal . . .

"The great sages of the time taught human beings how to cope with the misery of life, transcend their weakness and live in peace in the midst of this flawed world," she concludes. "They looked for greater inwardness in their spiritual lives."

The 5th century BCE was a period of transition in India. The India of the Buddha's time was not a single political unit but rather a collection of independent countries, often vying with each other for supremacy. Old tribal republics were breaking up under the impact of predatory and autocratic kingdoms. Not surprisingly, there were frequent turf wars of varying levels of intensity.

Cities were becoming larger and more sophisticated. People were leaving their villages and farms and flocking to urban centers. With the formation of monarchical states and capital cities that became the hubs of mercantile activities, there emerged a class of absentee landlords who lived largely in the cities but had vast landed properties in rural areas. Such absentee landlords are mentioned in the Pali text (Pali, the language spoken in the Buddha's region at that time, eventually became the accepted language of Buddhist scriptures). Also, not surprisingly, graft and corruption in politics were the order of the day.

Indian society was divided very sharply by the caste system. The caste people were born into determined what work they did, their status in society, who they married, where they lived and who they ate with—in fact, almost every aspect of their lives. The highest caste was the Brahmins, the hereditary priests of Brahminism, the educators and the scholars.

In Brahminism, the prevailing religion during the Buddha's time, there was a supreme creator named Brahma and many lesser gods: Aggi, the god of fire; Indra, the king of gods; Yama, the king of the underworld; Suriya, the god of the sun; and others. But there was widespread dissatisfaction with Brahminism and many people, including many Brahmin intellectuals, were becoming interested in new religious ideas. Parallel to Brahminism and much older was the tradition of unorthodox ascetic teachers (samana) who were beginning to attract increasing interest. The most famous of these ascetics was Nataputtā, known to his disciples by the title Mahāvīra Jain, the founder of Jainism. Many smaller religious factions also came and went.

It all sounded familiar: disillusionment with the predominant religious movements, spiritual experimentation, political graft and corruption, rampant wars, societal hierarchies, overcrowded urban centers, the growth of capitalism.

I couldn't exactly put my finger on it but something resonated with me about the life and times of Siddhartha, despite the differences of two millennia and 10,000 miles plus the fact that he was a prince by birth and I was a Jewish prince by self-proclamation. Now, though, Armstrong's observations about the Axial Age rang a bell. Some of the phrases, verbatim, easily could have been in reference to—even made by—my generation of postwar baby boomers. We were the antiestablishment Beatniks, the antiwar peaceniks, the antinuke activists who saw the world coming unhinged by assassinations, nuclear proliferation and military buildup. "Flawed world" would be an understatement from our perspective. Disillusioned by hypocritical and increasingly irrelevant religious institutions that were wracked by self-aggrandizing TV evangelists and sex scandals, we launched the so-called New Age movement in the 1970s. We explored Asian philosophy, Judaism's esoteric kabbalah, shamanism, Native American ritual—anything but our own white Anglo-Saxon and eastern European Jewish traditions. We thought we had written the book on alienation, reveling in nihilists like Sartre, loners like James Dean and a folksinger who also craved answers that were, alas, my friend, "blowin' in the wind."

In the years since then, ensuing generations would tell you those sentiments have only been exacerbated. Thus, Mr. Cobain and an endless assembly line of cultural antiheroes from the music, art, film and other worlds.

There were so many similarities between that time and this that I wondered if we could ourselves be in the midst of the New Axial Age, recognizable only a century or five from now. One can only wonder who would be this age's Axial icons. Freud? Stephen Hawking? The Dalai Lama? Or some relative unknown, like UCLA computer scientist Leonard Kleinrock, who created the basic principles of packet switching, the technological underpinning of the Internet? I even speculated that perhaps I had uncovered in the Buddha the world's first baby boomer, so prescient that he preceded the actual boom by some two and a half millennia.

This would partly explain why interest in Buddhism has grown recently. This became my working theory: In times like these, as in times like those, times when people have lost faith in existing spiritual institutions, social structures, cultural constructs and intellectual paradigms, there is something inherent in Buddhist doctrine that makes it appealing. What that essential quality is became part of what I hoped to learn. And I was not willing to have my insight blurred by such enigmatic expressions as Antoine de Saint-Exupéry's "What is essential is invisible to the eye."

I saw the burgeoning engaged movement as another piece of the puzzle. Buddhism has always found a way to be contemporary and relevant, no matter what culture it's in. Was engaged Buddhism the latest wrinkle on a very old, perpetually smiling face? Was this trend part of what contributed to Buddhism's popularity? Did people even know about it outside the in-gathering of Buddhists? Was it strictly a Western phenomenon, influenced by that good ol' Christian do-unto-others good-works ethic? Would the Buddha have approved?

Gate gate paragate parasamgate bodhi svaha.
(Gone, gone, gone all the way over, everyone gone to the other shore, enlightenment. "Hallelujah!")

    —THE BUDDHA, FROM THE HEART SUTRA, ALSO CALLED THE
       Prajnaparamita Sutra

We were all delighted, we all realized we were leaving confusion and nonsense behind and performing our one and noble function of the time, move.

    —JACK KEROUAC, On the Road

In an interview at his home in Berkeley, California, just before I left the country, world religions scholar Huston Smith told me the community of Buddhist monks, known as the Sangha, is "mankind's oldest continuing social organization." He explained that the Buddha and his followers began taking three months of meditative seclusion together during India's rainy season, from July to September; those annual so-called rains retreats have continued unbroken for 2,500 years in some form or another, in some time zone or another. Now, even laypeople who participate in Buddhist activities are considered part of that Sangha, an uninterrupted chain linked by generation after generation in search of truth, meaning and happiness.

The pilgrimage in the footsteps of the Buddha is a tradition that goes back almost as far. Despite the fact that the Buddha was emphatic about not becoming just another Axial superstar—"If you see the Buddha in the road, kill him," goes a famous Buddhist saying reinforcing this point—he told his closest followers of four places "which the believing man should visit with feelings of reverence and awe." Where he was born, where he became enlightened, where he gave his first lecture and where he died—to visit these places would be to gain merit, which could translate to a few less rounds of suffering.

Since that time, it would be impossible to estimate how many millions—or billions—have made their own arduous journey to pay homage to the Buddha and his teachings. And not just Buddhists: Hindus, Jews, Christians, Muslims and atheists all come, if only to visit a site of historical importance and archaeological significance, or simply to visit a tourist attraction. Some come simply out of curiosity. "Who *is* this guy who so many people revere?" Even the curiosity seekers, some Buddhists believe, benefit in ways they might not be aware of or acknowledge.

John C. Huntington, professor of Buddhist art and methodologies at Ohio State University, goes to great lengths explaining the phenomenon of pilgrimages in the Indic context. In "Sowing the Seeds of the Lotus: A Journey to the Great Pilgrimage Sites of Buddhism," a five-part series published in *Orientations,* a magazine of Asian art based in Hong Kong, he elaborates on the Hindu word *darśana,* which "literally means 'seeing' or 'viewing' but also carries a more profound concept of essentially identifying with the events that one 'sees.' "

> The idea is much more than just witnessing or observing an important event in the sense that one who experiences *darśana* of an event becomes part of it and the merit or other benefits that

might be gained by the principal participants are also gained to a lesser degree by the observer. In other words, when a great Buddhist teacher gives an initiation, he gains merit *(punya)* for benefiting others. At the same time, the initiate gains merit for making the commitment to Buddhism; those who participate in the ceremony gain merit for helping others make the commitments; those who attend the ceremony gain merit; and even those who simply pass by in a casual manner gain merit. In Buddhism, even beings in the most unfortunate of births can accrue merit simply being present and observing events surrounding the teachings of the Dharma.

That last sounded like a Merit Plus program of some astral airline. Aha, I thought, there is hope even for me.

Huntington adds, "This concept of accruing merit is the underlying motivation behind the pilgrimages. . . . The ultimate desired benefit is, of course, to positively affect one's own rebirth into a higher real."

My own desired benefit did not relate to rebirth, in which I did not believe. I was hoping higher realms could be achieved in this lifetime, so as to cash in my merit chips at least before my next back event made me a cripple again.

Not that I couldn't use merit wherever it came from, but I had my own reason for visiting the famed Buddhist sacred sites. I thought that being where the Buddha had been I might get the full gestalt of what it might have been like to actually be this man, perhaps helping me in some way unpack the enigma in the box that most biographies leave you holding.

But I took the concept of Buddhist pilgrimage even further. There is a Buddhist ritual of circumambulating sacred places known as stupas, special reliquaries where the Buddha's relics are believed to be enshrined. I took the globe as my stupa, undertaking a worldwide pilgrimage in the footsteps of Buddhism, if you will. I had the rare opportunity to walk through the pages of a Buddhist history book. As the weeks unfolded, I witnessed the sometimes subtle, more often blatant, shifts in the teachings and the practice. I saw, tasted, deeply felt Buddhism east and west, Buddhism old and new—at times awkwardly juxtaposed with my own values.

"Where are we really going? Always home!" the 18th-century German poet Novalis is quoted as saying in Hermann Hesse's *The Journey to the East,* one of those books that got many of my generation to re*orient* our ideas. That—along with Jack Kerouac's *On the Road* and *The Dharma Bums,* Shunryu Suzuki's *Zen Mind, Beginner's Mind,* Ram Dass's *Be Here Now* and an underground guide book called *Overland to India*—were on the syllabus for the late '60s and '70s wave of Westerners making their own "journey to the East." Iris, my young bride of 18 months, and I, post-hippies, pre-yuppies, were among that wave who went to India. Iris wanted to find Ram Dass's Hindu guru, a fat unshaven old man in a plaid blanket named Neem Karoli Baba. I, ever the romanticist, was up for a Kipling-esque adventure, the more exotic the better. So Hindu-tunnel-visioned were we at the time that when we were in Sarnath, one of the four most sacred sites of Buddhism, despite being surrounded by images of the Buddha, we didn't even visit where he gave his first sermon. That pilgrimage was about discovering the road, about fathoming the scope of the world and the billions of lives lived every day somewhere without—imagine this!—me knowing about them. Though we didn't come back and don saffron robes or take on Hindu names, that trip suggested there might be answers to questions I didn't then have the wisdom to even ask.

Now, 30 years later, I'd get to go again armed with some of those questions—this time older, somewhat wiser but still miles from attaining a degree of insight into myself that would make me happier. Meanwhile, Radio Dharma, that static station only I seemed to be able to tune into, continued sending me cryptic communiqués, channeling the Buddha through the most unlikely messengers. Who would have thought, for example, K. D. Lang, the Canadian-born openly gay singer-songwriter, was into Buddhism? Yet . . .

Constant craving
Has always been. . . .

Ultimately, any pilgrimage is a metaphor. Pilgrimage, like meditation itself, inevitably becomes an inner expedition. Henry David Thoreau proved you could go on pilgrimage in your own backyard. The Buddha showed you could do it in your own head.

It was both the worst and (I suppose therefore) best time to look inside my head. Clearly, there were some personal issues I was facing—rather, refusing to face: my relationship with money, my relationship with women, my relationship with family, my relationship with writing, my relationship with my body, my relationship with my own psyche, my relationship with relationships. But with a complicated itinerary to set up, it was necessary (and easier) to focus on the outer journey than the inner. I rationalized that I must have done something right along the way to exchange those Merit Plus coupons for this assignment. And don't think that every day on the road, even on those nightmarish days that accompany any long-distance travel, I didn't pinch myself. Sitting on a beach in Sri Lanka, or interviewing the Dalai Lama, or gliding down the Ganges River, or standing atop one of China's most beautiful mountains accompanied by one of China's most beautiful women, I had only one explanation for how I got there: *good karma!* This would be as close to journalism nirvana as I was ever going to get. But as Dr. Kabat-Zinn put it so well, "Wherever you go, there you are." And "I" would pop up in the most undesired places at the most unexpected moments, trailing myself like voracious, if schizoid, paparazzi. Eventually, I would have to deal with my issues, but the magic dusk had just been sprinkled and I had no intention of distracting myself from what I thought was my "real" objective, which was, in the time-honored tradition of my profession, to "get the story."

The night before I left New York had to be one of the coldest in the city's history. I had had a good-bye dinner with my daughter Ariana and my future son-in-law Ryan. Now I stood at a lonely corner in Lower Manhattan, braced against a bitter wind, trying without success to hail a cab back to my hotel. It was so frigid I thought my cheeks were going to crack and fall off my face.

"Great start," I howled out loud to no one standing next to me. My flight was the next day and those Big Questions I so loftily had posed seemed as essential as the proverbial bicycle to the fish. I could see the headline now: "Itinerant travel writer freezes to death trying to get uptown."

"I am so out of here," I shouted to my invisible companion.

three

Finding the Buddha's Truth of Suffering in Poland

Holding on to anger is like grasping a hot coal with the intent of throwing it at someone else; you are the one who gets burned.
—THE BUDDHA

I have learned two lessons in my life: first, there are no sufficient literary, psychological, or historical answers to human tragedy, only moral ones. Second, just as despair can come to one another only from other human beings, hope, too, can be given to one only by other human beings.
—ELIE WIESEL

It sounds like the setup for a politically incorrect joke: Did you hear the one about the journalist who began his journey in the Buddha's footsteps in Poland?

Siddhartha Gaumata was born nowhere near eastern Europe. And though the Buddha's entire itinerary is not certain, with some of his life completely unaccounted for, we can, however, safely say he never stepped foot west of what is now India. And with perhaps no more than 7,000 Buddhist practitioners among 38.5 million Polish countrymen (95 percent are Roman Catholic), one hardly could call this an important Buddhist center even in Europe.

So what was I doing in Oświęcim, a small unremarkable industrial city that straddles the Sola River in the southwest corner of Poland, not far from the former Polish capital of Kraków?

It might make some sense knowing the German name by which Oświęcim is better recognized: Auschwitz. If the connection to Buddhism is still not evident, consider the first of the four pillars upon which the Buddha built a system of belief. In what came to be known as the Four Noble Truths, he posited that, first and foremost, the human condition is rife with suffering.

Then where better (or worse, in this case) to stare suffering in the face, to confront what horrific pain one man can inflict upon another, of a magnitude that numbs the heart and tilts the brain? And, in the illogical logic of Zen Buddhism, where better to come to terms with such suffering, and perhaps turn that anguish—and all the other emotions the Holocaust evokes—into compassionate wisdom?

That, at least, was the theory when Bernie Glassman, a former McDonnell Douglas aeronautical engineer turned Zen priest and social activist, organized a Zen meditation retreat in 1996 at the Auschwitz concentration camp and Birkenau death camp across town. Under the auspices of Peacemaker Circle International, Glassman, whose ordained name is Roshi Bernard Tetsugen Glassman, called them Bearing Witness Retreats. "Bear," to carry. "Witness," from the French *wit,* for mind or intelligence. Carrying mindful intelligence to the experience. To be present there—or anywhere—is to have a clearer intelligence and deeper understanding of that experience, and one's own reaction to that experience.

Roshi Glassman, who was born to Jewish immigrants in Brooklyn in 1939, began studying Zen in 1967 under Taizan Maezumi Roshi, who founded the Zen Center of Los Angeles and established the White Plum Sangha in the United States. Glassman became Maezumi Roshi's first dharma successor in 1976. He moved back to New York in 1980 to establish the Zen Community of New York in Riverdale. In 1982, Glassman founded Greyston

Bakery in New York as a means to employ a handful of his Zen students. As the bakery grew, Glassman expanded its mission to provide jobs for residents of the neighboring inner city deemed "hard to employ" due to a lack of education and skills, and histories of homelessness, drug addiction and incarceration. From this social mission, the umbrella Greyston Foundation has evolved into a community development organization based in Yonkers, New York, serving the economically disenfranchised through housing development, jobs and enterprise creation, social services, child care and HIV-related health care. Since then the organization has expanded further with projects in the Middle East, under the umbrella of the Zen Peacemaker.

One of the "practices" that Glassman started was called "street retreats." They were 48-hour immersions in which people with jobs and suits and roofs and families voluntarily gave them all up—plus their wallets and credits cards and all other forms of identity—to become homeless. The rules were you fended for yourself, found shelter or any warm crevice, foraged for food or found soup kitchens. The experience offered a chance to free-fall without a net, without an ego. Participants reemerged into their "selves" with greater compassion and a sensitivity to what the homeless actually went through every single day, and it couldn't help but reward them with a there-but-for-the-grace-of-*whomever*-go-I renewed appreciation for their lives.

Given the level of self-deprivation bordering on masochism, this program was surprisingly popular, both with people who wanted to undergo this harrowing experience and with the media. In those years, with increasing economic instability in the United States, there were more and more homeless people crowding the sidewalks of New York and other major American cities. I lived and worked in midtown Manhattan from 1990 to 1992, and close to 20 people lined the two blocks I walked to my office, including several who took up "permanent residence" on the steps of the Fifth Avenue Presbyterian Church. Each time I walked by them was a painful struggle for anyone with a conscience; you had to relive a complex ricochet of emotions. *Do I give some money? Will it help their lives? I feel guilty not to spare some change. Damn these people, such a nuisance! Certainly I can afford a quarter? Get your life together, man! I go to work every day; why can't you?*

Glassman had a genius for touching people's nerves, for getting them where they lived, and where they didn't have to live—namely, on the street. Then came the Bearing Witness Retreats at Auschwitz, which also proved so popular that now they're an annual event, attracting hundreds of people from every country and religious background. Staying in dorm rooms at a Carmelite convent across from the entrance to Auschwitz, over several days participants tour the buildings and barracks that now have been turned into painfully poignant memorials to human suffering. In the children's barracks, the latrine, the crematorium and various other locations, they then gather and sit cross-legged on the ground in circles, light candles and incense, recite Buddhist chants and meditate in silence in the Soto Zen tradition. In the evening, after quietly dining together in the dorm commissary, they gather again to debrief on the day's effect on them. Borrowing from a Native American tradition, they sit in a circle and, one by one, each picks up an object placed in the middle, signifying they have the platform. Each speaker then tries, often with great trouble, to put into words the tangle of unspeakable emotions. The first night, after hearing people—including myself—falter, I thought, "These things are impossible to talk about, much less write about." I was almost ready to get on a flight back to New York.

Several days and nights of this and one cannot help but be overwhelmed with mixed feelings—of sadness and anger and grief, of course, but also, as I discovered, a surprisingly cathartic release from that same sadness and anger and grief.

It was not my plan to make this the first stop on my journey. I had hoped to start where the Buddha was born, in the village of Lumbini, now at Nepal's southern border with India, and chronologically follow his life and then the history of Buddhism. Logistics dashed that hope; my round-the-world ticket allowed me to make countless stops so long as I kept traveling east. Leaving from New York, that meant Poland before India. The retreat usually occurs in November with some occasional midyear additions; my Polish hosts rounded up an assortment of young Poles and Germans and organized this February mini-retreat to accommodate my schedule. I figured I'd fudge it a little in the writing so you, dear reader, would never know I didn't start at the Buddha's birthplace. But once I got there, I realized it was the most logical place to begin.

The American representative for Zen Peacemakers who escorted me from New York to Poland was Grover Gauntt III, who'd been involved with the Auschwitz retreats since the beginning and who also led street retreats for the organization. Those Roman numerals after his name—along with a certain refinement to his persona, the cowboy boots that peaked out from the bottom of his tight and well-pressed blue jeans, the turquoise jewelry and his involvement with the Native American movement—made him a walking cultural anomaly, but somehow he pulled it off without pretense. Though it never became clear to me exactly how he makes a living, his commitment to finding a way to use Buddhism as a catalyst for social change was clearly not some fashion statement for him.

We arrived in Warsaw in the late afternoon. Andrzej Krajewski, who heads the Polish branch of Zen Peacemakers with his wife Malgosia Braunek, met us at the airport and took us directly to the couple's house. Driving through the city, I felt as though I had passed through the looking glass and in my own way belatedly broken down the Iron Curtain. This was my first time east of the mythic barrier, and, even though the rest of the world had celebrated its rusting away with the fall of the Berlin Wall in 1989, I noticed I still carried old biased baggage and expectations of life "behind the Iron Curtain." Those expectations would have included adjectives like "depressing" and "dreary." So I wasn't sure if

I had prejudiced my perception or it really *did* seem depressing and dreary. The buildings were gray and brown, people dressed in gray and brown—even the air was a grayish brown. People I saw on the streets didn't walk; they plodded, hunched over. Maybe it was just me, shifting time zones, and nervous on my first day of "work." Maybe it was just February. Maybe it takes a people a very long time to unshackle themselves from many years of oppressive government.

On the way, I got a little history lesson with quick stops on the typical Warsaw sightseeing tour: the memorial to the Jewish ghetto revolt of 1942; the memorial to the Polish Resistance movement's Warsaw uprising against the Germans in 1944; the Monument to a Child Insurgent, a statue in front of the city walls commemorating the children who fought in the '44 uprising. In fact, although the resistance movement took place throughout the country, the largest number of war memorials is found in Warsaw. The city itself was almost totally destroyed after the tragic failed revolt of '44. The rebuilding of the city, especially of the Old Town Square with its buildings from the 15th to 18th centuries, is itself a monument to the Polish will to survive.

This has been Poland's plight for some 200 years. Russia, Prussia and Austria basically carved up the state for themselves in partitions of 1772, 1793 and 1795, the last one dissolving any sign that a Polish republic ever existed. No wonder these people seemed downtrodden; victimization was part of the national character. And, of course, then came Hitler and Stalin, and once again Poland became a pawn in someone else's political chess strategy. Now, since 1989, there is hope that Poland and Poles will be able to exercise their freedom.

Once at their house, a small but charming wooden building in a maze of streets that passed for a suburb of Warsaw, we settled around the kitchen table while they told me the stories of how they got involved in Buddhism and in this particular activist aspect of it. Out the back window across their small lawn I could see another wooden structure: the *zendō*, or Zen meditation center, where they sat regularly with members of their Kandzeon Sangha, one of about 30 such Zen centers in Poland.

Andrzej is a translator and an interpreter, a handsome six-footer in his mid-60s with curly graying hair and a strong jaw. He immediately struck me as warm and congenial with a wry and ready sense of humor. In 1974, he met Malgosia, one of Poland's most well known film actresses who dropped out of the film world at the height of her popularity just about the same time she became interested in Zen Buddhism. Now one of Poland's most well known Buddhists, she ordained as a Zen Buddhist teacher in 1999. That evening of the day I arrived she appeared on a taped TV talk show, which featured a panel of three Poles discussing why Buddhism was growing in popularity among young people. As we chatted, she seemed a bit more guarded, even shy, preferring to stay at the stove.

Except for a few differences of cultures, their odyssey basically paralleled my own and that of my fellow Americans in search of something other than what our societies and our religions were offering us.

Andrzej was living in Sweden in the early 1970s, meeting American Vietnam War veterans, objectors and deserters who introduced him to jazz and Beat poets and Hindu gurus.

In this way, he said, "The East was coming through the West for us.

"The sixties showed us this new system doesn't work, we were in a psychic depression," Andrzej went on, referring to the Communist stronghold on Poland. "In the seventies we just kept going down and down. We couldn't find hope in politics. We feared the Communist takeover; they were making headway throughout the world. There was no hope for change. 'Where is hope?' we wondered. For Poles, religion had always kept us together. But now we weren't looking to the church for spiritual hope anymore."

After "sniffing like a dog" at various Hindu gurus, as he put it, he and Malgosia found Rajneesh, a controversial Indian whose philosophy was a hybrid of Hinduism and a couple of other isms, including (or mostly, in my opinion) egotism. "He blew my mind," Malgosia said from the kitchen. He blew many minds. After being attacked in India, he moved to rural Oregon in the early 1980s and oversaw a giant ashram, continuing to attract followers and controversy. Of the many gurus who made their mark in the west, he did not seem the type to appeal to this rather sensible couple.

But Hinduism failed them as Catholics for the same reason it failed me as a Jew. She explained: "This is a Catholic country. I am a Pole. The background in me is Catholic or, you could say, Christian." As with the Judeo-Christian traditions, with Hinduism eventually you need faith, whether it's in the one God or the many. "You have to believe," she said as she prepared kasha, a buckwheat dish my Polish great grandmother had passed down to my mother. "In Buddhism, there's nothing about belief. You experience it."

Also, as Andrzej said, Hinduism was full of myth and magic and mystery. Those elements are present in Catholicism, with its belief in resurrection, and in Judaism, with such Old Testament phenomena as the parting of the Red Sea. Such miracles provided entertaining distraction but in the end could not obscure the reality: the poverty and pollution that were engulfing the Iron Curtain countries at the time.

By the end of the 1970s, they had been introduced to Zen via Phil Kapleau, the American author of the seminal *Three Pillars of Zen,* who had given a series of talks in Europe. Then they began serious study with the Korean Zen master Seung Sahn. That was it; they had found a spiritual practice that not just promoted but embraced "freedom—freedom from an oppressive political situation, freedom from an oppressive church," Andrzej said. When they met Dennis Genpo Merzel, a European-based successor of Maezumi Roshi, who died in 1995, they deepened their practice. Genpo Merzel established Kandzeon Sangha in Poland in 1983.

"Now we have another oppressor," added Malgosia. "Wild capitalism. Young people are under so much pressure now to make money—consumptionism. They are like rats on a wheel. They've traded one oppressor for another. Buddhism offers them some kind of balance that they are not finding in churches or in the arts."

When they met and learned about Bernie Glassman's work, they realized it didn't make sense to practice Buddhism sitting on a cushion but *not* practice it in the rest of their lives. "Bernie said, 'Go out and see what you can do—don't be shy.'" Kandzeon Sangha was the first Buddhist group in Poland to begin social outreach in a country where you don't have to go far to find a need.

The next morning, before driving to Oświęcim, Andrzej and Grover took me to see one of Kandzeon's socially engaged projects.

About an hour out of the city, we stopped at what looked like an abandoned old farmhouse. This was where an organization called the Slawek Foundation had established housing and a therapeutic center for recently freed prisoners trying to transition to independent living. Inside, it was musty and dingy; large rooms were barely furnished. The stagnant air mixed with the smell of men who hadn't washed for a long time, their hair permanently greased to their foreheads. As we were shown around the premises, men hunkered down on cots barely made eye contact. I tried to smile and look impressed, but I wanted to cry for these guys, for all of Poland. I could not imagine what Buddhist trick Andrzej and Grover had up their sleeves that could assuage their suffering.

Shortly, about seven or eight of the men filed into a large room and sat in metal chairs in a semicircle. Andrzej spoke, telling them he would translate as Grover introduced them to a little technique they might find helpful. With that, Grover proceeded to lead them through a short meditation, encouraging them to simply focus on their breaths, let thoughts come and go without attachment. I kept my eyes open and watched the men. They fidgeted like schoolkids, their attention spans about as long as a puppy dog's. "What could they be thinking about," I wondered. "What thoughts or sad memories would they even want to remain attached to?" Were they thinking, like me, that this exercise was about as useful to them as a subscription to *GQ*? It seemed like a Band-Aid to cancer, considering all they'd been through, all they lacked, all they desired. But on the way home, the Buddha Brothers, as I jokingly had nicknamed them, seemed heartened. "It's a start," Grover summed up his impression. "We'll keep going back," said Andrzej. "It takes time. It takes building trust. This is good."

I admired their optimism.

The four-hour drive to Oświęcim passed all too quickly, mainly because I was in no hurry to get there. I approached our destination and this episode with no small degree of trepidation.

My worst nightmare was that the reminders of the suffering here would be unbearably palpable—reinforced by seeing the wooden watchtowers, the barbed-wire fences and the sadly iconic brick gateway the trains passed through carrying prisoners. I feared sitting cross-legged on those infamous tracks, silently bundled up against the cold under a polluted, monotonic gray sky, trying to watch my breath, but actually "watching" my back spasming.

The nightmare was realized. But there was another "truth" that slapped me in the face harder than the bitter winds: the truth that I am of Polish descent (both my mother's parents were born in Poland). The truth that many of my grandmother's family died in the Holocaust. The greater and more well-concealed truth that I am in denial of these Polish roots. Prime example: Until I got there, I did not know Auschwitz was in Poland. I had told people I was going to do a retreat in Germany. Being a Polish American was not something one boasted about when I was growing up. All those Polish jokes.

"Knock, knock?"

"Who's there?"

"Polish burglar."

For most of my youth I thought "dumb Pollack" was one word. It's a fact of my life I rarely acknowledged, much less faced. But here there was nowhere to hide. Nor was it possible to hide from the suffering. It's in the air still, a dark cloud permanently hanging over the Auschwitz entrance: *"Arbeit Macht Frei"*—"Work Will Set You Free." That Nazi slogan arching over the gate was not, I gathered, related to the freedom to which Andrzej and Malgosia had referred earlier.

Entering the Auschwitz grounds, now a museum, Andrzej explained how Hitler's knee-slapping sense of the ironic extended, perhaps unwittingly, even further. "There's one explanation in a local history guidebook that some historians trace the name Oświęcim to the times when Christians more than a thousand

Steve McCurry

Grover Gauntt III stares down the Buddha's First Noble Truth at the Birkenau death camp outside Oświęcim, Poland. He coleads Bearing Witness Retreats, sponsored by Zen Peacemakers, at the former Nazi complex.

years ago threw the pagan figure sculpture of the god Swiatowid into the Sola River," he said. "Then the place was made holy—*oswieconę* or 'blessed.' But it also means 'strong' in the ancient Polish. For us Buddhists *oswieconę* means 'enlightened.' Light, holiness, power. There's the little tricky comma that hangs down the *e* in the word, like a tail. That comma makes us sound it slightly different and brings a slightly different aspect: without the comma it's *oswiecic,* to enlighten; with comma, to make holy, blessed."

This bit of etymology is more ironic when juxtaposed alongside the new definition of this town, as taken from some of the museum literature:

> Established around spring 1940, Auschwitz was both the most extensive of some two thousand Nazi concentration and forced-labor camps and the largest camp at which Jews were murdered by means of poison gas. Very soon Auschwitz became known as the harshest of the Nazi concentration camps. In March 1941, Himmler ordered the erection of a second, much larger section of the camp, which was located near the original camp. This was called Auschwitz II, or Birkenau. In Birkenau, the gas chambers and the crematoria of the Auschwitz killing center were operated. Auschwitz was the largest graveyard in human history. The number of Jews murdered in the gas chambers of Birkenau must be estimated at up to one and a half million people: men, women, and children. Almost one-quarter of the Jews killed during World War II were murdered in Auschwitz. Of the 405,000 registered prisoners who received Auschwitz numbers, only about 65,000 survived. Of the 16,000 Soviet prisoners of war who were brought there, only 96 survived. According to various estimates, at least 1,600,000 people were murdered in the killing center at Birkenau.

It's the little details that get to you. Yes, 6 million—the number is burned into every Jew's conscience—but that only obfuscates the reality on an individual level. That illusion was crushed seeing the glass-encased displays of prison life minutiae—one whole display filled with people's spectacles, another holding stray shoes. In the children's barracks, I projected being a frightened kid cowering in the darkest corner of my bunk bed, with only my imagination to buffer the harsh reality just feet away.

Like a walking mummy, my body felt so heavy I could hardly lift my legs through the exhibit halls and barracks. A perpetual frown overtook my face. I found myself shaking my head all the time, unable to look the other participants in the eyes, at a total loss for words—then, and even now. Watching other groups walking through, apparently in the same numb state, I wondered why anyone voluntarily would put himself or herself through this experience.

It hit hardest when we walked single file into a large chamber the Nazis called the Sauna. The Sauna, we learned, was a comprehensive installation in Birkenau to disinfect prisoners. Here the women were herded together every four weeks to be deloused. On these days they were beaten out of their cages, then led to the Sauna, where they had to sit naked all day long until their clothes had been disinfected. In the evening, they had to march back naked to their blocks under the supervision of SS guards; not until night were their clothes returned to them. The death rate increased greatly after each day in the Sauna.

Now the concrete flooring is covered with thick, highly reflective dark-tinted glass. Several exhibit walls have been erected and are covered with pictures salvaged from confiscated luggage: sepia tones of families sitting for formal portraits, or casually on picnic blankets or hamming it up in someone's backyard. Those prominent noses, those eastern European high cheekbones—features that reminded me of my own family.

The ritual we had been conducting in locations throughout the grounds now began again. We gathered our cushions in a semicircle on the glass floor, and sat facing a wall with one of the photo exhibits. The candles were lit. But this time, we departed from the ritual. We were handed a page with a list of names, each page different from the other, and simultaneously we read from our list. "Israelevitch, Abraham. Israels, Salomon. Issakowitsch, Alexandre. Issler, Ichel . . . ," I recited, naturally falling into a familiar Hebraic rhythm of incantation. One name blending into the next, one voice harmonizing with another, all our voices bouncing off the empty walls, an overlapping chorus of death.

A bell rang and we sat in silence. Long after the bell stopped resonating, the names still echoed in my ears. In the Soto tradition, you sit with eyes slightly open but faced downward, focused on one point. My stare landed on a photo reflected off the flooring of a fair-haired woman in her 20s, clutching her two children. In her 20s, my mother was a blonde beauty with a strong jaw and a strong nose, like Meryl Streep in the film adaptation of William Styron's *Sophie's Choice.* Suddenly, it dawned on me: We not only bear witness to those who died here but also to those who never got to live, the unborn children and those children's unborn children—to ourselves reflected into the future. History may have lost unscored musical compositions, undiscovered medical cures, unwritten novels and potential Nobel Peace Prize winners, but I lost unborn aunts and uncles and cousins: memories, experiences, love, wisdom. I had lost my past, my present, my future. When it touched this close to home—*my home*—it sunk in. In that microcosmic moment, I fathomed the magnitude of loss. But rather than get more angry or go numb, this time suddenly I felt an inexplicable release from it all. Granted, this lighthearted elation was fleeting, quickly followed by guilt, and then a string of the usual man-made emotions.

True, in this tradition I was not supposed to be thinking at all, much less emoting. In my defense, I had reached that path to forgiveness only when, in meditation, I was able to separate "me" from me. In other words, by staying focused on this moment, in the midst of such internal tumult, I could separate two experiences: what happened here and my reaction to what happened here. By simply bearing witness to what happened, without layering it with *my* feelings, *my* opinion, *my* reaction, *my* judgment, it just happened.

It reminded me of a brief exchange I'd had with Grover earlier.

"This must have been a literal purgatory for these people," I said, thinking also that purgatory is a theological view held especially strongly by Roman Catholics living here in Poland. Purgatory (Latin *purgare,* "to make clean, to purify") is a location or state of temporal torment, of which Gregory the Great wrote "that the pain be more intolerable than any one can suffer in this life," through which one supposedly passes until his soul is purified and then can transfer to Heaven.

"What would it be called in Buddhism?" I asked Grover.

We were walking among rows and rows of barracks, some of dark wood, others of brick more brown than red. I thought I could still smell death in the air. The afternoon sun cast long shadows; it felt like death row.

"Is this the *bardo?*" I tried. I had confused my Buddhist traditions, he corrected me. According to Tibetan Buddhism, the *bardo* is the phase between one life and the next, literally meaning "that which lies between" or "intermediate state."

"In Zen, there is no in-between state," he explained. "Between now and now there is only now." It was a succinct distinction that would come back to me throughout my travels.

The Bearing Witness ceremony at the Sauna ended with a reading from the Mourner's Kaddish, the Jewish prayer for the deceased, first in Hebrew, then in English: "Let there be abundant peace from heaven, with life's goodness for us and for all Israel. And let us say: Amen. May the One who brings peace to the universe bring peace to us and to all Israel. And let us say: Amen."

Amen, too, that that feeling of release—of a moment of peaceful coexistence with the utter atrocity of Auschwitz and all of our losses—returned to me the rest of that day, a fragrance that covered the smell of death.

That evening, when I told others with an almost confessional spirit about this experience of liberation from so many hellish thoughts and feelings, I was surprised but relieved that some of them nodded in understanding.

"I feel more alive here than anywhere else," confided Aleksandra Kwiatkowska, a 24-year-old photography student. Her comment was rendered all the more incongruous because she was a vibrant, upbeat, intelligent and compassionate striking blonde with a quick smile. In her spare time, she volunteered at a children's hospice in her hometown of Wroclaw, Poland. This was her second Auschwitz retreat, she told me.

Why submit yourself to this emotionally wrenching experience twice, I wanted to know. "Surrounded by death at every step?" I asked, incredulous. "How could you feel *more* alive?

"How could that be?" I insisted. "How?"

"I don't know," she replied, taken aback by my interrogational tone, as was I. "It's . . . just . . . true."

And she left it at that.

This answer provided me with no comfort; it perplexed and frustrated me. People often ask how this happened. How did we let 6 million people get killed? Who could be so cruel as to commit such a horrific act? The Buddhist replies, "I don't know." It sounds like a cop-out.

I wondered if she was thinking with what Zen practitioners call the "don't-know mind." The phrase suggests that there are things we can never understand, and that make sense only when we stop trying to understand them. In other words, when we let go of presumptions and assumptions, when we give up trying to comprehend and fathom everything intellectually—in short, when we put our minds on hold and "just sit," as Buddhists put it—we see things as they are. Why? Because we've let go of judgment, of discrimination and distinction, of "us" and "them"—and perhaps more to the point, us versus them.

I don't know about the don't-know mind. Where I come from, they'd call it denial. I do know that earlier that day in meditation, the sheer intensity of emotions coursing through my blood triggered my fight-or-flight hormones and flushed me of anger, grief, blame, revenge. At that moment I had three choices. One was to remain angry and revengeful, which only generates more pain. The second was to run and hide from those feelings—impossible! The third was to accept them as an incomprehensible part of the life spectrum, including death and suffering as well as vitality and happiness. In that third way, I, too, could "feel more alive."

Hermann Hesse had written some lines about suffering that seemed like a Hallmark card when I first read them. Now I read them with a new respect: "You know quite well, deep within you, that there is only a single magic, a single power, a single salvation . . . and that is called loving. Well, then, love your suffering. Do not resist it, do not flee from it. It is your aversion that hurts, nothing else."

It was a difficult lesson—for a Jew, for a Pole, for a person who thinks he needs answers—and I honestly still haven't gotten it. But I made some peace with my feelings about that blackened page in history, and I was willing to live with not knowing, for the time being, for I knew there would be time in the coming weeks to keep practicing.

four

In the Land of
the Buddha's Birth

India Reawakens to the Awakened One

You cannot travel on the path until you become the path itself.
　—THE BUDDHA

*He gave expression to truths of everlasting value and advanced the ethics not of
India alone but of humanity. Buddha was one of the greatest ethical men of
genius ever bestowed upon the world.*
　—ALBERT SCHWEITZER

The first International Conclave on Buddhism and Spiritual
Tourism, organized by the Indian Government's Ministry of
Tourism and Culture, was set to begin in February 2004, just
when I arrived in New Delhi. The president of India, Dr. A. P. J.
Abdul Kalam, would give an inaugural address. His Holiness the
14th Dalai Lama, whose Government of Tibet in Exile is based in
the Indian state of Himachal Pradesh, India, would deliver the
keynote. There would be seminars on such topics as "Relevance of
Buddhism and Buddhist Philosophy in the Modern World" and
"Buddhist Pilgrimage to India: Issues and Prospects."

It sounded like just the kind of event I ought to cover, but I hesitated signing up, partly because it didn't exactly fit my definition

of engaged Buddhism, partly because I imagined it would all be presented very Indian style, meaning lots of bureaucratic pomp with very little substantive circumstance. But beyond that, I was ambivalent about the whole promotional campaign.

On the one hand, one could say Buddhism was once again being recognized in the country of its birth, where it had basically ceased to exist roughly by the 13th century. So even if it was being mixed in with pie charts and demographic spreadsheets profiling the potential "spiritual tourist," a bit of Buddhist ideology surely would be introduced to people who would never have heard of it otherwise. On the other hand, the whole commercialization of Buddhism seemed to be in counterpoint to the very thing it was promoting. Eventually, I couldn't help but thinking, corporate interests would want their piece of the action, like many American sports arenas that have brand-name prefixes. I could imagine being hired to write the promo copy: *"See the inspirational Kmart Mahabodhi Temple! Sit under the world-famous Microsoft Bodhi Tree!"*

Now that the government saw big bucks in the burgeoning spiritual travel trend, they were ready to jump on the Buddha bandwagon. But it seemed to me that the government was a little late to the party. The way I saw it, the Buddha had already spearheaded this campaign. Twenty-five hundred years ago, when he encouraged people to make pilgrimage to those sites that were significant to his life, he launched what has become a multibillion-dollar international industry called tourism. Pilgrimages in the Buddha's footsteps were the first themed travel packages. In the last 2,000 years, countless people had traversed millions of miles to walk where the Buddha walked, to sit where he sat, sip tea where he might have sipped. And in those places, little tea shops, inns and souvenir stalls must have erected signage announcing, "The Buddha slept (sipped, walked) here!"

And one thing more that bothered me: The government was undertaking this despite the fact that Buddhism had experienced a long relentless decline from the 4th century to the 12th, victim of wave after wave of conquest by Muslims, finally all but dying in the country of its birth. Today, of 1.05 billion Indians, less than 1 percent are Buddhist (there are more Christians than Buddhists in India). Was the government hypocritical? Was it overcome by a new enlightenment? Or just enlightened self-interest? I should have attended just to see how they would handle this delicate subject.

But instead of attending the conference, I spent a day interviewing several tourism officials at their offices on the 7th floor of the Ashok Hotel in New Delhi. In a small conference room, an urban planner named R. K. Safaya, chief of the Design and Development Department at India's Housing and Urban Development Corporation (HUDCO), ran a slide show outlining progress and plans for the development of India's most famous Buddhist pilgrimage sites, eventually turning them into destinations that would be more easily accessible and more visibly appealing to the hoped-for increase in visitors. He showed the before-and-after of several sites, with descriptions and apt quotes by the Buddha written below. As each panel came up, Mr. Safaya read the words out loud, even though they were in English, which is my mother tongue. But he spoke them nonetheless, and in that wonderfully singsongy but often incomprehensible Indian English to which my ear was just beginning to readapt. I noticed, too, that each time Mr. Safaya alluded to the Buddha, he called him "Lord," which I first interpreted as his own devotion to Buddhism. I asked if he was indeed a Buddhist. He said no, he was Hindu. But it was a first indication that in Asia the reverence people show for this man doesn't necessarily have to do with religion or theology. To him, and many other Hindu Indians, the Buddha is more a historically significant figure, sometimes a Hindu deity, sometimes a human being whose ideas, values and actions deserve the highest respect, like a really good role model.

Buddhism is called the ecological religion, he said, citing the Buddha's words: "Like a bee gathering nectar, a human is required to make appropriate use of nature so that the continuity of a beneficial pattern of man/nature relationship is not threatened. Ask a householder to accumulate wealth in ways similar to the one adopted by a bee in collecting nectar to turn into sweet honey without harming either the fragrance or the beauty of the flower."

Mr. Safaya added, "I cannot today imagine any better definition of sustainable development than this clear statement."

This philosophic credo, he said, was the guiding inspiration by which he and his staff hoped to design the important Buddhist sites in India. The project they were hastily working to complete, even as we sat there, was Bodh Gaya, the most sacred of all Buddhist sites, where the Buddha attained enlightenment. The sacred grounds were declared a UNESCO World Heritage Site in 2002, the 23rd site in India to be so honored. The reason for the urgency was that the Buddhism and Spiritual Tourism conference would be bringing delegates there for a visit in a few days.

We were then joined by Amitabh Kant, joint secretary for the Ministry of Tourism. Mr. Kant was less poetic; he spoke in tourism-babble. "In terms of tourism, the Buddhist circuit is one of the core competencies of India," he said. "Prior to September 11, our long-haul tourism was developing." (Translation: People were coming from very far away to visit India with more frequency.) "After 9/11, the trend changed. Long-haul was falling and short-haul was on the rise." (Translation: Tourists from Europe, Japan, North and South America, even Australia, stayed home. But they were still coming from the Asian region known as BIST-EC—Bangladesh, India, Myanmar, Sri Lanka, Thailand Economic Co-operation—plus Nepal, Bhutan, Laos, Cambodia, Vietnam and Indonesia.) "Their interests are complementary to this thrust." (Translation: The majority of people from that part of the world are Buddhist.) "We realized the huge market. We've got terrific inventory, sites, relics, art, architecture, and we've done a lot of work on the infrastructure to enhance travel there."

My translation: That remained to be seen. What they did show me were photographs of some areas where work had been completed. One was the very famous Ajanta and Ellora caves, a couple of hours from Mumbai, which date back to the beginning of the first millennium. I would be going there later in my travels. The slides I saw at that point were not encouraging. The results of the infrastructural face-lift there looked very sanitary, very un-Indian, perhaps more acceptable to Western tourists but decidedly devoid of any charm or sense of antiquity. Three kilometers from the actual caves, an "eco-tourism green belt" had been established, with a central shopping area, consistent signage, concrete shops of the same drab green color, a parking lot with ample space for tour buses, and a green bus that shuttled visitors to the caves. In America, there'd be faux antique signage to denote this is really old stuff. Here there was just concrete painted the same color. We try to antiquate; they try to modernize.

The Bodh Gaya plan involved 100 acres surrounding the central attraction, the Bodhi Tree and the Mahabodhi Temple, which was erected next to the tree in about 250 BCE. They would reorient tour buses and visitor traffic to a location outside town, and regroup vendors as they'd done at Ajanta and Ellora. In Bodh Gaya, a town of 30,000 that sees 30,000 to 40,000 tourists and pilgrims every day from October to early February, the diversion of buses would greatly reduce human suffering caused by traffic bottlenecks. I told them I was heading for Bodh Gaya and was looking forward to checking it out firsthand.

"Are you Buddhist?" Mr. Kant asked. I knew it was a question I would be asked often but as yet hadn't developed a pat reply. I didn't want to take sides, especially if it would offend these Hindus, and I didn't want to launch into my whole cosmological quandary.

"I would say . . ." I stalled and equivocated. "I dabble. I've practiced Hindu meditation and Buddhist meditation. I really respect Lord Buddha and think he was certainly one of the three or four greatest human beings who ever lived. Well, yes, then, I think you could say I'm a Buddhist. I would be proud to say I am a Buddhist. But I grew up in the Jewish faith. That would make me a Bu-Jew."

It was a tired line Jews who practice Buddhist meditation use in the United States, but these Indians laughed riotously as though I had just imitated Robin Williams in his hyped-up comedy club days.

"Are you?" I now turned the tables on Mr. Kant.

"Oh, no," he quickly retorted as though I might have called him a mutant with pimples. But then he proudly explained that his own first name, Amitabh, was one of the childhood names of Siddhartha and also the name of the Buddha of Infinite Light, said to bring calm, peace and contentment. Why would a Hindu family give their son a Buddhist name? This strange disconnect— between claiming the Buddha as their homeboy but distancing themselves from Buddhism as a religion—was evident elsewhere in Indian culture. Hindus claim the Buddha was simply the reincarnation of the Hindu god Vishnu, thereby making Buddhism a sect of Hinduism. The flag of India, designed at its independence in 1947, features a wheel, known as the Wheel of the Law, the *Dharmacakra,* set in motion when the Buddha gave his first sermon at Sarnath, in modern Uttar Pradesh. Also from Sarnath, a noble statue of a four-headed lion atop a pillar erected around 250 BCE by the great Indian Buddhist King Ashoka is the national emblem of the modern Republic of India. All of India's coinage and currency notes have this four-headed lion symbol on it. To fathom this inconsistency, I feared, would require an in-depth analysis of the endlessly mystifying Indian mind-set, a feat even those scholars gathered at the International Conclave on Buddhism and Spiritual Tourism would not dare attempt.

The next day I flew 500 miles east from New Delhi to the city of Patna, and then took a car service along 50 bumpy miles south to Bodh Gaya, where I joined a group of 14 Americans on an organized Buddhist pilgrimage tour, an if-it's-Tuesday-this-must-be-Buddha's-birthplace whirlwind of eight sites in 16 days. We would travel by chartered bus to visit the four major sacred sites—as well as several of the lesser sacred sites. In all, this tour would cover about 1,500 miles in the northeast Indian states of Bihar and Uttar Pradesh, as well as crossing the border into Nepal.

I had found this group in a manner that I had begun to call Zen journalism, the Buddhist spin-off of Hunter Thompson's madcap gonzo journalism of the 1960s. Zen journalism was a kind of karmic random access, driven by Google and other search engines, ramped up by coincidence and luck, inspired by jazz improvisation, necessitated by an incurable case of procrastination. It meant your sources could come from anywhere: from watching late-night TV while you were supposed to be reading Buddhist sutras, from reading *Mad* magazine on the toilet, from stealing ideas from *Buddhism for Dummies*. It also meant you could land in a foreign country unprepared, with barely a few connections, with a map issued from the hotel front desk. In your room, you'd do some quick reading from guidebooks, from your own scribbled notes and copies of e-mails, then start dialing and see who was available once you had a good meal and a stiff drink. Then off you went on the serendipitous trail to find truth, meaning, happiness—and a good interview.

In this case, I had Googled "In the Footsteps of the Buddha," and among the first hits was this group, at www.buddhapath.com, led by an Indian man named Shantum Seth who sounded fairly well informed and reputable. I started e-mailing him, mostly to extract some information on whether I could do this alone and to simply pick his brains. Impressed, I called him from New Jersey to get a better sense of his veracity. When my mother got the $144 phone bill later, I realized I had to join his group: It was the only way I'd be able to justify the phone bill as a legitimate expense.

For the next 10 days, I was sucked into the vortex of an experience I had scrupulously avoided in my career like the Ebola virus. I had wanted my tombstone to read: "And he did it all without ever joining a tour or travel writers junket" (for the record, I am still a TW junket virgin). Why? Basically, I have a problem with two aspects of such experiences: I hate following other people's agenda, and I hate following other people's agenda. Not that I am a leader, but I am *not* a follower. Neither am I a joiner—of associations, of book clubs, of bowling leagues and certainly not of tour groups. The Lone Ranger, the Marlboro Man, Han Solo—these are the archetypal American male heroes after whom I model myself. Add the other usual suspects of alienated antiheroes and social separatists.

I mention this because it has serious downside implications for a neophyte Buddhist. And, because of that, here might be as good a place as any to share my personal struggle with at least one of Buddhism's tenets. The Three Refuges—vows that both Buddhist lay practitioners and monks take to express their commitment to the Buddhist teachings—are the following:

> *I take refuge in the Buddha.*
> *I take refuge in the Dhamma.*
> *I take refuge in the Sangha.*

You chant these three times, in that order, as you bow before a statue of the Buddha. You can say them before, after and even during meditation. Or whenever you feel temptation creeping in. Or when more lonely than alone. When nothing is stable or secure, the Buddha, the Dhamma and the Sangha offer a place of protection and comfort. Also called the Three Jewels, the Three Treasures and the Triple Gem, they are the Buddhist shelters from the storm, refuges from our own suffering. The Christian equivalent might be Jesus Christ, the "good news" message Jesus brought from God and the church congregation, according to the Benedictine monk and longtime Zen practitioner Brother David Steindl-Rast, coauthor with Robert Aitken Roshi of *The Ground We Share: Everyday Practice, Buddhist and Christian.* The Buddhist vows were developed several generations after the death of the Buddha as part of the ordination ceremony for hard-core practitioners prepared to give up their domestic and material possessions and go monastic.

The Buddha is the prime source of authority and inspiration.

His own experience shows that there is an escape from the world of suffering and that it is achievable through one's own efforts.

The Dhamma is the body of the Buddha's teachings. They are the compass by which we steer our way through that storm of suffering. (When spelled with a small *d*, dhamma means "the law," or "the way things are.")

The Sangha is one's spiritual community, the group of monks and nuns and teachers of Buddhist wisdom, as well as their students. I interpret that to also mean one's family and one's network of friends, since all are one's teachers if you do this Buddhism thing right.

I admit I have a problem with authority, so deferring to the Buddha could inherently be against my credo. Whether by profession or inclination, it's my habit to look for the falsehoods behind the truth. But it was the third refuge—the Sangha—that gave me the most trouble. The journalist stands at the edge of the crowd, looking in. He turns the subjective into the objective, eventually objectifying even himself, in effect separating himself from himself. To achieve that perspective, the writer pulls back and away, makes of himself an island. I take that even further; I choose to live on an actual island. So I am on an island (my mind) on an island (this glorified sandbar). I write at home so there are days that I do not talk to or see anyone; if it weren't for e-mail, I could be completely cut off from humankind, or any Sangha, and not be unhappy. Or so I convince myself.

My willingness and ability to suspend judgment on this Sangha matter was put to the test, and I fared better than I thought I would, despite some early faux pas. This group turned out to be fairly interesting but even interesting people can become cloying and tedious after a very short while. Among them was a 37-year-old Seattle man who matter-of-factly allowed that he had recently retired and who also let us know he was bipolar (as if his fidgeting and erratic behavior didn't telegraph it); a former Catholic nun, a delightful woman who had eventually married and then, as they say, divorced well; a woman whose husband's family had founded a liberal arts college in Maine, who was regal in demeanor but extremely naive; and the very successful Portland attorney whose clientele, he let us know on more than one occasion, included various nonprofits (as though that forgave his control issues). There were also several East Coast psychotherapists, two recently widowed women and a photographer, as well as several retired women. Socioeconomically, they were a group with ample disposable income; spiritually, most had had some exposure to Buddhist practice in the States. A few were quite involved with Buddhist practice. This was exactly the sort of high-end demographic cross section over which Mr. Kant & Co. would have drooled.

The most interesting to me, though, was the tour leader, Shantum Seth, a thin, handsome man in his late 40s with delicate features and a mellifluous voice that blended Indian and British accents. Shantum was born to a prominent Hindu family— "Hindu for as many generations as we know," he said as we sat in a tea shop near the monastery we stayed at in Bodh Gaya. His father, Premnath Seth, is retired from a successful career in the shoe-manufacturing business. His mother, Leila Seth, is a retired barrister, the first woman to sit as chief justice of a high court in India. Her autobiography, *On Balance,* was published while I was in India and she was getting quite a lot of press over that. His brother is an accomplished writer, Vikram Seth (*The Golden Gate, A Suitable Boy,* etc.). Now living in London, he, too, was in the Indian papers, having been named as a trustee to the British Museum.

Shantum had followed a path that should have led to a successful business career like his father's, but along the way his conscience kicked in. He recalled once staying in a hotel and realizing his night's rest cost the same as a shoe cobbler's salary for a week. Hinduism, with its rigid caste system, seemed to perpetuate such social injustice, he said. He had followed some Hindu gurus, but in the end, he said, he "got too blissed out—my feet were not on the ground. And in Hinduism, the attitude is 'everything is fine, as it's meant to be.' It's too much faith-based. I was brought up with more of a Western, practical, scientific, rational way of looking at life." Then, after doing his thesis on Mahatma Gandhi and sustainable development, he got involved in social actions and

Shantum Seth glides tranquilly down the Ganges River, with the holy ancient Hindu city of Benares (now Varanasi) in the background.

the peace movement, but "instead of being peaceful I was becoming more agitated and in a fighting mode. You become part of the problem." For the past 20 years he has been working in the development sector, most recently as an adviser to the United Nations Development Programme on volunteer promotion, livelihood and tourism. He is also actively involved with a group called Ahimsa Trust, which addresses peace and development issues.

Ironically, it took an extended trip to California for him to discover Buddhism and find a spiritual teacher he felt was worth following. "I heard some of the best teachers in the world were on the West Coast. Plus there was all this protest music; this was during the anti–Vietnam War period. Dylan, Joan Baez, Peter, Paul and Mary, Country Joe and the Fish." With the mention of Country Joe, in unison we chanted one of the most memorable mantras of that era: "Gimme an *F* . . . *F!* Gimme a *U* . . . *U!* . . ."

This was also at the height of the human potential movement. Shantum visited the spots that had been on every countercultural American's version of the sacred pilgrimage: Esalen, Taos, Boulder and the Ojai Foundation. It was at Ojai, 90 miles northwest of Los Angeles in the Los Padres Mountains, that he encountered the Vietnamese Buddhist monk and peace activist Thich Nhat Hanh. "He reminded me of Gandhi, plus Buddhism gave you a chance to actually *touch peace*. It's not like doing something now to get somewhere later, like other religions. It's all around us now, if we stay in the present." Now he is a student of Rev. Hanh, has been ordained as a teacher *(Dharmacharya)* and, with his wife and two young children, spends several months a year at Rev. Hanh's Plum Village retreat center in the south of France.

When he returned to India after that California trip, he invited Rev. Hanh to India for a Buddhist pilgrimage. That was 1988; it was Shantum's first, and he has been leading them ever since. "It makes me understand myself better," he told me. "It's become part of my practice. Like, how do I handle difficult situations when they arise."

✿

While Siddhartha Gautama was born in Lumbini, you could say the Buddha was born here in Bodh Gaya. It was in this dusty village, in the middle of the vast plains of the Ganges River—a landscape patched with rice fields, dotted with pipal trees and forest groves, and sprinkled with tiny thatched-roof villages—that the 35-year-old mendicant sat under a tree until he found what he'd been looking for, and emerged from under its shade as "the awakened one," the Buddha.

It had taken him six years to get there from the time he left his family palace at the age of 29, a night Buddhists call "the Great Departure." Exactly what transpired that night, and for the next six years, leaves even leading Buddhist scholars scratching their heads. As with the entire life of Siddhartha, the facts intermingle with the fictions. In *The Buddha: A Short Biography* (the title must be meant to be ironic), John Strong, chair of the department of philosophy and religion at Bates College in Lewiston, Maine, explains:

> [Buddhists] narrate many tales that have been remembered and revered, repeated and reformulated over the centuries, and whose episodes have been accepted as inspiring and worth recalling, whatever their grounding in history. Together these stories make up a sacred biography, or rather, several sacred biographies, for we shall see that there are many versions of tales about the Buddha. These narrations may contain "fictions" about the Buddha—legends and traditions that have accrued around him— but these "fictions" are in many ways "truer," or at least religiously more meaningful, than the "facts." They are certainly more plentiful, more interesting, and more revealing of the ongoing concerns of Buddhists. We may know very little about the "Buddha of history," but we know a great deal about the "Buddha of story."

Why the two versions? There are two reasons. One, as most of the Buddha's biographers agree, is that "we have little information that can be considered historically sound," as Karen Armstrong explains in *Buddha*. The first "external evidence that a religion called Buddhism existed," she notes, comes from the inscriptions made by King Ashoka, the Mauryan ruler and Buddha-phile, on the stupas he built, such as the aforementioned Mahabodhi Temple.

The problem is these came some 200 years after the Buddha died. Until then, his life and his philosophy were passed from one generation to the next in the oral tradition. The first most useful texts are those written in Pali, a North Indian dialect whose origins are uncertain but it seems close to Magadhan, the language that Gautama himself spoke. The so-called Pali Canon was orally preserved until it was actually written down in approximately the 1st century BCE. That would be about 400 years later. Can you imagine, for example, the word-of-mouth heroic spin that would be put on the achievements of George W. Bush in 2406 if we didn't have books and newspapers to document his actual achievements, or lack thereof?

The other reason, I believe, is human nature. In short, we have trouble with reality. As a result of our discomfort with things the way they are, we want superreality. Or suprareality. We are not just satisfied with heroes; we want—we need—superheroes. The Buddha, if we believe any part of the story, was a human who achieved a superhuman feat. He realized human potential long before the movement reached the hot tubs of Esalen. We cannot accept that a human achieved a state that most of us don't believe we can reach. It's the catch-22 of Buddhism. So naturally we must endow him with supernatural, superhuman powers. It's either that or make him a God, which the Buddha discouraged. Thus begin the fantastic stories, of flying one night to Sri Lanka, of appearing in two places at once, of stopping wild elephants dead in their tracks, of being born fully cognizant. The Buddha became a blueprint for perfection, or at least man's fantasy of perfection, over which men laid their own projections of what an "enlightened being" could accomplish.

I wondered what the Buddha would think of all these embellishments and amplifications on his life. He, the empiricist, who so fervently recommended that we base our thoughts, feelings, actions and assumptions only on what we see, smell, hear, taste or touch. I need not wonder. Once, it is told, a householder named

Kevattha, who was an ardent follower of the Buddha, suggested he perform superhuman feats and miracles. In this way, said Kevattha, even more people would come to believe in him. The Buddha replied, "This is not the way I teach *dhamma* . . ."

Let us return to that fateful night, which some sources actually narrow down to a full moon eve sometime in June or July, which began what is also called "the Great Renunciation," the first steps Siddhartha took on his own pilgrimage to becoming the Buddha six years later.

So there he is, a man with everything imaginable in the material world, servants at his beck and call, a beautiful wife who also happens to be with child, and yet he is disillusioned and dissatisfied. On a rare visit outside the palace grounds, he first sees the ravaging effects of what all others knew simply as the facts of life—illness, old age and death—and this affects him deeply. Something else he sees moves him as well: a man dressed in the yellow robe of a monk, probably a wandering renunciant. The man's demeanor and serenity impress Prince Siddhartha, giving him the idea that there is something this man knows that the prince doesn't know that has brought him such peace. Some versions tell us these eyewitness observations occurred on the same day; others say the sightings were over a short period of time. As becomes clear in reading about the life of the Buddha, for the sake of good storytelling time is condensed or given no regard.

The Sanskrit texts tell us that when he returns to the palace, the women of his harem seductively entertain him with dance, song and probably more. Distracted and tired, he ignores them and falls asleep. When he wakes he finds them in various stages of undress, wantonly flailed on the floor around him. They do not make for a pretty picture, as portrayed by Ashvaghosa, a 1st-century historian, in *Buddhacarita* ("The Acts of the Buddha"):

> [They] lay in immodest attitudes, snoring, stretching their limbs, all distorted . . . Others looked ugly, lying unconscious like corpses . . . the fastening knots of their dresses undone . . .

Another lay as if sprawling in intoxication, with her mouth gaping wide, so that the saliva oozed forth, and her limbs spread out so as to show what should have been hid.

This is the final straw. So disgusted is he with this sight—we're told it appears to him as "a charnel ground full of corpses scattered here and there"—that he realizes the inherent impurity and impermanence of the body. The texts tell us he summons his personal groom, Chandaka, who rounds up the prince's horse and they prepare to leave the palace in the quiet of the night. But not before he goes to take a last look at his sleeping wife, Yasodharā, and his newborn son, Rahula (which meaningfully translates to fetter, chain, obstacle or impediment). Biographers and modern Buddhists, especially feminists, have a field day trying to interpret and explain this behavior of the Buddha-to-be. Was he just another unreliable husband and father, callously abandoning his wife who would be left to raise the baby as a single mother? Was he being true to his higher calling? There are, not surprisingly, at least two versions here. One is he peeks in, prefers not to wake them, then leaves. The other is he stays, makes love to her one last time, then leaves. In the end, the result is the same. He answers his karmic call, and Buddhist feminists are left to ponder one more inconsistency of his life.

That night the prince and his groom leave the city of Kapilavastu. By dawn they have reached the banks of the Anoma River, where he shaves his head, takes off his princely jewels, exchanges his clothes for monk's robes and sends Chandaka back to Kapilavastu. Now he has become a bodhisattva, which literally means wisdom being, a seeker of enlightenment who works to aid others to overcome suffering.

From there the ascetic goes south to Rajagriha (modern Rajgir), the capital of the ancient Magadha kingdom, known as a center of spiritual learning, in search of a teacher. While there, he meets the king, Bimbisara, who is impressed by this charismatic new mendicant. After discovering that he had been a prince, the king suggests that he stay with him to share his kingdom. Gautama, however, rejects the king's offer, stating his mission. Bimbisara then requests that if and when Gautama attains enlightenment, he return to Rajagriha again, to which Gautama agrees.

We hear of two teachers, or gurus, from whom the young monk learns practices that he adds to his repertoire. One guru is Álára (or Arada) Káláma, a renowned sage from whom Gautama learns the "sphere of no-thing," a trance state. The other is Uddaka Ramaputta, another great teacher, who teaches him to attain the "sphere of neither-perception-nor-nonperception," a higher state than the sphere of no-thing. Gautama masters both—in fact, so impresses his teachers that they invite him to teach with them—but the bodhisattva wants something more than a trance. So he moves on.

Where exactly and how long are not made clear in the biographies, but it is during this time that he begins the rigorous practices of austerities, depriving himself of food and even air at times. These practices are typical of spiritual traditions popular in that day. The logic was that if their bodies were the gross obstacles to transcendence, then by depriving them the yogis would transcend the base needs of those bodies. If their physical forms were causing the pain, and therefore the suffering, of being human, then if they could up the dosage of pain and survive it, perhaps that was the path beyond. Today we might simplify the theory to "no pain, no gain"—minus the StairMaster. In one of the Buddha's autobiographical discourses (or sutras), the "Mahasaccaka Sutta: The Longer Discourse to Saccaka" from the *Majjhima Nikaya, or the Middle Length Discourses,* he recounts to a monk named Saccaka the details of two such extreme self-deprivations. One is breath control, which consists of clenching his teeth and pressing his tongue to his upper palate to block his respiratory passage. With mouth shut and nose closed, he holds his ears to block the loud noise of air he hears escaping through them. What he gets for his efforts is a really bad headache. Then he tries systematically to reduce his food consumption, finally allowing himself only a few drops of soup a day. In the *Majjhima Nikaya,* he describes its effect on his appearance:

. . . All my limbs became like some withered creepers with knotted joints; my buttocks like a buffalo's hoof; my back-bone protruding like a string of balls; my ribs like rafters of a dilapidated shed; the pupils of my eyes appeared sunk deep in their sockets as water appears shining at the bottom of a deep well; my scalp became shriveled and shrunk as a bitter gourd cut unripe becomes shriveled and shrunk by sun and wind. . . . The skin of my belly came to be cleaving to my back-bone; when I wanted to obey the calls of nature, I fell down on my face then and there; when I stroked my limbs with my hand, hairs rotted at the roots fell away from my body.

As a consequence of these severe bodily austerities, Gautama becomes so weak that he once faints and is believed by some to be dead. He continues in this manner alone, according to some accounts, in the area around Uruvela, near modern Gaya. Then he is joined in this seemingly one-pointed devotion to masochism by five other ascetics, whom he had met earlier with Uddaka Ramaputta. They inhabit a group of caves, the Mahakala Caves, set into the hills that overlook the village and rice fields along the Neranjara River (today it is called the Phalgu or Falgun River).

And then one day, while sitting in meditation, Siddhartha is struck by the realization that self-mortification is getting him no closer—perhaps even further—from his intended goal. And just as suddenly a memory comes back to him, of the first time he experienced a sense of peace and oneness in meditation. It had occurred in his childhood, spontaneously, as he had sat under a rose-apple tree during a seasonal plowing festival. His nurses, who had left him to enjoy the festivities, suddenly realized their duty. Hastening to his side, they were amazed to see him sitting cross-legged absorbed in deep concentration. Effortlessly and instinctively, with a child's innocence, he had attained the one-pointedness of mind known in Hinduism as samadhi, thus reaching the first level of trance called jhāna (ecstasy). His father, King Suddhodana, hearing of this, hurried to the spot and, seeing the child in meditative posture, bowed at his son's feet.

Perhaps, Siddhartha thinks, this wisdom he seeks is innately within us, a part of human nature that we obscure with too much stimulation, whether self-induced pleasure or pain. But he goes a step further, realizing that avoiding the "five prohibitions" believed to obstruct enlightenment (violence, lying, stealing, intoxication and sex) is not enough. Or more precisely, too much of the "nots." What about the positive attitudes that might help cultivate an atmosphere conducive to that state called *nibbana* (or nirvana, enlightenment)? To be helpful, wholesome, skillful, persevering, to develop loving-kindness. To practice these virtuous traits, he surmises, one could "feel within himself a pure joy" similar to that boyhood experience.

With these insights, he bathes and begins to take nourishment and regain his strength. Hearing this, his fellow seekers assume he has given up the pursuit and turn away from him, taking off for caves unknown.

Siddhartha begins to build his body back into shape for what he assumes will be the marathon meditation retreat he will undertake to achieve his target. Here again, time is contracted in the various renditions. It could have taken several weeks or months. Some claim this occurred overnight. Armstrong's version makes more sense. This is what we're told happens:

He "probably started to develop his own special kind of yoga," Armstrong writes. Then he begins to focus on his mind, deconstructing and scrutinizing his every thought. He called this attention to the workings of the mind "mindfulness." In Pali, it's *sati*, derived from the verb *sar*, which means to remember, to recollect—but more. It also means contemplation, reflection, recollection, heedfulness, carefulness, collected attention, awareness and vigilance. The practice of *sati* consists of moment-to-moment mindful contemplation, heedfulness, attentiveness and recollection of all of the activities of the body, all feelings, all thoughts and all objects, sounds, smells and so on.

Now he undertakes what I think of as a precursor to Freud's psychoanalysis. He pays excruciatingly careful attention to his thoughts, but rather than react to any of it, he simply notes it without judgment as the focus of this minute attention rises and then, inevitably, fades away. That's it. There is no hocus-pocus to it, no levitation, no out-of-body experience, no astral travel. There are no parting seas, no bolts of thunder, no booming James Earl Jones voice-over. This nonjudgmental analysis allows him to observe mental phenomena without guilt, without blame, without the desire to change, lament or regret. In this way, he dissects the chain reaction of thoughts, a psychological domino effect that eventually feeds into his theory of "dependent arising." Simplified, it means things, including thoughts, do not happen in a vacuum. Each action is connected to each other action. Similarly, each person—indeed all living things, creatures, plants, mothers-in-law—are interconnected. When you hear people use the word "karma" in casual conversation, whether they know it or not (and most likely they do not) they are actually referring to dependent arising, also called dependent origination. Many years later, physicists defined this same law of nature as cause and effect.

And, he saw, the effect of that cause would not last. All was *anicca*—impermanent. This transitory quality of life was one of the causes of the suffering. This suffering—*dukkha*—was not necessarily the sweat-the-big-stuff sort. It was the daily indignities, disappointments and disillusionments, hang nails, misplaced keys, social slaps, the minute-to-minute ups and downs of one's own emotions between the red light and the green. As he later wrote, "Pain, grief and despair are *dukkha*. Being forced into proximity with what we hate is suffering, being separated from what we love is suffering, not getting what we want is suffering." Clinging to anything—hopes and dreams as well as a craving for a mocha Frappuccino—causes suffering.

As the texts tell it, after some time a local woman named Sujata, seeing the young man washing by the river, offers him a bowl of rice milk. It is, according to the legend, the last meal he will eat for the next 49 days. He walks from the banks of the Neranjara River toward Uruvela (today called Urail). There, he notices "an agreeable plot of land, a pleasant grove, a sparking river with delightful and smooth banks and nearby a village whose inhabitants would feed him," according to the *Majjhima Nikaya* of the Pali Canon. Shortly, he settles under a pipal tree, and chooses a place to sit at its base facing east, ready for a long haul. As he famously vows, "My body may shrivel up, my skin, my bones, my flesh may dissolve, but [I] will not move from this very seat until I have obtained enlightenment."

In one long night, said to be spring, he deals with the final obstacle to his enlightenment, his own ego. If Freud had been couchside that evening, he might have conjectured that he was doing battle with the triple-headed monsters of self: the id (filling one's basic pleasure principle needs), the superego (the moral conscience) and the one that balances the two, the ego (reasoning and problem solving). In this story, they take the form of Māra. In Vedic mythology, Māra is a god of love—though in Sanskrit, the name literally means death. It is the act of love (sex) that brings a person into the world; death terminates a person. Thus, this god of death and love could be interpreted as a symbol for samsara, the birth-death-rebirth cycle that prohibits us from enlightenment (which, among other perks, removes us from that endless cycle). By conquering Māra, the Buddha is in effect conquering samsara.

The Buddhist Māra reviles man, blinds him, guides him toward sensuous desires; once man is in his bondage, Māra is free to destroy him. Māra had already visited the Buddha-to-be several times earlier at turning points in his life. But here Māra makes a last-ditched attempt to woo him back into the world of sensual delights. He tempts him with the promise of power, offering him the kingdom to rule that he had passed up before. He threatens him with arrows. He sends his three daughters—Tanha (desire), Raga (lust) and Arati (aversion)—to seduce him and break his concentration. Māra assaults him with the most fearful beasts he can conjure. Headless trunks, eyeless two-headed monsters without arms, others with many arms, some carrying knives and swords, others breathing fire—they represent the ugliest, darkest sides of human nature that keep us from happiness. Māra then tries to claim that he himself should be the one to attain the divine enlightenment, pointing to his armies behind him as witnesses to his merit. Asked who would testify on his behalf, Siddhartha invokes the earth to bear witness and the earth responds in the affirmative with a resounding roar. He gestures to the ground with his right hand. This hand gesture—or mudra—is called "touching the earth," or *bhumisparsha mudrā*. One of the most famous mudras, it is depicted in many statues and paintings of the Buddha.

None of it works, of course. Steadfastly, Siddhartha stares down these demons—the demons within himself—and keeps his eye on the prize. This rite of passage is reminiscent of the Christian Temptation stories of Jesus, in the Gospels of Matthew and Luke. They too "are legendary," Brother David Steindl-Rast told me. "They were created by the early Christian community to convey some important insights about the life and message of Jesus."

With the temptations of Māra behind him now, the Buddha-to-be passes through several levels of deep trance states. Achieved in "watches" through the night, each level reveals a world of knowledge that informs his philosophy. During the first part of the night, he gains the knowledge of his former existences. During the second, he attains the "superhuman divine eye," the power to see the passing away and rebirth of beings. In the last part of the night, he realizes the Four Noble Truths that are the pillars upon which his dharma ("truth") are built.

Having realized these truths, he utters, "Destroyed is rebirth for me; consumed is my striving; done is what had to be done; I will not be born into another existence!" Or words close to them.

That full moon in the month of Vesakha (May), at the age of 35, the Buddha was born. He had attained the stillness of mind called nirvana. In a state of amazed bliss, he remained under the tree and continued to sit for a week. This spot, most sacred to Buddhists of every sect, is called the *Vajrasana* (meaning "diamond throne"); a stone platform has been erected there. The *Vajrasana* was also sometimes called the Victory Throne of all the Buddhas *(Sabbabuddhanam Jayapallankam)* or the Navel of the Earth *(Pathavin-*

abhi). Still awestruck by his own accomplishment, he spent the next six weeks wandering the grounds that surrounded the tree. He stood at one spot on a rise on the west side of the pipal where, we read, for one week he unblinkingly stared back at the tree under which his enlightenment occurred. This spot came to be known as the "shrine of the steadfast (or unblinking) gaze" *(Animeshlochana Chaitya)*. In the third week, we learn, he walked back and forth in deep meditation; this short path is called the "shrine of the jeweled meditation walkway" *(Cankamana)*. Legend has it that lotus flowers sprang up where he walked. In the fourth week, the Buddha meditated in the jewel house *(Ratanaghara)*, said to have been built for him by the devas. He contemplated on metaphysics *(Abhidhamma)* and developed his philosophy on the laws of cause and effect *(Paticcasamuppada)*. As he meditated, blue, red, yellow, white and orange rays emanated from his body—colors that wave on the Buddhist flag, created in 1880 to mark the revival of Buddhism in then Ceylon and now the banner of the World Buddhist Sangha Council.

In week five, the Buddha meditated under a banyan tree *(Ajapala Nigrodha)*, realizing that good karma, not birth, make a brahmin. We're told he had a conversation with Brahma, the Hindu god of creation. The discourse given here is important, because it shows the Buddha breaking away from the caste system prevalent in that society. "Not by matted hair, by lineage, nor by birth (caste) does one become a Brahman. But the one in whom there abide truth and righteousness, he is pure; he is a Brahman," he says in *The Dhammapada,* the collection of his sayings. The Buddha spent the sixth week in meditation on the southern side of the temple, near Muchhalinda Lake; here, during a severe rain, Muchhalinda, the cobra snake king, covered the body of the Buddha to protect him. The seventh week was spent at the foot of the *Rájáyatana* tree, where he met his first lay disciples, Tapussa and Bhallika, two merchants en route to a business trip.

Today, each of these spots is marked on the Mahabodhi Temple grounds. The origins of the temple itself are veiled in obscurity.

The first edifice honoring the site was believed erected by the Indian King Ashoka (304–232 BCE), who had been one of the country's most ruthless and aggressive conquerors and then gave up his warring ways when he found Buddhism in approximately 250 BCE. As a devotee, Ashoka placed stupas throughout India containing relics of the Buddha and even sent some (along with a sapling from the original Bodhi tree) to Ceylon (now Sri Lanka) with his son Mahinda, in 251 BCE. The two great Chinese Buddhist pilgrims who traveled to India to learn firsthand about this new religion they had heard about, Fa-Hsien in the early 5th century and Huang Tsang in the 7th century, both recorded seeing the temple. The structure would have been much smaller and more modest—akin to a high primitive pyramid—than the 172-foot stone monument we see today covered with ornate carvings. For many, many centuries after Moguls had swept Buddhism from India, the tree and the temple were eliminated from the consciousness of the majority of people, though committed Buddhists continued to make pilgrimage to the most revered site. It wasn't until the mid 19th century that General Alexander Cunningham, working for the British Archeological Survey of India, removed the cover of wild shrubs and vines and reconstructed the remains of what was probably a 5th-century structure.

The pipal, the Bodhi Tree, is not actually the original tree, either. According to Ceylonese chronicles, legend has it that the first was ordered destroyed by Ashoka's wife, who was jealous of her husband's nearly obsessive devotion to it and feared he would leave her, as Siddhartha had left his wife. Dr. Huntington, at Ohio State, who is an amateur botanist, believes the tree was restored by Ashoka himself, while the Ceylonese claim it was grown from a seedling sent from their tree, itself grown from the original. The Indian tree is said to have been destroyed twice after that—once by marauding Shivites in the 7th century, once by a lightning bolt in 1876. The current tree is approximately 135 years old.

The first time I heard of Bodh Gaya was in 1975 from friends in

Cambridge, Massachusetts, who were part of the late 1960s and early 1970s wave of Western pilgrims who'd rediscovered Bodh Gaya yet again. John Bush, known as Krishna when I met him, was among them. He and his then wife, Mirabai, had a small silk-screen cottage industry, producing transparent stick-on images of the Buddha and Tibetan mandalas. They called them Dharma Seals. Sometime around then they created a rainbow Dharma Seal and suddenly the small business became a very big business. Those rainbows graced the rear window of nearly every VW Bug and Bus at the time. John and Yoko put Dharma Seals on every window of their apartment at the Dakota in Manhattan; I recall pointing them out to friends from the corner of Central Park West and 72nd Street in 1976. After selling the company and splitting up with Mirabai, John became a film director and producer.

In the first few years of the 21st century he traveled throughout Southeast Asia with a broadcast-quality Sony digital video camera in hand. His resulting *Yatra Trilogy* is a documentary feature film series that takes viewers on a Buddhist pilgrimage to Laos, Thailand, Burma, Bali, Cambodia, Java and Tibet (*yatra* is the Sanskrit word for sacred journey). Along with shows at such places as the Rubin Museum of Art in New York and film festivals throughout the world, his Tibet film, *Vajra Sky,* toured the United States with His Holiness the 14th Dalai Lama in 2005. When I saw the films, I was astounded by the long, almost painfully slow pans, the patience of his lens. Like no other films I'd seen of those places, they give the feeling of being there—standing on a hilltop at, for example, Borobudur Temple, the 9th-century Buddhist mandala monument in Java, the heat and pungent smells almost palpable, the sounds of birds and flies in your ears, the human accomplishment mystifyingly incomprehensible. When I asked John to recall his memories of Bodh Gaya from 1970, his vivid recollections brought us both back to a time laced with myth and magic. He traces the beginnings of his own life pilgrimage to that time in Bodh Gaya.

"Mira and I had left a commune in British Columbia and then

traveled overland from London to India. I'd wanted to learn Buddhist meditation. In New Delhi we immediately bumped into Sharon Salzberg, who I knew from the State University of New York at Buffalo, where Mira and I had gone to school." (Sharon later went on to help found the first American *vipassana* retreat center, Insight Meditation Society, in Barre, Massachusetts.) "She mentioned a meditation retreat in Bodh Gaya, led for Westerners by a Burmese teacher named Goenka. That sounded like what I wanted to do. We arrived in Bodh Gaya on Christmas Day, 1970. Back then it was a dusty stop on the road in what seemed like the middle of nowhere. Water buffalo and cows in the streets, one government rest house, beggars, flies, a few chai shops [tea houses] with Westerners hanging out at them. We dropped our bags at the Burmese vihara, where the retreat would take place, and walked into town. I looked into one chai shop and I saw Richard Alpert, who I'd seen at Buffalo giving a lecture in the chemistry department." Alpert and Tim Leary, both psychology professors at Harvard in the 1960s, had been dismissed for submitting psychology grad students to experiments with LSD. Alpert later embraced Hinduism and came to be known as Ram Dass, author of *Be Here Now* and one of my personal teachers.

"He was signed up for the Goenka course, too. Right then I knew a new chapter in my life was about to begin. We stayed in Bodh Gaya for a couple of months, did about five 10-day Goenka courses in a row. On the day between courses, we'd gather at chai shops, then walk where the Buddha walked and wandered around the grounds of the Mahabodhi Temple. This became our sacred topography.

"The Buddha was a huge role model," he said, chuckling at his own lack of irony. "Bodh Gaya represented the beginning of my own *yatra,* my sacred journey. It was my first profound experience; it fed my understanding of sacred. It turned me on to a more classical way of understanding who we are as people, as seekers in an archetypal way. My spiritual journey has gone out from there and then."

The description made me realize how much Bodh Gaya had changed in the 35 years between his time there and mine. I could not fathom how desolate it would have been 2,500 years ago, how tranquil and still.

Today, this spiritual epicenter for Buddhists everywhere is more like a spiritual three-ring circus, and it is anything but still. Along with many hundreds of other people, our Buddha Path group circumambulated the Mahabodhi Temple three times, as is the custom with any Buddhist shrine (or stupa). Then we sat in meditation beside the tree. My back flush against the cool base of the temple, I tried to simulate the Buddha's mind-set hoping some of the serenity and happiness he found would rub off on me.

Fat chance.

For about 25 seconds I tried to focus on my breath, to reach down into that place where there is no I. I tried to imagine the quietude the Buddha experienced in this very spot, hearing only the rustle of wind in the leaves, the chirping of birds, his own heartbeat.

But it was impossible. The sensory bombardment could not be ignored. The deep voices of a hundred Tibetan monks, their mesmerizing chanting amplified by tinny speakers assaulting my ears. The pungent smell of cheap incense clinging to the hairs of my nostrils. The sight of saffron-robed monks repeatedly throwing their bodies to mats in front of them in perpetual prostration. The veritable parade circumambulating the temple: wide-eyed American neophytes, stern Japanese Zen priests with their entourage walking gingerly behind, curious Indian Hindus following a bullhorn-wielding tour guide, ebullient Sri Lankans gracefully wrapped in long white attire.

My thoughts turned to my current obsession; isn't there always some obsession to distract us from enlightenment? Shantum had told me he was heartened to see birds and squirrels had returned to the Bodhi Tree. Recently, he explained, it fell victim to a type of

mealybug, which an agricultural expert speculated may have pro-
liferated due to the oils and carbon dioxide that had infected the
bark at the base of the tree where fervent followers place incense
and candles. Shantum and I stood in the shade under the venerated
tree speculating whether the infestation was a result of overzealous
spirituality, an ironic twist at which the Buddha might have
smirked. Was this too the price of the Buddha Boom? Or would it
have happened anyway, a result of the natural arising and falling of
all things, a hypothesis at which the Buddha also might have
smirked?

We agreed that it matters not: Bodh Gaya is no place for intellectual nitpicking. All one can do is surrender to the senses—and
the sense of peace that nonetheless manages to transcend even the
chaos here.

Meanwhile, I wasted my meditative moment under the world's
most hallowed hunk of wood deciding to track down an expert
entomologist at Patna University to get the real scoop. Pulitzer
worthy, I thought; maybe this meditation wasn't wasted after all.

The Mahabodhi Temple is the property of the state government of
Bihar. According to the Bodh Gaya Temple Act of 1949, the state
established the Bodh Gaya Temple Management Committee to
manage, protect and monitor the temple and the 14-acre property
surrounding it. The advisory board consists of the governor of
Bihar and 20 to 25 members, half of them from foreign countries.
Burma, China, Japan, Thailand, Bhutan, Nepal, Vietnam and
Tibet all have temples in the town. The nine-member committee
consists of five Buddhists and four Hindus to make sure the Buddhists can overrule the Hindus in locked voting. Indians are highly
political people, and this does not exclude the management of
spiritual destinations, especially when they are about to become
income-producing tourist destinations as well. The bureaucracy is
also necessary because of the high rate of graft and corruption

here. According to an article in the *Hindustan Times,* police records from 2001 cite Bijar second only to Uttar Pradesh in state crime statistics. In the region of the Buddha's wanderings, now the average citizen must worry about murder, kidnappings, robbery and riots. Records of political graft and corruption are not kept, but the prevailing attitude here is anyone and anything can be bought and sold—whether at gunpoint or gavel point.

Perry Garfinkel

A Tibetan monk sits in reverence at the Mahabodhi Temple, beside the Bodhi Tree in Bodh Gaya, India, most important of the sacred Buddhist pilgrimage sites.

The man whose job it is to be both caretaker of the property and diplomatic liaison among all the various factions was one of the funniest, most wry and intelligent monks I met in my travels—the temple's head monk, Bhikkhu Bodhipala.

"It's difficult to find balance, yes," he giggled. "It's a nice practice for me." He has tried to get the chanting Tibetans to tone down their loudspeakers and the Hindus selling souvenirs to turn down the volumes of their blaring music, with some minor success. "I try to maintain a touch of sanctity here," he said. He wishes there could be more security, to protect the tree and the temple. That's not easy either. "When I locked the gate that surrounds the Bodhi Tree, worshippers who want to leave sweets and light incense and oils protested," he told me. "But I have to explain to them: 'Do you need to get your blessings or do you need the tree to be there and be able to sit in its shade in years to come?' "

Bodhipala was the Buddhist equivalent of Solomon. Just as I was beginning to earn his trust and build up to touchy questions about his reaction to the Indian tourism department's plans for Bodh Gaya, our interview was interrupted when who should show up but HUDCO's Mr. Safaya. He had come to examine firsthand how his proposed bypass roads could actually be implemented—"to see the ground realities," as he put it. Bodhipala suggested I follow him. I jumped into the front seat of one of several cars and joined him and a band of local city authorities for a site inspection. A couple of kilometers out of town we stopped under an arch that welcomed visitors to Bodh Gaya. Out of the cars tumbled a handful of men, like circus clowns squeezed into a Volkswagen. I counted three men in ties, clearly the higher-ups, another six who looked local and six men in green military uniforms carrying rifles. Mr. Safaya and the others walked into a small cluster of shacks just off the road, a makeshift little village that looked like American Depression-era Hoovervilles. As I trotted behind him with my tape recorder, he explained that plans called for a parking lot for tour buses here.

"So what will happen to these people?" I asked, scurrying to keep up.

"Who?" he asked.

"Who?" I repeated indignantly. I could feel my outrage building as Joni Mitchell's line echoed in my head: '*They paved paradise/ And put up a parking lot . . . ooo, la, la, la.*" "All these people living here."

"Oh, them," Mr. Safaya replied matter-of-factly. "They will be relocated somewhere." I figured there was an Indian equivalent to eminent domain. (Later, Bodhipala assuaged my concern—sort of—explaining they were squatters who has no legal right to live there anyway. "Maybe the government will provide low-cost housing for them," he said. "If they could afford low-cost housing, they wouldn't be living in that squalor," I thought.)

We rushed to the other side of town, to an open field where they said the bypass road would be built. The whole objective was to avoid downtown congestion, as he had explained in New Delhi, but now that I saw the reality, I had serious doubts. A lot of local "merchants"—that's anyone who threw out their mats and squatted on the sidewalk selling their trinkets and statues and posters at the entrance to the temple grounds—would not appreciate being relocated from their strategic point-of-purchase locations at the temple gates. Perhaps these sacred selling spots had been passed down from generation to generation. Now, to ease the egress of traffic, they would be robbed of their livelihood. I am sure they could have cared less about "tourism infrastructure."

I had seen this tourism development tug-of-war before—in Baja California, in Hawaii, in Napa Valley. It's the classic double bind of tourism: Developers promise locals that their personal economic lot will improve as they decimate their environment. But the very thing that attracts tourists there ends up being diluted and sterilized by the need to clean it all up to attract tourists.

I am sure that in 10 to 20 years, Bodh Gaya will have less traffic, less noise and less air pollution—and less character—than when John Bush was there and than when I was there. Will it be the better for it? Buddha only knows.

On the day before we left Bodh Gaya, Shantum led our group to the Mahakala caves that Siddhartha sat in—for weeks? months? years?—while he beat up his body before he got to that pipal tree. (In Sanskrit, Mahakala is a fierce deity who protects practitioners during their journey toward enlightenment, a powerful demon who conquered even the greatest gods by means of a special boon from the supreme god Brahma. He had been subdued by the bodhisattvas Manjushri and Avalokiteshvara and subsequently devoted his powers to the service of the dharma.)

We walked across the mostly dry bed of the Neranjara River on a very hot day, then in single file along the footpaths separating paddies of rice that stretched along the hazy horizon. Siddhartha would have walked here, too, probably oblivious to the raw beauty as he fought against hunger, thirst and enjoyment itself. It was hard to accept that this place is virtually unchanged visually, culturally and economically from 2,500 years ago. Having grown up in the suburbs of New Jersey in the late 1950s and '60s, I found the concept unfathomable. I was used to the landscape of new split levels and malls changing every time I rode my Schwinn around the neighborhood.

Walking through this extremely poor agricultural region with this group—the women protecting their pale skin with wide-brimmed hats from Neiman Marcus, the men wielding their Nikon cameras—I could have sworn there was a neon sign hovering over our heads, flashing "Rich Americans here!" We seemed, to me, as conspicuous as a row of Rockettes high-kicking across the rice paddies. I lagged behind the group, as if that might have concealed my affiliation with them, but it was of no use. Indians glonged onto us like flies to water buffalo dung. *"Baksheesh, sahib!"* they whined, aggressively thrusting their hands, palms up, into our faces in that mudra known universally as the sign of street beggars. These Americans had experienced nothing like this and it affected them deeply. Their do-good hearts bled. It made them feel guilty at the disparity between how *much* they had and how *little* these people had. Having traveled in Third World countries— and particularly in India, where the pushiness and persistence of beggars is without parallel—I knew how to put up a wall of seeming indifference, almost hostility, without letting it get to me too much, though that pang of guilt works its way into even the most stone-hearted. By the time we reached the hill that ascended to the caves, some of the women had established practically familial relationships with kids who were relentless in their appeals for money, hair bands, candy, scarves—whatever.

We then reached the two small caves. We sat in a semicircle outside one as Shantum told stories of what transpired here. I sat next to him, tape recorder leaning on my elbow, the better to capture his voice amid the noise of chanting pilgrims around us. I tried to sit there inconspicuously, so as not to draw attention to myself and distract the others from the spiritual experience for which they had paid handsomely. I had already been told that they discussed my participation in their tour. Would they feel inhibited from speaking freely, knowing they might be quoted in the magazine? Would I dominate the situation with my constant questions? It's been my experience that people have approach-avoidance issues with the media. They want the publicity; they don't want the publicity. They want the notoriety, but they don't want to be portrayed in any other way than in a complimentary light. Then, too, if someone is going to get quoted, they want it to be them. It comes down to—surprise, surprise—ego. Only one person came up to me and said that under no circumstances did she want to be interviewed or quoted.

Then, in small groups, we sat inside the cave. Outside there are reminders of modernity: some cement infrastructure, the steps up to the caves, the Tibetan-run temple, tea and souvenir shops nearby. But once inside . . . well, it's one thing to walk in the footsteps of the Buddha, to sit under a tree or by a river, or cross a field where he too had been. But a cave is a confined space with poor (read no) ventilation. It's almost as if you are breathing the same air he breathed. The interior is virtually unchanged from the time he was there. It's not hard to imagine him sitting right next to you— *now!* It took several minutes for my eyes to adjust to the darkness, for my nostrils to ignore the dank smell, to forget the presence of my fellow sojourners. Then, instead of peacefulness, I felt anxiety. I sat there, claustrophobic, antsy to jump out of there—to jump out of my own skin. Why? I was not sure. It was too close for comfort—literally. To walk in his footsteps, okay. But to go through what it took to become the Buddha? Thank you, but *no thank you.* And to think that he did this for hours, days, weeks, months on end. Today, we would institutionalize him. The guy must have been certifiable. To retreat from society for a while is one thing; but to willingly submit to this kind of deprivation and isolation made me wonder if he suffered from some kind of pathology. Just sitting there, I experienced what I would diagnose as "situational insanity," a condition you won't find in the American Psychiatric Association's *Diagnostic and Statistical Manual of Mental Disorders* nor any of the Buddha's sutras.

I suspect this intensity of emotion was shared by others who sat with me in that cave, and I want to believe that's what precipitated the next interaction. Leaving the cave, as we retraced our steps down the hill, one of the men turned to me and said, "You know, you don't have to tape these talks. You can get the same information right out of one of Thich Nhat Hahn's books."

"I don't think *National Geographic* sent me all the way over here just so I could lift some pages from a book," I responded, perhaps with a little too much bite and attitude in my voice. Who was this guy to tell me how to do my job? Could it have been my own insecurity that I didn't know how to do my job?

"Well, excuuuuuse me," he bit back and walked off. "Sorry for trying to help."

"You're excused." I wasn't going to let him have the last word. And there you had it: a typical testosterone-driven male-to-male face-off. Two men who thought they knew more than each other and hesitated not one second in asserting it. It was ugly, and the more so having just come out of a cave where the Buddha-to-be had earnestly tried his darnedest to shed himself of such flawed human behavior. I immediately felt both terrible and indignant about the interaction. This was just the sort of reason I loathed joining these groups: As I said, I have trouble with relationships. And, knowing myself (or pretending to), I was pretty sure I was going to avoid this guy like the plague for the rest of this trip, while at the same time obsess about him to myself for quite some time. It reminded me of an old Buddhist story. The Buddha and a monk were approaching a river and saw a woman washing some clothes along the banks. As they reached her, she asked if they could help her ford the river.

"Ah, we are sorry, kind lady," said the monk. "You know a monk is not allowed to touch a woman."

But the Buddha, having compassion for her, offered to carry her on his back and, lifting her, proceeded to wade across the water. He put her down on the opposite bank. She thanked him profusely, and the two men went on their way. Walking in silence, the Buddha realized the monk was upset.

"What is wrong, brother?" he asked.

"Lord, you know we have taken vows and are not supposed to touch women," said the monk. "How could you?"

"My friend," the Buddha replied, "yes, I did pick her up and carry her across the river. But there I put her down. You, however, are still carrying her."

How long would I carry this bad exchange on my shoulders?

Walking back, I ended up strolling with the lovely but naive woman who seemed in over her head, culturally speaking. Yet she had an elegance and pristine quality that attracted me. I could tell she came from money, and I would have found her innocence somehow charming if it hadn't been so sad that someone could still live such a cloistered life in the United States (who was being naive now?). We walked through a village that may have been the actual Uruvela of the Buddha's time; if not, for sure it was exactly like the one Siddhartha would have passed to get from the caves to the river. Thatched roofs, water buffalo, women thrashing wheat by hand, stacks of dung to be used for heat and building material, snot-nosed kids running amok—the same set, the same props, the same players since 500 years before the birth of Jesus, the plots of their lives unchanged and unchanging for millennia, and for millennia to come.

"Isn't this quaint?" said my walking companion. "Look how ingenious they are!" To her it was like we were visiting those living-history museums of early American life: 17th-century Plimoth Plantation in Massachusetts or the restored 18th-century village in Williamsburg, Virginia.

Half of me wanted to shake her out of her cushy American coma. The other half wanted to be her, to be that oblivious to the harsh realities of the Third World. As we stood at the edge of the village, we realized we had lost sight of the others; either we had walked ahead of or fallen behind the rest of the group. In the distance, I could see my antagonist from before approaching us, probably also lost. But I did not wait to find out. I walked right past him, with as much indifference to him as my body language could speak.

That evening, after dinner back at the temple where we stayed, Shantum convened what he called "strucks," during which participants shared one experience during the day that struck them in any way. That night, the majority of people talked about their reaction to the beggars—the guilt, the pathos, the blah-blah-blah. Frankly, I was bored by their preoccupation, and it fed my sense that I was with the wrong group. Why weren't they talking about Buddhism, the Buddha, the Mahabodhi Temple, *enlightenment?* Why were they letting themselves be distracted by a situation they could do nothing about, that had not changed since the time of the Buddha and would not change by the time of the next Buddha? As they talked, I stole sideways glances at my nemesis to see if he was catching sideways glances at me. Either he was too cool or the whole interaction had floated off his back unnoticed. If the latter, that irked me even more.

When it came to my struck, I felt my pulse beat faster and the blood rush to my face. "I have something I want to share . . . ," I began, careful now *not* to catch the gentleman's eye, "that I'm not proud of." I stopped to collect my thoughts, and to give my announcement dramatic impetus.

To my own amazement, I outed myself, recounting the day's noxious incident and confessing that it had left me in a state of personal conflict for the rest of that day. Now looking straight at him, I took responsibility for what happened and apologized to him in front of everyone. I immediately felt a great burden lift from my shoulders and a cloud pass from over my head. I had freed myself from my own imprisonment simply by bringing the truth of my petty preoccupation to light.

From then on, the group took me in. I had earned their trust by admitting my flaw, my humanness. Though it did not necessarily bring this man and me closer (that was not really my intention), it brought me closer to me. And it assuaged my own guilt at being such a rude donkey's rear end.

Something else happened that night that bode well for me, both professionally and personally. Toward the end of that evening, Shantum checked his cell phone messages and said, loud enough for all to hear, that I had gotten a message from my literary agent in San Francisco. I suppose I had given her some contact information in case there was any news on my proposal circulating to publishers for a book based on my *Geographic* assignment. It sounded so impressive: "Perry, your agent rang and wants you to call her." Not only did I have an agent, but also she'd tracked me down in the middle of India. I went to a local international phone booth on the dark streets of Bodh Gaya and placed a call to her. She told me there was a good offer, good enough to elevate me to cloud nine. Only later did it dawn on me that this momentous turning point in my life occurred in the town of the Buddha's enlightenment. A more auspicious place could not have been chosen to receive the news of my redemption from the literary abyss.

❧

After the Buddha attained enlightenment, he faced a dilemma few of us will ever have to confront. He could luxuriate in his One-ness, savor the bliss of nonattachment, without a care in the world—in the truest sense. Or he could go out and teach others how to get there, too. In your own life, the comparison would be that once you reached a goal—the promotion, the wedding band, the house in the country, the retirement party—you have "arrived," as the saying goes. There would be nowhere else to go, no one else to be. So why do anything else? Just wallow in your Such-ness and your gin and tonic.

Indeed, the Buddha considered "checking out." He could have lived up to one of his names, Tathagata, which means "thus gone." Furthermore, he lamented that his Truths were much too compli-cated to teach and much too difficult to follow. But in his first act of selflessness—and the one people in the engaged Buddhism movement point to as the very first example and the model they follow—he decided to accept the challenge and responsibility to pass on what he had figured out. He chose to give back to society.

The first five students, he decided, would be the renunciants who had abandoned him at the Mahakala caves. He found them in Sarnath, where many seekers often gathered near Benares (now Varanasi), the Hindu holy city along the Ganges. Their first re-sponse was to rebuke him, but upon listening they immediately could tell he had reached the goal they all had sought. There, in a park where deer roamed on an open, grassy meadow, he gave his first sermon, elaborating on the Four Noble Truths, the Eightfold Path and the Middle Way. His initial discourse, in Deer Park, is called "Setting in Motion the Wheel of the Dharma," or *Dharma-cakrapravartana Sutra*. The monks, later known as "the Fortunate

Five," listened intently to his explanation and, it is said, attained instant enlightenment, so powerful and penetrating was the Buddha's message. They became his first disciples. We hear stories over the next months of similar encounters and similar realizations upon hearing the Buddha's talks. Very quickly he had a following of thousands. And thus his career as an educator began and continued right up to the moment of his death.

In the recounting of his life, a curious thing occurs that confounds the Buddha's biographers. "Even though the last 45 years of his life were passed in the public eye, the texts treat this long and important phase rather perfunctorily, leaving the biographer little to work with," writes Karen Armstrong in *Buddha*. "The Buddhist scriptures record the Buddha's sermons and describe the first five years of his teaching career in some detail, but after that the Buddha fades from view and the last 20 years of his life are almost entirely unrecorded." Even in the first teaching years, she continues, "the texts tell us nothing about the Buddha's thoughts and feelings, but use his activities to show how the early Buddhists related to the urban, commercial, political and religious world of north India."

This seems appropriate. The Buddha had become an archetype, a blank slate on which future generations could paint the portrait of perfection according to their needs. He himself was never the object; his teachings were. As a result, we are left with little sense of his personality; he had no "self" anyway.

Shantum took us to Sarnath, where we toured a local museum. We sat in the park. We even saw deer. We circled the giant stupa where it is believed he gave that first dharma talk. From there, over the next days we also traveled to the place of his death at Kushinagar, and of his birth in Lumbini, across the border into Nepal. But, as with the Buddha's life after his enlightenment and the first years of his teaching, I, too, must admit that my memories of those travel days with the tour group faded. Even as I later listened to tapes of that period, I had trouble inserting myself into the experience.

This was quite odd for me, because I am quite like a camel who, over the years as a journalist, has mastered the art of storing impressions and the sense of "being there," later to call upon them when necessary—that is, on deadline. It was as though his enlightenment and the turning of the wheel were the climax; the rest was interesting but less compelling to me. I had gotten my "story"—a few good quotes, anecdotes and encounters—and, typical journalist with the attention span of a tsetse fly, I was ready to move on to the next experience.

The Reclining Buddha statue in Kushinagar, India, where the Buddha passed away, achieving the ultimate nirvana, Mahaparinibbana.

If not a changed man, I had, however, changed my opinion on one count. I had joined Shantum's group reluctantly, as I said, thinking that I could have or should have done it alone. A tour group had nothing to do with engaged Buddhism, as I had defined it. But I realized that even at this early stage of my travels my definition would have to be a little more fluid than I had planned. I recognized that these Americans had been engaged in a

Buddhist educational process that changed them. I could see them change in front of me already. They would go home and talk to friends and family about their experiences, and those people would be engaged, and they, too, would change, if only subtlety. There would be a chain reaction of change that would—or could—ripple through the small societies they inhabited. And on it would go. When I got back to the States many months later, I stayed in touch with the woman I had thought too naive for my taste. She turned out to be so much more substantial than I initially gave her credit for; I could tell she was struggling to adjust to her comfortable life, to come to terms with the separation between what she had and what others had so much less of. She tried to hold on to the meditation practice and to the Buddha's teachings in a culture that gave her little reinforcement to do so. I wondered how things would turn out for her now that she had been engaged. What I did know was that life as she had known it would never be the same again.

"Jai Bhim," a voice called to me from across the airport terminal upon my arrival at Nagpur, a city of 2.1 million people in the geographic center of India.

"It means 'Victory to our great leader, Bhim Ambedkar'—a way of greeting by our people," explained Dr. S. K. Gajbhiye, a lecturer in the Department of Dr. Ambedkar Thought at Nagpur University, as a welcoming committee laid a garland of marigolds around my neck and my fixer's, a slight but strong and unbelievably competant woman named Neha Diddee, from Bangalore. "Our people" are the millions of former Hindu untouchables in India who have converted to Buddhism since 1956.

If the epicenter of Buddhism for followers from around the world is Bodh Gaya, then Nagpur is the epicenter for a new Buddhist movement based on social equality and a rejection of the country's oppressive caste system.

The term "engaged Buddhism" had not been coined in 1936 when Dr. Bhim Rao Ambedkar—a social psychologist, political activist, Gandhi colleague and architect of the Republic of India's constitution—wrote his famous treatise, *Annihilation of Caste*. Yet his efforts would certainly fit my definition. In effect, he used Buddhism not so much as a spiritual vehicle to attain enlightenment but as an instrument of social change to attain independence and self-worth. That terse 1936 manifesto condemned Hinduism for basically institutionalizing class-based oppression 2,000 years ago with the Laws of Manu, a document written by Hinduism's highest priests that established the hierarchy: Brahmans at the top, the *achuta* (meaning "untouchables") below the bottom.

Dr. Ambedkar spent most of his life fighting for the rights and humanity of the people variously called depressed classes, scheduled castes, outcastes, Harijans ("children of God"), untouchables and, now, Dalits ("broken," "oppressed"). Realizing that the obstacles to alleviating their suffering were deeply entrenched Hindu beliefs now tightly woven into India's social fabric, thereby assuring untouchables subsubservient status, he decided to convert to Buddhism, a belief system that presupposes, like the American Declaration of Independence, that "all men are created equal."

On October 14, 1956, less than two months before his death, he orchestrated a mass conversion of an estimated 500,000 Dalits to Buddhism in Nagpur. Dr. Ambedkar had said he chose this city because the Naga people, after whom the city is named, were once staunch Buddhists who for a time successfully fended off wave after wave of Aryan aggressors opposed to Buddhism, but, in the end, succumbed.

Of the 22 vows they took that day, nine commit them to a complete renunciation of Hindu gods, Hindu rituals, Hindu beliefs— "to denounce Hindu religion which is harmful for my development as a human being and which has treated human beings as unequal and lowly." Instead they swore to accept the Buddha's Dhamma.

Some call them Ambedkar Buddhists, or New Buddhists. I call them Buddhists. Today, there are an estimated 6 million of them.

There would undoubtedly be more, but with Ambedkar's death, and without a charismatic leader to fill the vacuum, the movement is factionalized, and the wave he touched off that could have grown into a tsunami of anti-untouchable sentiment has become a small ripple in relation to India's vast population.

Those I met here made up in enthusiasm for any lack of numbers. I had met several young men of the same background in New Delhi several days earlier. They were all bright-eyed men in their early and mid-20s. Several were students at the Indian Institute of Technology, the now-world-famous IIT, from which India's best and brightest techies are reproduced like so many chipboards. They call themselves "digital Dalits." When I asked one very serious 24-year-old what he hoped to become after completing his studies, without a second of hesitation he replied emphatically with a single word: "Technocrat." A Buddhist technocrat? It sounded like an oxymoron, but then again, I thought, maybe a corporate raider with a Buddhist foundation could turn "hostile takeover" into an oxymoron.

Though a bit timid, still growing accustomed to the fresh taste of freedom and their first feel of enfranchisement, all the converted Buddhists I met radiated a contagious joy and happiness. Why not? They were rising from the lowest class to a humble but emerging middle-class existence. And all were ferociously fervent about their cause and their hero. In Nagpur, my welcoming party was giddy that I was going to write about them and that word of their movement would be published so widely outside of India.

A man with an energetic bounce in his step and a quick smile, Dr. Gajbhiye was born several months before the mass conversion, but he and his generation are its beneficiaries. After earning his PhD, he worked in the business sector for 10 years. On the tiny plot of land where he grew up with his parents in a hut made from materials salvaged from the dumps, he has built a concrete home, extremely modest by American standards but a castle in his family's eyes. By the time my new friend Gajbhiye was earning what he boasted was four figures a month (equivalent to about $100), he decided it was time to give back to his community and turned to teaching. An itinerant entrepreneur, he also owns a retail shop so chockablock with Ambedkar memorabilia—books, watches, banners, statues, portraits that flicker between him and the Buddha— I could hardly turn around once inside. I told him it was his "Ambedkar tchotchkes shop," translating the Yiddish word (which means trinkets and other little ornaments), but my brave attempt to bridge that cultural/linguistic divide was in vain.

"Every year on October 14, now celebrated as our Independence Day, hundreds of thousands of converted Dalits come to Nagpur—I do a very good business then," he beamed. At Dr. Gajbhiye's home, as at others I visited in Nagpur, Dr. Ambedkar's image is on the walls, on their prayer tables, everywhere. Usually pictured in a smart blue business suit, a copy of the constitution under his arm, with his thick black glasses almost obscuring a roundish stern face, his visage is more prominent, in fact, than that of the Buddha.

"There are more than three hundred statues of Dr. A in Nagpur," Dr. Gajbhiye proudly told me as we drove around the city to meet a number of people in his community. One was a woman who cried with joy as she recalled the day she attended the conversion half a century ago. I met another woman in her 80s who also attended the conversion. "I was speechless and spellbound," she said at witnessing the largest gathering of people she had ever seen in one place. After 10 years of study, this woman made the full commitment to become a Buddhist nun.

"My parents used to say, 'Do you think eating once a day you will find God?' " she told me through Neha. "They called me crazy, but I was not bothered."

At her monastery in a run-down section of Nagpur, she teaches the Buddha's *Dhamma* mostly to women Dalits, who in India would probably be perceived as the underclass of an underclass.

"We explain to women in simple language they can understand that this is the time, this is *their* time, to be equal to men," she said. "Buddha's teachings are for women as well as for men. Sometimes the senior male monks try to contradict that, but I am confident Buddha meant it that way."

"What about you?" I asked. "What enabled you to hoist yourself out of where you came from, to overcome so many obstacles?"

The question stopped her, but not because she did not have an answer. "No one has asked me that before," she smiled. Her face grew solemn and memories of oppression darkened her eyes. "Meditation," she said simply. "I got strength from sitting."

From there we made our way to Deeksha Bhoomi ("conversion ground"), the grounds where the conversion took place. In the center of a large barren field, now considered a sacred pilgrimage

The author with a group of New, or Ambedkar, Buddhists at Deeksha Bhoomi ("conversion ground") in Nagpur, India. This giant modern stupa is on the site where Dr. B. R. Ambedkar converted half a million untouchable Hindus to Buddhism in 1956.

site to these Dalits, stands a monstrously large, modern circular edifice that took 20 years and an estimated 50 million rupees to build (US$1.1 million). I had read that it's the largest stupa in India. Dedicated in 2002, made of granite, marble and sandstone, its dome is 120 feet in height and diameter. Five thousand worshippers can sit in meditation on each of the two stories. Inside an ornate box on the domed third floor, in a room so large my echo reverberated for a full 30 seconds, are the ash remains of Dr. Ambedkar.

Yet another bubbly group met me at Deeksha Bhoomi, and they invited me to meditate and chant the Buddha's Three Jewels with them inside the temple. As we sat cross-legged, my wandering eye caught sight of a woman worker dressed in a shabby sari, squatting in that way Asians can with such ease, her butt almost touching the floor, swooshing a straw broom back and forth as she moved across the floor at the foot of a giant Buddha statue in the center of the cavernous hall. She did her work and kept to herself as people brushed past her, never acknowledging her or making eye contact, rendering her almost invisible. Even in a Buddhist-inspired social revolution, I thought, some would be left behind. Even among this class, there is a lower class.

As we left, they bowed and wished us *"Jai Bhim"* again. Neha, by habit, said, *"Namaste,"* back to them, which is the Hindu salutation, meaning something close to "I salute the God within you." Dr. Gajbhiye and his friends reminded Neha that that address reinforced entrenched Hindu values, which they wanted no part of now, not even as a kindly gesture. Neha, a truly gentle soul, responded indignantly, pointing out that Ambedkar might be their leader, but he was not hers, so why should she "jai" him? " *'Namaste'* is a universal greeting in India," she said. They agreed to disagree as we got into the van. It was the one tense moment of the Nagpur trip, but it showed us both how dearly they held on to their belief, and it made me realize how much more work there might be to do to "convert" Hindus so that they would accept these Ambedkar Buddhists on their terms and vice versa.

Several days later in Mumbai, I met another converted Dalit who also reminded me of the class difference even within the class. The life of Dr. Narendra Jadhav is so beyond the wildest dreams of most Dalits that, while he must be an inspiration to many, he invokes jealousy and some disdain from others. A principal adviser in the Department of Economic Analysis and Policy for the Reserve Bank of India, he lives with his wife in a large apartment in a section of Mumbai he himself described as "tony." Tall and erudite, sporting a scholarly tightly cropped graying beard, he is best known to Indians as the author of two successful and controversial books about being a Dalit, *Our Father and Us,* published in 1993, and *Outcaste,* published in India in 2003 and in the United States in 2005 under the title *Untouchables.*

He was not short on self-confidence, and over breakfast at his apartment he retold the story that begins with his father, living in a former municipal labor camp that I had visited coincidentally earlier that day. It remains as it had been in his father's time: rows of wooden barracks, each domicile consisting of one small front room and a tiny kitchen area. Common toilet facilities were behind each barrack. "It was absolute poverty," said Dr. Jadhav. "Before that, my father had slept in rail stations.

"I still carry a chip on my shoulder," he confided. "Not only

Admiring Dr. Narendra Jadhav's awards at his apartment in Mumbai. Born to a poor untouchable family that converted to Buddhism, he is now a principal adviser for the Reserve Bank of India and author of the autobiographical Untouchables.

were others looking down on us for hundreds of years but we ourselves were looking down on ourselves."

His wife prepared our meal in the kitchen. I implored her to sit and join the conversation, but she declined.

"To me," he continued, "conversion means the right to live like a human being—conversion gave us that opportunity. As far as Buddhist practice goes, this is the most important thing I have to tell you: The significance of religion to me doesn't lie in the rituals we follow—it's the change in mind-set."

He gave me an example that hit home. "Before conversion Dalit children were given names like *Dagdoo* and *Kacharu*," he said, giving the Hindi names. "Do you know what they mean? Stone. Dirt. I mean literally—*stone, dirt*." He practically spit the words out. "Now we give them names like *Siddharth,* which means 'one who reached fulfillment,' and *Pradnya,* which means 'intellect,' and *Neha,* which means 'love.' "

I knew well the significance of children's names, and the impact they can have. Iris and I chose the name Ariana for our daughter in 1976 because we liked the association with the mythological Greek princess Ariadne, meaning "very holy one," and "most holy" in Old English. And, indeed, Ariana has lived up to her name to those who know and love her.

For the Dalits, I understood that the new nomenclature spoke volumes about a new self-esteem that Dr. Jadhav and every other converted Dalit attribute to that other Siddharth and to Dr. Ambedkar, their own Siddharth.

There was one 24-hour period in India during which I witnessed the almost breathtaking adaptability of *vipassana,* a meditation technique practiced in the Theradava tradition of Buddhism and the one I have practiced since the mid-1970s.

The day began in New Delhi—in jail.

"I'm not doing time, I'm doing *vipassana,*" a prisoner named Hyginus Udegbe told me.

Having waited four and a half years for his case to be heard on charges of cocaine possession, he remains at the Tihar jail complex in New Delhi. With almost 13,000 inmates, more than twice its capacity, Tihar is perhaps the largest prison in Asia. To the overcrowded conditions, add inadequate sanitation and a staff that previously had been trained to oppress, deprive, physically punish, isolate and dehumanize prisoners—in short, to make it their living incarcerated hell.

But for Hyginus and thousands of others in jails throughout India, "doing" *vipassana* meditation has transformed prison if not exactly into paradise, then at least into an oasis for self-reflection and rehabilitation.

The first silent *vipassana* 10-day retreat took place at Tihar in 1993. Along with 96 prisoners, 23 jail staff also participated. It proved so beneficial—for both inmates and jailers—that one section of Jail No. 4 was cordoned off as a permanent retreat site. Now two 10-day courses are offered every month. Prisoners can repeat retreats every three months, and many do. In prisons around the world run by enlightened administrators, Buddhist meditation groups now meet regularly. In practicing Buddhist techniques, studies conducted by a professor at the Indian Institute of Technology show prisoners ease their own suffering and, upon release, inflict less suffering on others. Now *vipassana* is taught not just in jails, but also in schools, in government agencies and police departments, as well as among a wide cross section of individuals throughout India.

A barrel-chested six-footer with a scruffy beard, bald pate and a formidable brow that canopied his eyes, the Nigerian looked more like the American boxer Joe Frazier than the meditating type. Surrounded by prison officials and curious inmates and guards, we talked in front of a high wall; on it was painted a yellow wheel, the traditional symbol for the Buddha's teachings, the Wheel of Dhamma.

"I had high blood pressure and couldn't sleep," Hyginus said. "After my first ten-day retreat here, my pressure dropped and I could sleep ten hours. I saw immediate emotional changes, too. I used to have quick temper. I used to react—be so aggressive. Now I feel like a dove, very peaceful. I am so much happier.

"My case is not progressing," he went on, eager to share his experience, "but I am much more detached. It's the craving that causes miseries. This is what we learn. I actually feel blessed to be

Interviewing Hyginus Udegbe, a Nigerian incarcerated at Tihar Jail in New Delhi, where he has done several vipassana retreats in the permanent retreat center within the walls of one of Asia's largest and most crowded prisons.

at Tihar. Otherwise, I would never have learned about *vipassana*."

As impressed as I was speaking with several inmates who gave moving testimonials of personal transformation, I was more struck by a conversation with a 38-year-old Tihar prison officer of 14 years. He had been through three 10-day retreats here, all voluntarily.

"I just wanted to experience for myself this thing I had heard about, *vipassana*," he told me as we sat in an office within the retreat complex. "Before the course I was a very angry person. I used to beat the prisoners without much pushing. I felt so much stress it turned me into a monster. After the course, I felt more for the prisoners, a connection with them. I felt more human."

Now, he said, prisoners come to him for personal counseling. "Before I thought of prison as a penal institute. Now the concept has changed—it's a reformation ashram," he added, using the Hindi word for spiritual center.

"We are all prisoners—of our minds," said Satya Narayan Goenka, an 80-year-old Burmese businessman turned meditation teacher who has spearheaded the *vipassana* renaissance in India. This was several days later, when I had flown to Mumbai to meet him at his home. "So where better to recognize this than behind bars?"

"But I am not teaching Buddhism," he told me emphatically. He is a big but graceful man, with a booming bass voice. "I am not interested in converting people from one organized religion to another organized religion. I am interested in converting people from misery to happiness, from bondage to liberation, from cruelty to compassion. I don't call myself a Buddhist, but I am a staunch follower of Buddha's teachings."

The words could have been spoken by the Buddha himself. Goenka wanted to impress on me that he was not a religious proselytizer; rather, he was promoting Buddhism's end goal, the cessation of suffering.

"There's no mystery to it," he continued with a chuckle, his big belly shaking. "*Vipassana* means 'to see things as they really are.' After watching your breath for several days, you begin to pay close attention to your sensations. You realize very quickly that you are obsessed with cravings—food, warmth, all sorts of desires—as well as aversion to unpleasant things. Then you realize the impermanence of it all. Everything changes. The pain in the knee moves to the neck. One obsession replaces another, and another."

With that, he held his thick hands by his sides and made a gesture of a sinking feeling deep in his belly: "Impermanence," he bellowed. "Impermanence, impermanence." His hands sunk

Interviewing Satya Narayan Goenka, a former Burmese businessman turned meditation teacher, at his home in Mumbai. Through his efforts, vipassana *is now taught in Indian schools, government departments and jails.*

deeper with each repetition, as if to emphasize how penetrating this understanding needs to be internalized deep in one's gut. I remembered that gesture for a long time after I had forgotten much of what he said. "From these simple understandings—all empirically discovered by each person, starting with Buddha himself—an entire doctrine eventually unfolds."

Back in New Delhi, however, there was still time for one or two more visits before catching that plane for Mumbai later in the afternoon. Still following the trail of Goenka's *vipassana* movement, I crossed New Delhi to a suburban neighborhood. There, at the DLF Public School (actually a private school), I watched young, upwardly mobile 12- to 15-year-old students, all in their well-pressed blue school uniforms, fill a large hall, boys on one side, girls on the other. They sat on the floor cross-legged, facing a stage up front. On the stage, the presenter set up a tape recorder hooked up to a loudspeaker. Listening to a fuzzy tape through rumbling speakers, they giggled when they first heard a low bass voice. It was Goenka on a tape, guiding them through a simple meditation session. They tried to still their fidgety minds, their fidgety bodies belying their best efforts.

As I watched, I imagined myself at that age. If my mind seems like a wild monkey now, at 12 it was like the proverbial barrel full of them. The students tried to concentrate for 10 to 15 minutes at a stretch. It must have felt like hours to them. Between the sittings, they were directed to work on an arts-and-crafts project. The woman leading the session distributed popular magazines among the audience, then asked them to cut out pictures of people who looked happy and glue them to colored paper in collages. The kids gathered in small groups of four or five, happy to be doing anything rather than trying to do nothing. I scurried around, shoving my tape recorder in some of their faces, asking how they liked the meditation practice and how they thought it will be useful to them. One bright-eyed boy typified what I imagined was the overriding impression. He offered that this would help him achieve his goal: not enlightenment but acceptance to the Indian Institute of Technology. "I suppose it could help me focus better with my studies," he said as his classmates nodded in agreement. "That is very important to me to get good grades so I can get into a good university."

I left the school at first thinking that the real purpose of Buddhism was being lost here, that these kids saw it only as a means to move ahead, to keep up with the competitive rat race that Indian life was turning into. Later I rethought my position. A little bit of *Dhamma* is better than no *Dhamma* at all, right? Who cares what the motive is? Focus? Fine. It's better than Ritalin. Just give them a taste; if they like the taste, they will be back for more. Eventually, the *Dhamma* would catch up to them, even through this back-door approach, and hopefully before they became raving Type A workaholics. The idea that this methodology was infiltrating the schools, along with the prisons, seemed a surprising but good example of educationally engaged Buddhism. I would see other examples in educational institutions in other parts of the world, some of them equally surprising.

I dashed to the airport and flew to Mumbai to interview Goenka. Then, thanks to the friend of a friend, who had given me their names, I went to visit a wealthy couple who I was told were close students of Goenka. They had agreed to let me interview them and also offered to put me up for the night at their luxurious home. I was more excited about the latter than the former, addicted as I am to creature comforts, the more comfortable the better, especially in India.

My hosts were a congenial couple in their mid-60s, the Patels, a name as familiar in India as Smith in the United States. Rohit is a retired international construction engineer; his wife, Charu, is a gentle and thoughtful woman whom I immediately recognized as a fellow pilgrim asking those same compelling questions that itched me and the Buddha. Their home was in a neighborhood of Mumbai where Bollywood executives and stars live. We sat in the open-air patio, the marble floor so smooth and clean you could eat off it.

Rohit told me the *vipassana* practice had helped ease his incessant headaches. Charu seemed more intent on seeing how *vipassana* could bring her closer to understanding herself and the vast universe just over that high fence surrounding their home.

"*Vipassana* doesn't go far enough, though," she said. "How long can you just watch your breath?" She confided that she was losing confidence that the simple meditation practice could go deep enough or help her find answers.

Meanwhile, at a lull in the conversation, Rohit conspiratorially signaled me to follow him into the house. He led me to a shelf set into the wall, jammed with candles and incense and statues and colorful paintings. To Hindus, it's called a *puja*, or worship area. "You see," he said, "these are the gods we pray to." He pointed out his Ganesh, the elephant god, and other deities of Hinduism, along with the garland-framed photos of his guru.

Once a Hindu, always a Hindu, I figured. I had begun to think of them in the same company as a certain Beverly Hills psychologist I knew, who had taken up the latest spiritual fad because she'd heard about it around the pool at the Polo Lounge. But Charu's conundrum touched me. She was such an earnest seeker, but under it all she was dissatisfied. Despite the considerable material wealth she possessed, she was spiritually impoverished.

To Rohit, a 10-day *vipassana* retreat was an easier pill to swallow than an Advil. To Charu, it was less embarrassing than admitting to seeing a psychotherapist. I saw their involvement as Buddhism Lite in the land where Buddhism Heavy was invented. Nonetheless, I enjoyed an evening of convivial conversation over dinner served in their expansive dining room by a bevy of kitchen staff. Then I retired to an air-conditioned room, a bed protected by tight mosquito netting, a glass of Courvoisier and *The Dhammapada: Sayings of the Buddha* beside me.

The next morning I graciously thanked them and moved directly from the alpha to the omega of *vipassana* in terms of economic disparity. I went to one of Mumbai's most impoverished sections, the barracks I mentioned earlier that were once the railroad's municipal labor camps where Dr. Jadhav said his father had lived. My escort, a *vipassana* teacher assigned by Goenka's contingent, introduced me to a segment of society at the other end of the economic spectrum practicing the technique. But this low? I stooped into dark enclosures where families of six or more shared one room and a kitchen my mother would not have wanted to see, much less cook in. One particular family reached deep into my heart, which I thought had now already grown callous to such encounters. The wife recounted how her alcoholic, abusive, jobless husband—a man who disappeared for days on end—had gone to a 10-day meditation retreat and came back clean, sober and loving, much to her and their children's joy. He had a job now, and she felt ever so grateful.

The side of me that always thinks a little more is a little better asked, "So now that you feel your family life is a little more stable, with a little money coming in, is there something you'd like that would make your life a little easier?"

She looked at me quizzically, as though I had just suggested a more suitable mode of transportation to chauffeur her to the local market might be a stretch SUV.

"I have everything I want—I have my family, I have my Buddha," she smiled through tears, though I couldn't tell where hers ended and mine began.

five

Still Shedding
the Tears

Sri Lanka Before and After the Tsunami

Those who are suffering from some form of insanity cling to their own phantom Ego, and those who have an exaggerated idea of their own Egos are partially insane. Nirvana is for the sober scientific analytical student, who discarding all forms of theological metaphysics, priestly ceremonies and nihilistic ideas, exerts strenuously to lead an active life avoiding evil, doing good and purifying the heart.

—ANAGARIKA DHARMAPALA FROM "AN INTRODUCTION TO BUDDHISM,"
IN THE *Maha Bodhi Journal*, VOL. 15, JUNE 1907

All tremble at violence; all fear death. Seeing others as being like yourself, do not kill or cause others to kill.

—THE BUDDHA, *The Dhammapada*

Buddhism spread from India by two routes. To the south, seafarers and fishermen brought it to Burma and Thailand, then through Southeast Asia and into southern China. To the north, merchants carried word of it first to Gandhara in the northwest of India from the 2nd to 4th centuries BCE, then east across the northern Himalaya foothills and along the Silk Road into the heart of China over the centuries that followed.

But before all that, the seed of Buddhism was transplanted first to the country known then as Lanka ("resplendent land" in Sanskrit), later Ceylon (in the Sanskrit literature of India, it was sometimes referred to as Simhaladipa, "Island of Lions," or simply Simhala, from which the English adaptation Ceylon is derived). In 251 BCE King Ashoka, the Mauryan emperor who converted to Buddhism after a career as one of India's bloodiest rulers, sent his son Mahinda there as a missionary, according to 4th- and 5th-century monastic records called the *Dipavamsa* ("Chronicle of the Island") and the *Mahavamsa* ("Great Chronicle"). This makes the island country now known as Sri Lanka (nickname, "the fallen tear") home of the world's oldest continuing Buddhist community.

I choose to travel next from India to Sri Lanka to follow Buddhism's actual chronological migration; as well, there was a compelling contemporary example of engaged Buddhism I was eager to see.

Sri Lanka's importance to the history of Buddhism cannot be overstated. When King Devanampiya Tissa (250–c. 207 BCE) accepted the Buddha's Truth, he became a powerful patron of Buddhism and established the monastery of Mahavihara, which became the historic center of Theravada Buddhism in Sri Lanka. Subsequent events also contributed to Sri Lanka's prestige in the Buddhist world. It was on the island country, for example, that the Tripitaka—the oral teachings of the Buddha—were committed to writing for the first time. Devanampiya Tissa was said to have received the Buddha's right collarbone and his revered alms bowl from King Ashoka and build the Thuparama Dagoba, the first Buddhist stupa in Sri Lanka, to honor these highly revered relics. Another sacred relic, the Buddha's tooth, or *Dalada,* had arrived in Sri Lanka in the 4th century CE. The possession of the *Dalada* came to be regarded as essential for the legitimization of Sinhalese royalty and remained so until its capture and possible destruction by the Portuguese in 1560. The relic (thought by many to be a substitute) venerated in the Temple of the Tooth, Dalada Maligawa, in Kandy, links legendary Lanka to the modern era. The annual procession of Perahera, held in honor of the iconic incisor, serves as a powerful unifying force for the Sinhalese in the 20th century. Ashoka's daughter, Sanghamitta, is recorded bringing to the island a branch of the sacred Bodhi Tree from Bodh Gaya, India. According to legend, the tree that grew from this branch is near the ruins of the ancient city of Anuradhapura in the north of Sri Lanka. The tree is said to be the oldest living thing in the world, an object of great veneration to all Buddhists.

The connection among religion, culture, language and education and their combined influence on national identity has been a pervasive force for Sinhalese Buddhists that, as you can see, goes back to its earliest times. Devanampiya Tissa employed Ashoka's strategy of merging the political state with Buddhism, supporting Buddhist institutions from the state's coffers and locating temples close to the royal palace for greater control. With such patronage, Buddhism was positioned to evolve as the highest ethical and philosophical expression of Sinhalese culture and civilization. Buddhism appealed directly to the masses, leading to the growth of a collective Sinhalese cultural consciousness.

In contrast to the theological exclusivity of Hindu Brahminism, the Ashokan missionary approach featured preaching and carried the principles of the Buddha directly to the common people. This proselytizing had even greater success in Lanka than it had in India and could be said to be the island's first experiment in mass education.

Buddhism also had a great effect on the literary development of the island. The Indo-Aryan dialect spoken by the early Sinhalese was comprehensible to missionaries from India and facilitated early attempts at translating the scriptures. The Sinhalese literati studied Pali, the language of the Buddhist scriptures, thus influencing the development of Sinhala as a literary language.

All that, sadly, foreshadowed an inevitable conflict between the island's Sinhalese and Tamil populations. With 75 percent of Sri Lankans of Sinhalese descent, the Tamils are a clear minority, representing about 18 percent. The predominantly Hindu Tamils descend from the Indians of Tamil Nadu, the coastal state at the southeast tip of India, from which a close look at a map suggests a piece broke off in some long past geologic cataclysm and slipped 30 miles out to sea. This is confirmed by a study of plate tectonics that appeared in *A Country Study: Sri Lanka,* published by the Federal Research Division of the U.S. Library of Congress in 1988. It notes that most of south India was part of a single southern landmass called Gondwanaland. Then, beginning about 200 million years ago, forces within the earth's mantle began to separate the lands of the Southern Hemisphere, and a crustal plate supporting both India and Sri Lanka moved toward the northeast.

"It stands to reason that a country which was only thirty miles from India and which would have been seen by Indian fisherman every morning as they sailed out to catch their fish, would have been occupied as soon as the continent was peopled by men who understood how to sail," Sinhalese historian and Cambridge scholar Paul Peiris commented in the *Journal of Royal Asiatic Society, Ceylon Branch*.

Nonetheless, this has not dissuaded each of the two groups from claiming bragging rights as the rightful rulers of this land and waging war to prove it throughout the country's history.

The Sinhalese get credit for developing an innovative hydraulic engineering system of interconnected reservoirs (or "tanks") and irrigation canals in Sri Lanka's dry north-central regions that they settled as early as 500 BCE. Because early agricultural activity— primarily the cultivation of wet rice—was dependent on unreliable monsoon rains, the Sinhalese constructed canals, channels, water-storage tanks and reservoirs to irrigate their crops. Such early attempts at engineering reveal the brilliant understanding these ancient people had of hydraulic principles and trigonometry. The discovery of the principle of the valve tower, or valve pit, for regulating the escape of water is credited to Sinhalese ingenuity more than 2,000 years ago. By the 1st century CE, several large-scale irrigation works had been completed.

Occupied by the Portuguese in the 16th century and by the

Dutch in the 17th century, the island was ceded to the British in 1796, became a crown colony in 1802, and was united under British rule by 1815. As Ceylon, it became independent in 1948; its name was changed to Sri Lanka in 1972.

In 1956, postcolonial Sri Lanka legalized the establishment of Sinhalese as the sole official language (it had been English until then). This effectively excluded Tamils from holding public office and other key jobs, and blocked educational opportunities and other rights of citizenship. That the man who pushed through the legislation, Prime Minister S. W. R. D. Bandaranaike, scion of a noble Sinhalese family, was a converted Buddhist was irrelevant. Or was it? His change in policy coincided with the 2,500th anniversary of the Buddha's enlightenment, a cause for great celebration in Sri Lanka. Protesting that policy, disenfranchised Hindu Tamils erupted in street riots. Hard-line Sinhalese retaliated with wholesale violence. In 1959—and when I read this I almost dropped the book—Bandaranaike was shot dead by an apparently deranged Buddhist monk.

It has been a delicate balance since then. Tensions between the Sinhalese majority and Tamil separatists erupted into war in 1983. A secessionist group fighting for Tamil equality, if not independence, coalesced into the Liberation Tigers of Tamil Eelam (LTTE). (*Eelam* means "homeland" in Tamil.) Tens of thousands have died in an ethnic conflict that continues to fester. The LTTE's leader, Velupillai Prabhakaran, "is one of the most bloody-minded and effective warlords in today's crowded field," wrote Philip Gourevitch in *The New Yorker* in August 2005.

After two decades of fighting, the government and LTTE formalized a cease-fire in February 2002. When I arrived, that cease fire had been tenuously in effect.

Now these current events give "fallen tear" more than geologic meaning; it's the Buddha's tear now, crying for suffering in the land where his teachings were to be a role model. They can call it a civil war or an ethnic war, but it is hard *not* to see it as a religious war. The vast majority of Sinhalese are Buddhists; the Tamils are largely Hindus. This Buddhist-Hindu conflict shot to hell a theory of mine that had helped get me this assignment. In my proposal, I had suggested that Buddhism must be doing something right. As justification, I challenged my *Geographic* editors to name a war in the world today—a world, as others have pointed out, in which every war is, at heart, a struggle between religious factions—that Buddhists are fighting. Sri Lanka refuted my claim.

❧

I knew very little about Sri Lanka's internal struggles as my plane descended in the Colombo airport. I was simply taken by the change in scenery: the turquoise waters, the white sand beaches, the palms gently bowing with the winds. In stark contrast to the teeming intensity of India, it immediately evoked memories of tranquil tropical isles of my past and I naturally relaxed. *Yes! Bring it on!* All of it belied the turmoil roiling just beneath that beguiling surface.

Today, pilgrims and tourists travel what's called the Cultural Triangle, a popular circuit in the geographic center of the country defined by the three ancient capitals at each corner: the country's first capital, Anuradhapura (from the 5th century BCE to the 12th century CE), Polonnaruwa (10th to 12th century), and Kandy (16th to 19th century). I wanted to see them all, but first, after landing in the current capital city of Colombo, my own pilgrimage took me to the city of Moratuwa, an hour's drive down the coast. There I met a man who has been compared to Mahatma Gandhi, Martin Luther King Jr., and His Holiness the Dalai Lama. A former schoolteacher, Dr. A. T. Ariyaratne, a slight 73-year-old man with a childlike voice and cherubic face, demurely denies any of these comparisons—and then he will show you a room filled with citations, plaques and awards for his humanitarian work.

Dr. Ariyaratne is founder of the Sarvodaya Shramadana Movement. "Sarvodaya" is a word coined by Mahatma Gandhi, meaning "the awakening of all." Shramadana means "a gift of labor." Together: "to awaken all by sharing the gift of labor."

Its origins were a program he initiated as a science teacher in 1958 that brought students to rural areas for two weeks to learn about village life. Incorporated in 1972, it has grown into a "political organization at a grassroots level that's Buddhist based," he told me at Sarvodaya's Moratuwa headquarters.

Dr. A. T. Ariyaratne, founder of the Sarvodaya Shramadana Movement in Sri Lanka, a self-governance program based on Buddhist principles that serves the majority of the country's villages. He posed with the author in the gardens of the organization's headquarters in Moratuwa, an hour's drive south of Columbo.

It is a comprehensive system of self-governance that reaches into the smallest of villages, offering professional assistance for every social service imaginable—from technical training, to helping build and staff pre- and elementary schools, to prenatal care, to courses on setting up savings programs, to providing loans for building wells. In one village, I joined a group giving an actual helping hand, along with a helping scythe, to clear a grown-over path that led to a long-neglected tillable field.

Though one could view this elaborate system of everyone taking care of everyone else as a form of socialism, philosophically and organizationally it's all rooted in the Buddha's teachings. By explanation, as he showed me around the complex of buildings, auditoriums, computer labs, and central courtyards at Moratuwa, Dr. Ariyaratne pointed to an organizational chart on a wall, similar to what you'd see on the bulletin board in your high-school civics class. The overall thrust, and each program within it, corresponds to the Buddha's Four Noble Truths: the "decadent village" equaling the first truth of suffering, the cycle of ignorance and poverty in that village creating the cause of that suffering, constructive engagement being the third truth that affirms a way out of suffering, and a well-conceived plan on all fronts equivalent to the fourth, a community-building version of the Eightfold Path. I could see he had drawn on his educational background in building bureaucratic structures, and then making neat org charts.

Now, with funding from such international groups as Oxfam, UNICEF, and CARE, as well as corporate funders like the Novartis Foundation of Switzerland, the Nippon Foundation of Japan and Norad of Norway, among many others, Sarvodaya staff people and programs are active in some 15,000 of the 38,000 villages that the government counts. The organization estimates that 11 million of the country's 19 million are individual beneficiaries of various Sarvodaya programs—and that's whether they are Buddhist or not. The group distributes funds from a financial reserve bank of 1.6 billion rupees (US$16 million).

"We are the largest organization in the country," he said as fact, not boast. This would make him a potentially very powerful man in a country that seems to be perpetually struggling in a power vacuum.

"Yes," he conceded, "since 1982 with every national election, the newspapers consider me a dark-horse candidate." He was considered so threatening to the government during the administration of President Ranasinghe Premadasa that from 1989 to 1993 he was the target of attacks and threats on his life. "They decided it was too much of a risk to kill me straightaway."

He insisted, however, he has no political aspirations. "At the top you can organize greed, hatred you can organize at the top, ignorance you can organize, too," he said. "But you can always organize truth from the level of the community, from the bottom up.

"It's the moral power that we have," he added. And then, as if on cue, he was interrupted by a call from the government's Internal Security Ministry, asking for advice. It was campaign season, and a handful of Buddhist monks were running for Parliament seats.

"This would be good, right?" I asked. "Buddhist monks in office would assure no corruption . . . right?"

He disagreed. "We don't think they should. They should be above it. I was the first to oppose their campaigning for office. I am sure they would be corrupted by power."

At home, between sex scandals and power politics within the Catholic Church, we assume priests will fall into step with their legislative brethren. But from monks in a country with such deep Buddhist roots? It was a sorry comment on the seductive power of power.

With a map in front of us, Dr. Ariyaratne charted a cross-country tour for me that would combine firsthand looks at Sarvodaya village programs along with some sightseeing.

In Anuradhapura, a tall thin man named Vinsor Kanakaratne, Sarvodaya's district coordinator, met me at the Nuwarawewa Resthouse. The hotel is named after Nuwarawewa, the largest tank in Anuradhapura (four miles across), created in the 2nd century CE. I could see the reservoir from my hotel window, but a severe long-term drought had reduced it to a mere puddle.

As we headed for the rural villages, Vinsor told me Anuradhapura is the largest district in the country, with a population of 900,000. Of the 900 villages, half have a Sarvodaya presence. When a village accepts the Sarvoada concept, they elect a board consisting of president, secretary and treasurer. Each villager pays a pittance of a membership fee—two or three rupees a month— which goes partly into their own savings account and partly to the village's coffers. After six months of demonstrating that they can save money, villagers are eligible for an "instant loan" at a very low interest rate. In a year, they can get a bigger loan.

"Poverty is the biggest problem here," he said. "But we don't just give loans; our approach is holistic, including building both psychological and self governance infrastructure. We equip them with all the social services and trade training they will need to better their lives."

According to the Sri Lanka Ministry of Foreign Affairs, the average annual income of Sri Lankans is about US$870—about $80 a month. Life is hard here these days, Vinsor said. The violence and the drought have been a double whammy on people's livelihoods. As we drove, I could see that most of the fields looked a sad shade of brown and the lakes were bone dry.

"Rain is not predicted," he said.

"You mean for tomorrow?" I asked.

"No, for months."

Vinsor, who at 52 had been with Sarvodaya for 23 years, had spent some time in the United States, and he enjoyed practicing his English on me, speaking slowly and with precise diction. Every now and then he would spring a vocabulary question on me.

"What is the difference between 'perception' and 'perspective'?" he asked in the middle of one conversation as we approached the first village.

Intuitively, I knew the difference, but faced with the need to explain the distinction to a student of English as a second language, I was stopped in my linguistic tracks. As the authority, at least in that car, I gave it a try: "Perspective is the angle from which you look at something. Perception is how you see it, your own point of view." It sounded lame even to me; he looked at me as though I was Webster himself. "So perhaps 'perspective' is what you see and 'perception' is what you think of what you see."

Later I had to look it up: the real Webster says "perspective" is "the aspect in which a subject or its parts are mentally viewed, *esp:* a view of things (as objects or events) in their true relationship or relative importance." "Perception" is "awareness of one's environment through physical sensation" or "ability to understand: INSIGHT, COMPREHENSION **syn** penetration, discernment, discrimination."

In fact, I had gotten it backward. Or had I? I had thought it was a vocabulary lesson, but it was his Dhamma teaching to me. I made it my koan: "What is the difference between perception and perspective?" And it came in handy immediately. Though I knew we were going to villages, I had a picture of arriving at a tiny center, with shops and cars and even a small reception committee, to which I had already gotten accustomed and rather relished. But when we arrived at the village of Nawa Makulewa, I was taken aback. The road was a glorified cow path. There were two or three cottages—period. The village of 250 people has been with Sarvodaya for four years. We were going to attend a meeting to discuss the village's savings program, but we learned that there was a death in a family so the meeting was canceled. Instead, we dropped in on the village's treasurer, a furniture maker named W. W. Senewerathna Banda, who had just spent a week making a gorgeous ornately sculpted wooden chair. Sale price: US$85. Plus shipping and handling.

"We were completely disorganized before Sarvodaya came in," he told me through Vinsor. "Now we have a vision. We have hope."

Then we drove through the backcountry to see how the money was being spent locally. One 32-year-old woman got a loan of 10,000 rupees (US$100) to start manufacturing and selling bricks. That was two years ago, and she had almost repaid the loan. Another family got funds to put a roof over their heads—literally. Behind them their small cottage, otherwise looking run-down, now had a shiny new top.

Sarvodaya was helping supply the elemental basics. Several times Vinsor pointed out that a big priority was building latrines and wells. In one village, we saw a newly built well that would save women from having to walk a half mile each way for their day's supply. Was this in the same country that 2,000 years ago dazzled the world with irrigation systems beyond anyone's imagination at the time? What had happened to Sri Lanka in the intervening years? Gratefully, I didn't have to answer that koan. I was having enough trouble using my new koan to develop a skillful perspective on my perceptions about Sri Lanka. As mine shifted, my respect for Dr. Ariyaratne's daunting task only increased.

❧

The next day, before I left Anuradhapura, I circumambulated the Bo Tree, the descendant of the original Bodhi Tree in India. Before doing so, I bowed before a statue of the Buddha in a temple beside the tree. A monk standing there was collecting small donations. I gave 100 rupees, a single dollar, nothing, but a huge amount to them. In return, besides merit and blessing, the monk tied a small string around my right wrist, as is the custom. I had already collected several such strings of white and red in India. "You shouldn't cut them off," Shantum had told me. "They are reminders to be in the present and in the Dhamma." I liked them because I thought they looked sexy. Also, they were quick cultural identifiers to those who knew what they identified. I swore not to cut them off until they unraveled on their own accord.

Outside of town, in sauna-like heat I traipsed up 1,840 granite steps to see the ruins of a monastery Mahinda and his fellow monks had established and where in 247 BCE he met King Devanampiya Tissa, who had been on a royal hunting trip. Mahinda spoke of the Buddha's teachings and shortly thereafter the king— and most of the rest of the country—became ardent followers. The Chinese pilgrim Fa-Hsien recorded seeing several thousand monks in residence here in the early 5th century. I saw a lovey-dovey couple strolling in slo-mo down the steps and very few others the day I was there.

But when I got to the top, in one of the caves atop the hill known as Mihintale, I found myself swarmed by a group of students, bright-eyed and attractive in their school uniforms, on a field trip. They teased me and tried to engage me: "What country you are coming from?" they asked in a chorus. The Sri Lankan English has that same bouncy patois of the Indians, though they themselves would probably object to the comparison.

Ordinarily, I am up for such playful banter, but on that day I was distracted. I was an hour or two away from the Sarvodaya district office in Batticaloa, on the eastern coast, and my anxiety was increasing. On March 2, the day after my arrival in Sri Lanka, a one-column headline in the lower left-hand corner of page one of the *Daily News,* the country's largest English language paper, quietly announced, "UNP candidate shot dead in Batticaloa." A candidate from the United National Party, the country's main opposition party, running for the upcoming Batticaloa District general election, was gunned down in the first polls-related killing. The LTTE, the story said, was suspected of responsibility for the murder. The candidate was running against the LTTE's warnings; the LTTE was backing a Tamil National Alliance (TNA) candidate. The positioning of the story, and the scant reporting, suggested this was about as alarming as a cat-up-a-tree story. Above the fold was a teaser for a story more Sri Lankans would have taken note of: "Test cricket is a huge patience game."

The next day yet another campaign-related murder occurred. The delicate cease-fire in the 20-year ethnic conflict between the Sinhalese and the Tamils had been shattered. The war games were on again, and "huge patience" would be a much-needed but rare commodity here.

As I got closer to Batticaloa, I noticed more and more armed military guards standing in front of roadside army compounds, barbed wire and bunkers behind them. Even my driver was getting nervous.

The movement's district office, in a quiet residential area, was abuzz with activity—dedicated bushy-tailed staff mostly in their 20s rushing about, paperwork flying behind them. It was apparent that Sarvoyada Shramadana is a well-trained and well-oiled machine, Dr. Ariyaratne's organizational stamp quite evident. District office coordinator E. L. A. Careem, who Dr. Ariyaratne had advised of my visit, enthusiastically greeted me. He invited about eight top staff into his office to brief me on their efforts. The conflict had hit this local community hard, they told me. Jobs were scarce. Sometimes it was difficult to get provisions through the security areas, not to mention the constant psychological stress of impending violence hanging over their heads.

Then I watched as villagers appealing for funding paraded through the office, each making a strong case for a little financial aid for the simplest of entrepreneurial ventures. One young man requested a loan from the Sarvodaya reserve bank of 98,000 rupees (US$980) to buy a motor scooter. This would mean he wouldn't have to ride his bicycle 20 kilometers a day to pick up provisions to sell at his little streetside shop. He'd already demonstrated that he could save money. He'd have three years to repay the loan, at an interest rate less than a tenth of the government's lending rate. He easily was approved for the loan.

Later in the day, Mr. Careem took me with several staff to a village where youths from the region had been bused in for a weekend; it reminded me of youth camps I'd attended as a kid, combining spiritual awakening, volunteer community service and peer-group confidence building. The villagers all gathered under a spreading banyan tree in front of two temples, one Hindu, the other Buddhist. There was a contagious energy that Mr. Careem and his people spread. He had told me earlier that the whole strategy was to build trust, find out what the community considered its priority needs, then respond with an action plan right there and then. At the start, I noticed the villagers sat back on their haunches listening to the pep talk. I could imagine that though their needs were plenty, they had a built-in distrust of outsiders. Perhaps they'd heard it all before. Perhaps they had been betrayed. Perhaps, surrounded by civil war, their paranoia and suspicion were justified.

Apparently, they believed what they were hearing because several village leaders started to pipe in. The next thing I knew people were organizing into small groups. Mr. Careem pushed me toward one cluster of young people as they happily walked single file along a path that seemed to lead to nowhere. I found one of the Sarvodaya members who spoke English to explain as we walked. We were heading on this path that led to some fields that had been abandoned, he told me. Now the villagers were hoping to begin growing crops there again, as their population had been rising dramatically. This person said that from the Sarvodaya perspective, the bigger concern was population control—teen pregnancy and out-of-wedlock single mothers were rampant—but feeding crying babies was the higher need right now. I liked that Sarvodaya listened. That had been a complaint about the Peace Corps; they went in and did what they thought would be best for communities, as opposed to helping the communities do what they thought was best for themselves. Our job today was simply to clear the path that had been overrun by weeds. I grabbed a scythe and started thwacking away beside the nicely dressed volunteers. But I noticed something else: Though the villagers had walked out to this area with the volunteers, most of them stood by and gladly watched their visitors do the work.

"We don't expect them to jump in and do it themselves right away," my companion explained, "or they would have done this long before we came. But we think if we are role models, then their own pride will motivate them to take over." It was the Huck Finn strategy all over again: after Sarvodaya was gone, the hope was villagers would see that hard work results in personal benefit. These were almost embarrassingly simple lessons, but that's what the Sarvodaya movement is about: providing the fundamentals. And while the government fails to create real infrastructure, Dr. Ariyaratne and these staff and volunteers provide the brick and mortar to help villagers build their lives.

Though not a word about Buddhism was uttered, that message of self-sufficiency and self-motivation was the same the Buddha would have conveyed here. "Oneself, indeed, is one's own protector. What other protector could there be?" the Buddha says in *The*

Dhammapada. "You must each be a lamp unto yourselves," he said in the last hours of his life.

One particular program showed me just how tenuous life here really is, as well as how Sarvodaya's Buddhist approach transcends the need for a lesson in Buddhist philosophy.

Mr. Careem and a few of his colleagues from the district office took me on what seemed like a wild goose chase to the village of Eravur, down endless side alleys until even they appeared totally lost. At the edge of a small neighborhood abutting an open field, we stopped at an empty house and entered a room with no furniture. Suddenly the sound of giggling children broke the silence. From some back room, about a dozen kids, ages five to 18, filed into the room and formed a circle. Two 19-year-old girls, one a Hindu, the other a Muslim wearing a hijab (a head covering), led the group in animated songs and play activities. Muslims here are the minority of the minorities, representing about 7 percent of the population.

Then they showed the kids a series of posters illustrating land mines. This was the purpose behind this play group. They were being taught to recognize the deadly weapons that sit like forgotten debris throughout the countryside here. This mine-risk education class was funded by the European Union Humanitarian Aid Office (ECHO) of the European Commission and UNICEF, but staffed by Sarvodaya. They call the whole region an "uncleared area," meaning uncleared of such devices. Mines have cost both children and adults lives and limbs; this is the price of hatred, of religious intolerance, of xenophobia, of petty turf wars.

When the kids had arrived in the room, a group of eagle-eyed mothers entered from a back kitchen I hadn't noticed. They squatted, quietly but carefully watching to make sure their own child was paying close attention. This little game and these songs the kids were being asked to memorize could be a matter of life and death, and nobody knew it better than these women. Several rattled off to me the family members they had lost. Later, Rajani Kanagalingam, the director of the program, tallied the success rate of this mine-risk educational effort. Before the program was initiated in 2003, 21 people were injured; after its start, there were none. Before, three deaths were attributed to land mines; after, one. The mines, they told me wryly, do not distinguish whether their victims are Tamils or Sinhalese, Hindu, Buddhist or Muslim, old or young, fathers or mothers, Sri Lankans or visiting American journalists. In this way the mines are as undis-

A preschool in the Anuradhapura District of Sri Lanka, built with Sarvodaya funding and staffed by Sarvodaya-trained teachers. At right is Vinsor Kanakaratne, Sarvodaya's district coordinator.

criminating as the Buddha himself was. I tried to make this attempt at dark Buddhist humor but the comment fell flat, as well it should have.

This was no laughing matter. But I was getting confused, and perhaps a bit cynical. Monks in politics? Buddhists at war? A once avant-garde culture now so primitive, so divided? Buddhism was part of this country's cultural bedrock; if Buddhism "works," then Sri Lanka should be its best advertisement. Instead, it is a country hemorrhaging from within. Why? It was the koan I took home, the one that probably will never be answered.

The cute faces of the children were still etched in my mind the next day as I headed back to Colombo. It was my good fortune to arrive in Kandy on the eve of a full moon, auspicious by any measure but the more so for Buddhist Sri Lankans. Legend holds that the Buddha's birth, enlightenment and death occurred on full moons. Full moons, called *Poya,* are days of sabbath, a legal holiday when the city shops are closed, alcohol is not served, and killing—including fishing—is forbidden. On this night, at Sri Dalada Maligawa, the Temple of the Tooth, the veil is parted to the window that conceals a series of seven gold- and jewel-decked caskets, underneath which, legend has it, rests one of the Buddha's incisors. Once a year, in August, the whole casket is paraded through the streets of Kandy on the back of an ornately costumed elephant. In 1998, an LTTE terrorist suicide squad crashed outside the temple, killing 11 and wounding 23. The attack occurred days before the 50th anniversary of Sri Lanka's independence. There was massive damage to the building, but by my visit it looked mostly repaired. The accounts reported the tooth itself remained untouched.

The hallway outside the window was crowded with couples and families with children of every age, all crying, or so it seemed to me in the sweltering heat. This was not just a holy day; it was a ritual family holiday. I waited patiently, trying to watch my breath, but even when I could block out the wailing *babus,* the beads of my own sweat dripping into my eyes broke my concentration.

Finally, with my eyes focused on that little window, I saw some movement and, thinking I was the only one to notice, rose quickly, like any self-respecting New York native, to aggressively edge my way to the front. But I was not alone: with the synchronicity of a marching band, the throng rose en masse and inch by inch shuffled their way into position. A pushy New Yorker could learn a thing or two from these Sri Lankan Buddhists. Once in line, standing a full head above most of the others (except for the occasional Westerner also in line), I stuck out like an albino string bean. Slowly but surely, the line snaked around corners as it moved toward the highly anticipated window. I watched the drill carefully; you had only a few brief moments to see whatever there was to see, and then you had to move on.

Now, before I was truly prepared, it was my turn. There was spotlight glare bouncing off the window from the inside and a reflection from the outside so it took several seconds for my pupils to adjust. Then there was so much to see in such a small space in such a short time that I think I panicked. I didn't know where to hold my gaze; instead, I surveyed the whole picture in the window. It was like a little exhibit mounted on some tables covered with white cloth, and I could see walling behind it all. Just when I thought I recognized the casket and was staring closely to see any bit of white tooth, the man standing guard beside the window signaled me that my time was up. When I hesitated, he ever so gently but encouragingly invited me to leave. Those waiting in line right behind me, pushing at my elbow, were of a similar persuasion. I was whisked past the window so quickly, dazzled by all the flashing jewelry and lights and flow of humanity, I barely caught a glimpse of *anything*—much less the cherished tooth itself.

Maybe the realities are too harsh here. It's easier to cling to the illusion of a tooth, to parade it around on the back of an elephant and hope that paying obeisance to it will alleviate one's suffering.

I'm sorry—maybe I hadn't been immersed long enough in The Teachings—but I was having trouble connecting the dots here in Sri Lanka. Did praying to an ossified bicuspid bring back a whole arm or leg? Had Buddhism wandered so far from its roots in the first leg of its worldwide migration? Or was it I? Did I not "believe" enough? I thought faith in tooth fairies was not what the Buddha had in mind. I was, however, putting my faith in Dr. Ariyaratne's Sarvodaya movement.

Postscript from a former paradise:

On December 26 of that same year, while I sat safely on Martha's Vineyard writing, Sri Lanka experienced an event that literally swept away life there as I had seen it and, I suspect, made them question their own faith in the tooth. Sri Lanka was rammed head-on by the world's fourth-largest tsunami since 1900. It gathered force as it crossed the Bay of Bengal from its epicenter in northern Sumatra, seemingly setting its sights on a bull's-eye of Batticaloa and Sri Lanka's northeast coast. The tsunami caused more casualties than any other in recorded history. Of the more than 150,000 people killed in that part of the world, an estimated 35,000 were Sri Lankans.

On-the-ground news reports from that area were sparse. The best coverage came from my good friend Jeff Greenwald, an Oakland-based journalist, author of, among other books, *Shopping for Buddhas,* and founder of a respected organization called Ethical Traveler. He had volunteered to work in Sri Lanka as a media liaison for Mercy Corps, a Portland, Oregon, charity group. The reports he filed on his EthicalTraveler.org Web site were painfully difficult to read and touched on issues that plagued us all. Here, a clip.

> Our drive up the coast toward Batticaloa is interrupted by numerous detours and back-tracks. We'll pass through a town, and travel five rough miles up the half-collapsed road, only to find the bridge down. Illustrated with fierce clarity is the sheer breadth of the killer wave. The entire coastline of Sri Lanka is a wreck. Sometimes the damage lies right at the shore, sometimes it extends far inland, but it is nearly universal. Many houses of worship—Buddhist, Hindu, Christian and Moslem—were spared, but not all. Just north of Thirrukovil we find a Hindu temple hit by the tsunami. Colorful statues and bits of paintings lay scattered across the roadside like an exploded bouquet.
>
> It makes me wonder, again, if I would have understood—when the water rushed out, exposing the seabed—what was in

store. The truth is, I don't know. None of us had any sense of what precedes a tsunami, as there haven't been any during our lifetimes. Disaster movies don't show the water receding; a huge wave simply rushes in, tossing taxicabs and billboards down the street. Would I have run out to marvel at the exposed reef, or run in the other direction? There is no way to reckon whether I'd have been saved by my intuition, or killed by my curiosity.

For months I pictured the causeways I'd driven, lagoons I'd walked by, beaches I'd strolled—all washed out. But mostly I thought about the people I'd met and wondered how they fared, if they even survived. It took me awhile to build up the courage, but I finally called Dr. Ariyaratne, who happened to be in the United States speaking and raising funds for relief efforts. Miraculously, he told me, none of the Batticaloa staff I'd spent several days with died. "But yes," he said. "Lives were lost. One entire preschool we built—gone. Kids, teachers, all."

Reaching for some kind of positive spin, I said, "Well, it probably brought the country together and put the civil war in perspective, yes?"

"For the first couple of weeks, there was cooperation between the LTTE and the Sinhalese," he replied. "But then the Tamils claimed they were being discriminated against, accusing the government of shortchanging them on relief supplies. Actually, the tsunami widened the distance."

It was true. I stayed tuned to news reports: The number of politically motivated murders increased, not decreased, in the wake of the tsunami. The LTTE wasn't the only faction to seize the occasion of this great tragedy to add to the divisiveness. I read with utter disbelief, in a January 2005 dispatch from the Agence France Presse, that even the under-underdog Muslims couldn't resist pointing a finger of blame.

> God signed His name in the tsunami that battered Sri Lanka and other countries on December 26, and sent it as punishment because humans have been ignoring His laws, Sri Lankan Muslims say. Proof, according to Mohamed Faizeen, manager of the

Centre for Islamic Studies in Colombo, is a satellite picture taken seconds after the tsunami smashed into Sri Lanka's west coast near the town of Kalutara and as it was receding. "This clearly spells out the name 'Allah' in Arabic," Faizeen said, pointing to the shape of the waves—a gigantic "E" complete with whorls and sidewaves that do indeed appear to combine to resemble the Arabic script for the name "Allah."

Meanwhile, Sarvodaya had risen to the occasion. Within hours of the great wave, it opened a national operations center that over the next three months provided half a million dollars worth of humanitarian aid. For its efforts, it was named to the 2005 UN-HABITAT Scroll of Honour, whose recipients "shine out in their commitment to the cause of improving human settlements, their innovative ways of reducing urban poverty and bringing relief to the victims of disasters such as the Indian Ocean tsunami."

six

Tattoos, Pick-up Sticks and Mock Monks

The Creative Mix of Thai Buddhism

As long as there are monastics who delight in living in the forest, at the foot of trees, the way of the Awakened One will not decline."
—The Buddha, "Digha Nikaya II"

I believe a leaf of grass is no less than the journey-work of the stars.
—Walt Whitman, *Leaves of Grass*

Buddhism is sometimes compared to water. Water is pure and clear, transparent. But add a dye to it and it becomes that color. Sip it and it has no taste. Add flavoring and it tastes like that flavor. Grasp at it and it slips through your fingertips. It has no shape of its own. Pour it into a glass and it takes the shape of the container. So, too, with Buddhism. Buddhism is transparent: It has no dogma and is free from any theistic viewpoint. Over the course of its history, Buddhism has fit into the cultural vessel of each country to which it has migrated. Although it keeps some of the characteristics recognizable from the Buddha's era in India, Buddhism also adapts elements unique to each new place and new time. It is malleable, transparent, flexible, inclusive, not exclusive. This adaptability is why Buddhism has succeeded in each country and culture across Asia.

I began to understand more clearly what this means in Thailand, a country where 94 percent of the 64 million people are Buddhist, a country so committed to Buddhism that by order of the national constitution, the king is required to be Buddhist.

Here I also had to confront the difference between the American separation of church and state and the complete integration of it in a country whose name was changed in 1949 from Siam (*thai* means free, thus Land of the Free). My conclusion: Both countries are completely hypocritical. Why, for example, do American presidents end their State of the Union addresses with "And may God bless America"—as if God *would* sanction U.S. military actions throughout the world? And why was the phrase "under God" added to the Pledge of Allegiance in 1954, in effect contradicting the religious freedom the U.S. Constitution assures? American Buddhists, Muslims and Hindus who don't believe in that particular God might still be patriotic Americans. And how could Thailand, which requires its kings to attend a spiritual retreat as part of their training, have attacked Burma and Cambodia repeatedly in the 13th and 14th centuries, destroying the Cambodian city of Angkor Wat in 1389? Karma being karma, the favor was returned when the Burmese invaded then Siam in the 16th century, and in 1766–1767 captured the capital city of Ayuthaya and decimated its Buddhist temples and statues.

These inconsistencies aside, since Thailand's earliest history Buddhism has been inextricably tied to this beautiful country surrounded by Myanmar (formerly Burma), Malaysia, Cambodia and Laos. Whether you buy the legend that King Ashoka sent monks to "the golden land" in the 3rd century BCE or the archaeological evidence that Buddhist monastic communities were established southwest of what is now Bangkok as early as the 4th century CE, the consensus is the Buddhism that developed here was a mix-and-match of many practices.

"Buddhism in Thailand can only be described as eclectic," writes Donald Swearer, professor of religion at Swarthmore College, in *The Encyclopedia of Buddhism*. "As part of the Indian cultural influence into 'greater India,' elements of Mahayana, Tantra, and mainstream Buddhist schools entered different regions of Thailand. . . . These diverse Buddhist expressions, in turn, competed with Brahmanism, Hinduism, and autochthonous animisms. Rather than an organized sectarian lineage, the early religious amalgam in Thailand and other parts of Southeast Asia might be more accurately described as a syncretic collage of miraculous relics and charismatic monks, Hindu dharmasastra, Brahmanic deities, Mahayana buddhas, tantric practices, and Sanskrit Sarvastivadin and Pali Theravada traditions."

I wouldn't have recognized half of what he was referring to, but I *did* see some examples of this mishmash as soon as I arrived. It looked nothing like the Buddhism I had seen in the United States or up to now in Europe, India or Sri Lanka.

On my first day, outside Wat Maha Budre, a temple along the Saen Saep Canal in Bangkok, I saw a row of booths where astrologers and tarot and palm readers hawked their services, carny style. Each person I talked to confirmed he or she was a Buddhist and that their services were integrally related to Buddhism.

"How?" I repeatedly asked, but none could explain.

My fixer, Prasong Kittinanthachai, was put off by the fact that I was put off by the fact that these people actually thought this could be part of Buddhism.

"The Buddha was all about reality—seeing things as they are, not this sort of mystical mumbo-jumbo stuff," I said, as though now—after traveling in three whole countries—I was a renowned Buddhologist. It was, simply, a reasonable assumption, and I said it with such conviction. And yet, if Buddhism came from India, where astrology's origins derive from Vedic culture dating back to 3,000 BCE, then quite possibly it had a place in the cosmological understanding of the Buddha.

Prasong, a thin man in his late 30s who was working on a

master's degree in Buddhism, looked at me with an expression I would not get used to for the 10 days he traveled with me—a drooping of the eyelids that simultaneously conveyed patience and disgust with my ignorance.

Across from the Wat Maha Budre, there was another smaller temple, where I saw a monk inside alone.

"Let's go talk to him," I suggested.

"Okay, but you can't go in empty-handed," Prasong warned. "You must bring him some sort of gift."

Conveniently, just outside his door was a vendor selling white buckets full of the tackiest plastic Buddhas and other trinkets. They were in two piles; I smelled a scam. "Are you in on this?" I asked Prasong. He gave me that look. I bought the cheapest one and we entered. Inside, the scene resembled a stage set Sam Shepard might have designed after studying too many Hieronymus Bosch murals. As disheveled a monk as I had seen sat on a cushion in what looked like a crowded and messy fluorescent-lit storage room. Off to the side was a small TV, poorly tuned in to a station blasting nasal Thai pop music. Behind him were all those white buckets in two piles as well. One was the buckets he had collected that day; in the other were buckets going right back to that vendor's "in" pile, to be resold.

I gave Prasong my own look. "It doesn't matter," he said with theological certainty. "It's the gesture of giving something to the respected spiritual teacher that is important." I was thinking the money could have been better invested in getting him a good interior decorator and a savvy marketing manager.

The monk said nothing of value and in fact appeared to resent being engaged in any kind of religious Q&A.

From there, we went into another small temple in the same courtyard, where Prasong explained what looked like a game of pick-up sticks. This was fortune-telling without the teller. It's called *Sieng Seam See*. In a small box, there are about 10 to 20 numbered sticks, each number corresponding to numbered slips of paper on a board. You shake a box full of the sticks until one falls out (if more than one falls, it's a do-over). Match the number on the stick to the paper, on which is written a small prediction about your life, love or work. It seemed like a cross between throwing the I Ching coins, Chinese fortune cookies and, yes, pick-up sticks—but with giant life-altering implications. I tried. Here's the message I got:

"Keep trying hard, you will get rewards soon. Legal case is unfavorable. Patient condition is worsening. Good fortune and support is approaching."

Was that Eminem I heard channeling through the Buddha statue at the front of the temple? Maybe there was something to this after all: the impending rewards of this hard work, the predicament with my back, the ever-compelling hope that good fortune lay ahead in the form of a lovely and loving woman—all, and more, forecast with the simple flick of the wrist and a fallen stick. Is Buddhism amazing or what? I tried to suspend judgment and put my cynicism aside. But coming from a Western (insert implicit adjective "rational" here) culture where the cobwebs on superstition had been swept clean (except for the horoscopes in every newspaper and women's magazine), I found it hard to accept, harder still on Buddhist temple grounds. But to the Thai people, this was as integral to their practice as, say, ritually eating a dry, thin, tasteless wafer and calling it "the body of Christ" was to another religion.

The heat in Bangkok was punishing. I walked out of my hotel in the early morning and was smacked in the face by a steaming hot towel. Luckily, my hotel, the Four Seasons Bangkok, was one of the most beautiful I've ever stayed in, so I tried to sandwich my outings with frequent returns to my fully air-conditioned ecosystem. I had decided to blow my Thailand hotel expense wad and give myself a mini-vacation in the midst of my travels. This hotel could not have been a better choice. Centrally located across from the Sky Train, it had a long outdoor pool, an indoor spa with a waterfall in the Jacuzzi (for which my back bowed ever so gently in gratitude), and a great restaurant called Spice Market serving gourmet local cuisine. Plus that top-notch Four Seasons pampering, to which it is not hard to get attached. My press rate and upgraded room included access to the executive lounge. This meant I had unlimited use of high-speed Internet access, critical to setting up the next leg of my travels to Hong Kong, China and Japan. And if I timed my schedule right, I could nibble through breakfast, lunch and dinner at the complimentary buffet, attractive Four Seasons staff fussing over me. Though I had recoiled at hearing stories of old *Geographic* writers who would conduct interviews with aboriginal natives in the bar of their five-star hotels in outposts like Perth, Australia, now I understood on a primal level the necessity at times of making sure you had your creature comforts covered when you were on the road weeks and months on end, PC or not.

One early morning—after a swim, an e-mail check and a healthy sampling of gravlax—I ventured out of my paradise to a nearby multilevel mall whose anchor department store was called, quite imperfectly, Zen. The name aside, I could have been at the Livingston Mall in New Jersey or Fashion Island Shopping Center in Newport Beach, California. Shoppers were just as rabid and just as pointedly in sale mode as back home, elbowing each other as they shuffled around the discount bins. I could not detect a single Zen vibe in the place. In fact, all of Bangkok—a city strangled by traffic, suffering from noise and air pollution and appearing eternally under construction—reeked of commercialism.

"Yes, we have given in to commercialism, too," Sulak Sivaraksa, founder of the International Network of Engaged Buddhists (INEB), told me by way of implicating his country as well as mine in the Madison Avenue–ization of Buddhism. "You can't help it." He gave as a local example Wat Dhammakaya, touted to be the world's largest Buddhist temple, a tout I heard in reference to other stupas throughout the world as well. "Biggest and best acoustics, largest number of followers. I understand that the more contributions you pay, the more you can look at the Buddha there.

This mentality of Buddhism goes very well with the trend toward consumerism and capitalism."

As one of Thailand's most astute observers, Sivaraksa is, at the age of 71, allowed to conjecture on the sociology of Thai Buddhism. Along with Thich Nhat Hanh, Bernie Glassman, A. T. Ariyaratne, and the Dalai Lama, he is acknowledged as one of the world's most important proponents of socially engaged Buddhism. A prominent and outspoken Thai intellectual and social critic, he has been teacher, scholar, publisher, activist and founder of many nongovernmental organizations, and is the author of more than a hundred books and monographs. In 1976, Siam—as he prefers to call his country, rather than the current Anglicized adaptation—experienced its bloodiest coup. Hundreds of students were killed and thousands were jailed; the military burned Sivaraksa's whole bookshop stock and issued an order for his arrest. He was forced to remain in exile for two years. In 1984, he was arrested on charges of criticizing the king, but international protest led to his eventual release. In 1991, another warrant was issued and he went into political exile once more. He came back to fight the case in court in 1992 and won in 1995. He has twice been nominated for the Nobel Peace Prize, and was recipient in 1995 of the Right Livelihood Award, also known as the Alternative Nobel Prize. When we met at what had once been his grandmother's farmstead, now the headquarters for his international work, he had just returned from a month at Smith College in Northampton, Massachusetts, as a visiting fellow and participant in a conference with the catchy title "TransBuddhism: Transmission, Translation, Transformation." His lecture: "Buddhist Identity in the Modern World."

Alan Senauke, a director of the Buddhist Peace Fellowship (BPF), an international organization based in Berkeley, California, had recommended I meet Sivaraksa. His Sathirakoses-Naga-pradeepa Foundation, an NGO, was founded in 1968 to work at the grassroots, national, regional and international levels on issues of freedom, human rights, traditional cultural integrity, social justice and environmental protection—all within a spiritual context, mostly

Buddhist-based. It became the central foundation for several sister organizations, including the INEB, founded in 1987 as the first international Buddhist network linking engaged Buddhists worldwide. INEB deals with alternative education and spiritual training, gender issues, human rights, ecology, alternative concepts of development and activism.

A stocky man with smooth skin and a cherubic face, Sivaraksa is not modest. "Yes, if I may claim, the idea for the Buddhist Peace Fellowship came from me," he told me. "I challenged the American Buddhist community: 'You sit and become quiet and calm. You are 6 percent of the world population, yet represent 47 percent of the world's resources. If you don't do anything about the world's concerns, then you are not practicing Buddhism.' "

The BPF began in 1978 in Hawaii, spearheaded by a group of American and European Zen Buddhists "to serve as a catalyst for socially engaged Buddhism . . . to help beings liberate themselves from the suffering that manifests in individuals, relationships, institutions, and social systems," as its literature explains. BPF's programs, publications and practice groups connect a worldwide network of 4,000 members and 45 chapters.

Compared to the BPF or the Sarvodaya organization, the INEB is extremely decentralized. Sivaraksa said he has consciously kept the administrative side small. "As you know, I criticize everything," he began. "I have great respect for Goenka. *Vipassana* is wonderful. But for me the use of tape recorders to give Dhamma talks—well, I need a personal teacher. He must feel he has to change with the times, or he should get more teachers.

"The same with Ariyaratne. He has success on a quantitative basis, not qualitative. He claims so many villages, but also he has to compromise with the government sometimes. He doesn't challenge the monks who say they should attack Tamils, for example. He keeps quiet on that. Of course, he does peace marches and all the other good social service work. But to me, to be really engaged, you must always speak the truth.

"And Thich Nhat Hanh, who has been my friend for thirty

years, now he wants a bigger Sangha. He has his Plum Village in France, and his centers in Vermont and California now. But once he has all that, he can no longer criticize any government if he wants to keep his movement growing."

He was on a critical roll, though he might have called it constructive or challenging criticism, but I wanted to shift the direction. "And to what do you attribute this growing movement of Buddhism in the West?" I asked.

"The West has a life of materialism—but has found out materialism is not the answer," he said. "And scientific knowledge is not the answer. It goes back to the Cartesian philosophy."

He was referencing Descartes's *"Cogito, ergo sum"*—I think, therefore I am. But in a way, wasn't that what the Buddha had also said? In *The Dhammapada*, we hear him say, "We are what we think. All that we are arises with our thoughts. With our thoughts, we make our world."

But I let Sivaraksa continue without comment: "People think too much; individualism has become too much. We forget to seek something spiritual."

That *too much* answered the question I hadn't asked. As the Buddha might also have said, by taking the middle path someone would not have gone to the extreme that has resulted in the proliferation of so much self-involvement in the West.

"But why Buddhism? Why not other religions?" I asked.

"For me," Sivaraksa explained, emphasizing "me," "Taoism is not concerned enough with society. Hinduism—well, I'm not in a position to say since it's a rival firm." He chuckled. "But in Hinduism, you need to have faith. In Buddhism, you can be quite comfortable without faith. That is what appeals to people who, though raised on faith, still see no benefit."

"And what about Thai Buddhism?" I asked.

"It's sad," he said. "We have been uprooted from our own Buddhist traditions. My own teacher, Buddhadasa Bhikkhu, said, 'We follow the West so much; Sulak, if you want to do anything, plant Buddhism properly in the West and then the Thais will follow it.' "

The next day I saw an example that proved he and his teacher were right. I had already been to Boulder, Colorado, home of Naropa University, the only Buddhist-informed four-year fully accredited college in the United States, where one of the faculty members had told me a group of Thai academicians had come to observe how this American institution of higher learning integrated meditation into its curricula. Odd, I recall thinking: We go halfway around the world to bring home wisdom from the East, and they're coming here for the same wisdom they could have more easily gotten at their home, and less diluted. Now that I had learned something about Buddhism in Thailand, it struck me as even more odd that Buddhism wasn't naturally part of their educational system. While it is almost the national religion, it is at the same time separated. I had noticed the lounge areas roped off for monks in airports. The 227 restrictions they must observe by definition set them—and, therefore, any "serious practitioner"—off from the rest of society.

Now I sat in a newly renovated hall at Suan Sunandha Rajabhat University with about eight academicians from that institution, Mahachula Buddhist University and Mahamongkut Buddhist University, all in Bangkok. Representatives of each had visited Naropa for three weeks to study its "contemplative education," as they call it.

Group interviews are usually unsuccessful, as some people dominate the discussion. Often those people are simply the loudest or the highest ranking in the room. It's also hard to get someone to reflect on a much more personal level in front of his or her colleagues. In Asia, there is also the gender issue, meaning women tend to defer to men, even when they are higher ranking and may have more insight than their male counterparts. I had strongly advised Prasong that I wanted to meet with only two or three people at once, but that is not easy in Asia. Asians are used to being in larger groups. As well, there is the issue of honor and respect; those not invited would be insulted.

So I tried to adapt. Thai people speak very softly, a style I had thought singular to Prasong. Each was very eager to explain Buddhism to me, starting from the day the Buddha was born. But it was very hard to hear them. So I passed them my tape recorder as each spoke—but once they held the device, it intimidated them. Understanding cultural and gender differences did not seem to have made me any more compassionate; Prasong and I exchanged our "looks." Then, after a sumptuous and extravagant lunch they had prepared in my honor—they told me several times it was the first meal served in this new hall, each repetition making me feel more guilty at the impatience I was sure I had telegraphed to all of them—I grabbed one faculty member I thought would be best for a one-on-one interview. He agreed only if his boss, the president of the university, could participate.

I sat down with Chaiwat Tantarangsee, an assistant professor and director of the training and social services office at Suan Sunandha Rajabhat, and the university president, Dr. Dilok Boonruengrod.

I asked why they went to Naropa in the first place? "We know Americans are very powerful in terms of technology and so on," said Dr. Tantarangsee, "but why do they come to be interested in something so simple and easy?" Did he say meditation was "simple and easy?"

"In Thailand we teach religion as a separate course," he continued, "but when we learned that Naropa integrates it in everything, we thought it was weird. They invite rinpoches to give lectures. Students do chanting. And they do meditation at the beginnings of classes. Also, in Boulder they have Buddhist education like convenience stores—in shopping strips and malls. In America, it's easier to access."

I wanted to explain to him that Boulder is an exception, a little Lhasa in the Colorado Rockies. But it's also true that most anywhere in the United States now you can take Buddhist meditation classes upstairs from a 7-Eleven or a mandala-making workshop next to a Best Buy.

After watching the Naropa approach, Dr. Tantarangsee returned back home very enthusiastic about the possibilities. So he tried it as part of a warming-up exercise in one of the classes he taught.

"I explained, 'Today we are going to do something you've never done in a university before . . .' 'What?' they all wanted to know. So I went on, building it up like a good teacher: 'We can do anything we set our minds to but we have so much trouble keeping our attention to our breath. Why don't we try to breathe . . .'"

When he first suggested this to an English composition class, they looked at him as though he was kidding. Even though he was careful not to call it by its Buddhist name, *anapana sati,* "people could guess what I was going to do," he recalled. "I told them, 'This is not only for monks.'"

"Perhaps to humor me, they gave it a try. The result: I see more peacefulness of mind and their attention to learning is better. Even me! I think of students more as individuals, as humans, without being angry at them. It helps me to be patient." It almost echoed what the prison guard at Tihar in New Delhi had said.

President Boonruengrod, in turn, echoed Siravarska's comments: "We look to America as a model. So why not look to it for Buddhism? Our students follow American fads closely so this was our strategy: to tell them, 'This is the American way.'"

The so-called American way at Naropa had been borrowed from the East. Now, the Thais were borrowing it back again. Now, President Boonruengrod said, he has begun faculty brainstorming sessions with short meditations, and with favorable reception, he added, astonishment in his voice. And Dr. Tantarangsee now assigns his composition students to write essays addressing four questions he felt have resonance from a Buddhist point of view. I had to laugh to myself when he recited the questions.

Who are you?

Where did you come from?

What are you doing?

Where are you going?

To myself, I threw in a fifth question: Is there an echo in here?

I had one more stop before heading to northern Thailand. It was Wat Bang Phra, popularly known as the Tattoo Temple, in the city of Nakorn Chaisri, about an hour's drive west of Bangkok.

On the grounds was a cluster of temples. At one, about 15 young men, who looked to be anywhere from 17 to 30, crowded on a porch, squatting and sitting on the steps. This assortment of tough guys, Prasong told me, inhabit the margins of Thai society—drug dealers, petty criminals, pimps. They waited their turn, eyes hollowed with fear, as they watched a monk perched on a three-foot-high platform working on one man at the end of the porch. Cigarette dangling from his mouth, the monk dipped what looked like a foot-long blunt-edged silver needle into a cup of very dark ink and resumed jabbing at his canvas: the skin on the back of his subject. I moved around for a better look from behind the monk. A tiny trail of blood dripped from the reddened punctured area.

The pattern the monk was etching appeared to be letters of some sort. Later I was told they are words from Buddhist scriptures. Other images on this man and the others—they were all men, I was told, because monks won't touch women—included tigers, dragon heads, various Hindu gods such as Hanuman the monkey god, Ganesh the elephant god, the phallic *linga* of the destroyer god Shiva, as well as hieroglyphics, special numbers, letters and other indecipherable characters. Some of the men were covered with black ink from their necks all the way down to their waists.

This practice goes back to the region's historic roots in animism, imbuing animals with aspects of human nature and superhuman psychic abilities, and the reverse: imbuing humans with some animals' ferociousness and other traits. It is said that the Khmers who settled this region used tattoos as early as the 1st century CE. Historical documents have shown that Thailand's King Rama I used tattoos as identification markers for freemen. The Thai epic poem *Khun Chang Khun Paen* refers to soldiers wearing protective tattoos into battle. In the annual festival of Nakorn Pathom, those who have been tattooed go into trance states, writhing and shivering, their bodies and spirits taken by the animal or other powers those tattoos are said to represent. Now, that annual event, held in February, has become a big tourist magnet, a matter that does not please Sulak Sivaraksa. He was quoted calling for reforms by the Sangha Council, the monks' national governing body, which he said should never have allowed the situation to get to this point. "Buddhism has become mere form," he stated. "Buddhism for Thais nowadays has become a kind of superstition." But was he looking realistically at his own country's Buddhist history?

After one young man's turn, I asked to speak to him. Tentatively, he agreed. He said he comes every day, during his lunch break. As payment to the monk, he offered two packs of cigarettes, some flowers and a small donation to the temple—equal to about $2. "This gives me power, I am sure," he said, his eyes darting back and forth, as though he was watching for someone, or watching for someone watching for him. "I know I will be guarded against danger. No evil will harm me. I will suffer less."

Given the suffering I had just seen him withstand, I thought he had already gotten his money's worth.

The creativity with which Thai people have interpreted Buddhism is paralleled in the Thai art world. A vibrant contemporary arts community is inventing new forms to express their Buddhist sensibilities in, appropriately, a variety of mixed media. The examples are endless. In one, at her outdoor theater in Bangkok, nationally renowned director and choreographer Patravadi Mejudhon was producing *Eclipse,* a nine-act, 90-minute dance-music-drama morality play weaving Thai and Japanese dance traditions, intense percussion and neoclassical music with Buddhist philosophy. It's highly symbolic theater; the darkened stage, for example, reflecting humanity's struggle to overcome desire and fear. "Buddhism is not just ceremony," she told me over drinks. "Buddhism is freedom—freedom of thinking. But you use that freedom with discipline."

In Chiang Mai, that freedom of expression has run amok, as I found out when I arrived at this hub of northern Thailand, a popular destination. Prasong had picked out three artists he thought might represent the spectrum. The first was a prominent artist named Kamin Lertchaiprasert, who was successful both critically and commercially. The 40-year-old has shown throughout the world. His studio in a residential neighborhood of the city was the Grand Central Station of modern Thai artists; a sort of mentor to the next generation, he lends his space to them to work. A student of *vipassana* meditation—his teacher was Goenka—he took a year off in 1990 to do serious meditation practice.

"I believe that the process of creating art enables us to understand our own nature just as the process of practicing Buddhist Dhamma does," he said amid the chaos in a small room he reserves for himself. We were surrounded by small papier-mâché Buddhas that were a continuation of a series he called *Problem-Wisdom,* which he had shown from 1993 to 1995. But apparently he couldn't put it down. The *Problem-Wisdom* that toured was a large floor-based installation consisting of 366 papier-mâché sculptures. Lertchaiprasert sculpted each object in response to a problem affecting contemporary Thai society. Every day for a year, he selected an article from a Thai newspaper, pulped the paper and made a small hand-sized object that responded to the reported problem. The following year, he systematically revisited each object and meditated on a solution. The solution (or wisdom) was inscribed in calligraphy on the object. It seemed like a better use of yesterday's paper than as lining for bird cages.

"Inherent in this is the Buddhist belief that everything in life—good and bad, right and wrong—exists in balance," he said.

A highly politicized social activist who believes the canvas is mightier than the sword, he gave me a booklet entitled *Beyond Peace and War,* fancifully mixing fonts and typefaces and graphics in the spirit of a college art project. Half in English and half in Thai, it promoted a project called *Art Against War,* which he helped fund. He gave me another booklet of his own making, made of fine thin paper. One image captured my eye; it reminded me of the patterns and designs I'd seen on the skin canvases at Wat Bang Phra. It was a circle containing what might have been Thai lettering and an image that looked to me like the Buddha's thumb and first finger in a circle—the teaching-the-Dhamma mudra. Alongside it was this text:

> Senses awakened, receptors open, *Umong Sippadhamma* is a tunnel in the heart of Dhamma. It bores to the core of art according to the precepts of Buddha. Just take a look at the logo. At first glance it looks like a tribal tattoo. Lines weave in and out like a visual mantra. Is this a "Kamin?" The ink swirls, spirals and spins to its own laws. It's chaos incarnate. Take another look at the logo upside down. See it through rose-tinted glasses. A three-degree shift of perception reveals order in the eye of chaos. The third eye is the tunnel; the curvaceous contours are an abstraction of the words *Umong Sippadhamma.*

Umong means tunnel; *Sippadhamma* means arts and dhamma. So: tunnel of art that reflects the dhamma. Or, as Kamin explained, "Figuratively, it connotes digging for truth. Art and dhamma are the same thing. Generally, the arts are misinterpreted as beautiful things solely. A true piece of art is dhamma because it is about goodness, beauty and truth."

This was psychedelic '60s art meets Thai Buddhadelic art.

From the sublime to the ridiculous, Prasong then took me to Dhamma Park Gallery and Heritage Gardens, the invention of a wealthy British sculptor named Venetia Walkey and Thai woodworker Inson Wongsam. "A sculpture park and contemporary centre for spiritual development and the arts," the brochure explained, but it hardly grasped Ms. Walkey's whole vision, though after a personal tour by her I was still grasping for her vision—and gasping from exhaustion at her lecture. Her "work"—fairly literal expressions of her interpretation of Buddhist teachings—was less sophisticated than other work I had seen. As patient as I tried to be, I found myself attempting to expedite her lecture by suggesting that she didn't need to explain *all* of Buddhism or show me *all* of her work, or explain *so* specifically the association between the art and the Dhammic teaching. But with each interruption, she became more stubborn. I was in for the duration. I gave Prasong "the look," and this time he could only shrug behind her in apology to me. What was inspiring, though, was that somehow this locale encouraged such a freedom of self-expression and that she was so moved by Buddhism that she had given up what had probably been a quite civilized life in Europe to move to this outpost of outposts.

But it was standing in the middle of a fallow rice field on the outskirts of Chiang Mai that my own imagination was captured. Roongroj Piamyossak, who might be described as the Christo of Thailand, had taken me to see the outdoor environmental installation he calls *Temple of Mankind,* a triangle of black iron walls. On their inside he had painted six-foot heads of the Buddha in acrylics and other media. Interspersed among the faces were mirrors.

"What's it mean?" I kept asking, as the traffic whizzed by on the nearby highway. "Why here? Why a triangle? Why Buddha?" I unnerved him with my questions.

Roongroj is a soft-spoken man of about 40 with a ponytail and a thin mustache. I immediately liked him; his lack of ego was refreshing, especially compared to the last two artists I'd met. He said he'd rather let his art speak for him. But, I explained, that makes for a bad interview, so he struggled to explain. "Only a rich man can build a temple, but everybody should be able to," he said as we wove in and around the triangle. "The people of this region are very connected to the earth.

"This field is sacred because it's in the middle of a triangle of three important Buddhist temples," Roongroj continued, pointing to a mountain we could see from there. At the top was Wat

Phrathat Doi Suthep, which means "Royal Monastery of the Beneficent Angels, Containing a Holy Buddha Relic." When he was a kid, he used to go up there with his father, he said.

The installation also was meant to be a social and environmental statement; this field where we stood had been acquired from the farmers by developers. By the time you read this, there will be a high-rise condominium apartment complex that few in this re-gion—especially the displaced farmers who put their sweat and souls into the land—will be able to afford.

The mirror, he explained after much prompting, suggests that "here, in this natural environment, we can see ourselves more clearly." The triangle has multiple meanings. The Buddha is often depicted as a triangle, representing his perfect three-pointed sym-metry when he sits in meditation. Also, he said, there is a death theme: The hole within the triangle of black walls is death. I inter-preted that to also mean the death of this land as a producer of life-sustaining rice and any other edibles.

"Why such doom and gloom?" I asked.

"Not," Roongroj now said firmly. "Birth, sickness, death—all are part of life to Buddhists. All is oneness."

"Why Buddhism" required a long personal tale, so we sat under the shade of one wall. In short, he had suffered debilitating physi-cal pain that led to an emotional downward spiral, which in turn led to those fundamental questions of who/why/what. There were serious intestinal problems that sounded like colitis, then a rotator cuff problem, then a year of complete disability and the inability to work at his art or at anything else, then alcoholism. Then the questions . . .

"It started with 'why me?' " he said. "Eventually, it came down to just 'why?' Lying on your back is like meditation. I ran out of options—doctors didn't work, drugs and alcohol didn't work." Then he recalled accompanying his father to the Buddhist temples. But back then he bowed to the Buddha by rote. Now he went vol-untarily, open to whatever he could glean from the experience— "It was my only alternative, my last hope." And there he dis-

Perry Garfinkel

Roongroj Piamyossak, a modern artist, stands at the bottom of 290 steps that lead up to Wat Phrathat Doi Suthep, 3,000 feet above the city of Chiang Mai, Thailand. The temple houses relics of the Buddha.

covered a process, long forgotten or, he admits, one he never took in so deeply as a youth, by which he could accept his physical pain. "Even to my own bewilderment," he said, "in surrendering to it, I was freed from it." It reminded me of my own experience at Auschwitz, somehow released from anger by surrending to the inexplicability of the Holocaust.

Now his Buddhist practice is, simply, mindfulness. He would

not elaborate along the lines I had become used to: some long monologue on Buddha Dhamma and Thai history. He just smiled and looked at me unblinkingly. More than almost anyone I met in Thailand, he simply embodied whatever it is we all are looking for.

"Can you show me how it works?" I asked.

Roongroj stopped and became still; the wheels of time slowed down. Maybe three minutes of silence. *What am I supposed to be doing? Listening for? Feeling? Do I look at him? Close my eyes? Study the landscape?* He then, compassionately, broke the silence: "I hear the birds, I smell this earth, I witness the thoughts in my mind, I am here, with you." The sun slowly disappeared behind Doi Suthep Mountain. "This is my practice."

"Take me there," I said. He looked at me quizzically. I realized myself the question was ambiguous. What I thought I had meant was "take me up that mountain tomorrow morning." What I really meant was "Take me to that lovely and tranquil place where you just were."

But that place and that moment were impermanent. They passed, and my Mr. Journalist persona kicked back in faster than you could say "deadline."

Impermanence could be the operative word when it comes to Thailand's environment. Bangkok, like Asia's other major cities, has become an urban obstacle course of traffic jams and bad air. In the rural upcountry, the depletion of the country's green forested areas causes an ecological ripple effect of concern to all levels of the food chain. Since the end of World War II, the percentage of area covered by forest has dropped from 70 to about 25, according to Pasuk Phongpaichit, professor of economics at Bangkok's Chulalongkorn University, in *Thailand: Economy and Politics,* coauthored with Chris Baker.

That loss is due to commercial logging, a practice that was made illegal by the government but continues, according to local authorities I interviewed who asked not to be identified. The taking of trees for fuel and the clearing of stands for agricultural development by rural people are also responsible.

The environmental impact is inestimable—from silting that kills fish and leaves riverbeds dry, to the loss of nesting and feeding for birds and other wildlife. But there is also a metaphorical impact. When Buddhists think of trees, they think not only of a living organism that deserves to be nurtured, but also of the Buddha himself. They associate all trees with that tree he sat under in Bodh Gaya. For several hundred years after the Buddha's death, the only visual representation of the man was inanimate objects like a tree or leaf. They also connect forests with the place that wandering mendicants have retreated to for solitude, for protection and for spiritual sustenance since time immemorial, writes Southeast Asian historian Kamala Tiyavanich in *The Buddha in the Jungle*. In Thailand, there are "town monks" and "forest monks," as she points out in her other book, *Forest Recollections: Wandering Monks in Twentieth-Century Thailand*. To the forest monks, these trees are their walls and the roofs of their temples.

The Thai Buddhist response to the decimation of what they consider their sacred sanctuaries has been the mobilization of a group that has been dubbed the "ecology monks," who have launched a number of activities and initiatives to bring awareness to their country's environmental crisis and to try to reverse it.

To see a very moving example of the type of proactivity they engage in, I drove with photographer Steve McCurry five hours from Chiang Mai deep into the wooded high-country district of Santisuk in the northeast corner of Thailand, then to the village of Pong Kam. The head of the local temple, the Venerable Somkid Jarayadhammo, had invited us to witness a unique ceremony.

Since 1991, monks have been ceremonially ordaining trees as monks to protect them from being clear-cut. The idea is that since virtually the entire population in these rural areas is Buddhist, no one—not even those tempted by some quick cash offered by private sector interests—would take the life of even a mock monk.

So local monks and members of the community are called to officiate these ordinations in the forests.

The night before the ceremony, we sat and talked with the Venerable Somkid, a monk of about 40 who grew up in this area. He sat at the edge of the platform from which he conducts services for this small community of about a thousand people. The temple was a simple concrete building, two sides exposed to the outside.

"When I was a kid, that river was high," he said, pointing to the now-dry bed that paralleled the building. "There were catfish, twenty kinds of shell fish and many eel. In the forests we often would see deer, monkey, bear, boor—no more."

Now he was combining Buddhist wisdom with what he'd learned in the environmental-management program he was taking at Chiang Mai University. But it was a struggle, he conceded, both as a movement and on a personal level. On the positive side, though statistics are hard to come by, he did sense growing awareness and a slow reforestation. But his activities were causing disharmony: There were arguments with government agency representatives in the local community. Information from them was not forthcoming; he suspected they were lying. There was tension. To live a life according to Buddhist principles was not easy: to not harm one person may cause harm for another person. Sometimes when one person wins, another may lose. But, added the monk, for the sake of these people and the other living things here, inaction was not an option.

That evening, after dinner and a lovely informal performance by young dancers and folk musicians, Steve and I carried his photo equipment and our bags up a short trail to our "accommodations." I put that in quotes because earlier we had been shown where we would be sleeping: a concrete building that appeared in midconstruction. There was not a stitch of furniture on the two floors of the building. We would sleep in a small side room off a larger room on the second floor. I had stared at the hard, bare concrete floor, the bare dangling single lightbulb, the less than sanitary bathroom downstairs, the windows that had no screens or shades or even glass. I smacked my neck, killing a mosquito, not even worrying about the 10,000 more lives I had incurred with that one reflexive motion. Our bedding would be . . . nothing. We were told some straw mats would be provided later but I wasn't so sure they would materialize. And while I tried to be grateful for the little things, and even for the big thing—that I was still here, still on the assignment of a lifetime, still doing the Buddha's good works, my back still holding up—those earlier Eminem-inspired mantras of self-motivation had deteriorated into an incessant incantation that bounced from ear to ear deep inside my wary brain. My new mantra: *"What a fucking nightmare!"*

Now, walking to these sleeping quarters, I was dragging my butt behind Steve, the intrepid photog who had regaled me with stories the whole five hours we had driven together from Chiang Mai to Pong Kam of his adventures around the world, of traipsing through the jungles of Laos and Cambodia, of nearly getting arrested in Afghanistan while tracking down the girl he made famous, of the many times he had put his life in harm's way for the mere sake of a good picture. This kind of thing was his cup of tea, I presumed; he was in his element. So I kept my own mouth shut, while that mantra now beat more loudly against my ear drums.

Then I heard Steve muttering in a stage whisper loud enough for only me to hear.

"What a fucking nightmare," he said—*he said!*

Now I was really nervous. If the Great Steve McCurry was calling this a "fucking nightmare," it must be a real fucking nightmare, even worse than I had imagined in my own little mind. This gave me no solace whatsoever. But it did give me a different perspective on Mr. McCurry; maybe there was a sensitive and vulnerable soul lurking under that thick veneer of "veteran photojournalist."

That night would have been a nightmare, had I fallen asleep to dream at all. But how can you have nightmares when you lie awake all night, swatting at mosquitoes real or imagined? It's those mental mosquitoes that get to you on nights like that, lying in your own neurotic juices. *Would I find a fixer in China? How the hell was I ever going to condense this global expedition into a 5,000-word article? Could I do justice to all the people I'd interviewed, to the Buddha himself? Or would I once again successfully pull the wool over everyone's eyes, blinding them with a display of flashy words to distract them from the realization that I had so unsuccessfully mastered this material? What if I have to get up and take a piss? Ugh—that bathroom! Would I ever find lasting love? Forget happiness—would I ever stop beating myself up so ruthlessly? Would morning ever come?*

If I hadn't been so consumed with panic, I would have marveled at my mind's ability to reel off such a dazzling series of non sequiturs. One tiny island of comfort that loomed in this ocean of personal obsession proved just how desperate one's mind gets in dire situations. I pictured myself the following night back in Bangkok, back at the Four Seasons, back in that lush bed, wrapped in the 400-thread-count linen sheets, the air-conditioning so cool that I would need to pull up the soft blanket—in short, back where I belonged.

An hour before we had planned to rise, I finally sat up, allowing myself to leave my emotional shrapnel on that hard, damp floor. When Steve got up (I never asked how he slept), we rounded up the group and congregated at the edge of a wooded area several hundred yards behind the temple. Teenagers participating in a weekend of cultural education sponsored by the head monk had also been invited. In the clearing, a long Oriental rug had been laid. A dozen monks, from young to old, filed in and seated themselves in a row on the rug. A Buddha statue was carefully placed next to Ven. Somkid. String was tied around the trees, then around the Buddha, then around the monks' wrists, and then to those witnessing it—all of us now connected to each other. Harm one, harm all; this was a graphic demonstration of Buddhism's principle of the interrelated nature of all things. We're all tied seamlessly into one living organism.

Several trees were wrapped with saffron ribbons. For 45 minutes, the monks chanted in the traditional Pali language. All I could make out was the now familiar repetition of the Buddha's Three Refuges: "I take refuge in the Buddha, I take refuge in the Dhamma, I take refuge in the Sangha."

The mist that had blanketed us broke in time for Steve to take his photographs. While I waited for him, one shy monk approached me and handed me a booklet containing verses from a Buddhist text. Oddly, it was in English, a rarity in this remote region. I read:

"Ecology monks" in northeastern Thailand symbolically ordain trees with saffron ribbons to protect them from being clear-cut by illegal logging interests.

"To begin, then, with the Buddha's own words, we find this in the Gradual Sayings: 'He who has understanding and great wisdom does not think of harming himself or another, nor of harming both alike. He rather thinks of his own welfare, of that of others, of that of both, and of the welfare of the whole world. In that way one shows understanding and great wisdom.'—Anguttara Nikaya, Fours, No. 18."

The Anguttara Nikaya is part of a collection of discourses called the Sutta Pitaka, attributed to the Buddha and a few of his closest disciplines, written in Pali, and containing the central teachings of Theravada Buddhism.

Though I appreciated the idea, such highbrow Buddhist literature usually made my eyes glaze over. It was the kind of Buddha-babble I read in bed as a remedy for insomnia back in the States before I undertook this journey. But now, enhanced by the sweet smell of trees, the wet mist on my face, the sounds of birds chirping, the urgency of this community's needs, that "great wisdom" was beginning to penetrate my thick skull.

My *Go Green!* romanticism notwithstanding, my thick skull would not let me wax too quixotic in the face of the facts. The best I can report on the success of the tree-ordaining ceremonies is anecdotal, like Venerable Somkid's sense that the forests are slowly coming back. The Thai Forestry Department's statistics only reported to 1995, and in the Byzantine world of Thai bureaucracy, finding an authority to attribute anything to was impossible. But the actions serve several positive purposes, according to Susan M. Darlington, an anthropologist at Hampshire College in Massachusetts who has been tracking the success of the ecology monks since the early 1990s. In the 2000 edition of the *Journal of Buddhist Ethics,* she writes: "First, the action draws attention to the threat of deforestation. Second, the ritual provides the opportunity for the ecology monks and the laity who work with them (predominantly non-government environmentalists and development agents) to teach about the impact of environmental destruction and the value and means of conserving nature. Finally, the monks use the ritual to teach the Dhamma and to stress its relevance in a rapidly changing world."

In her paper, "Rethinking Buddhism and Development: The Emergence of Environmentalist Monks in Thailand," Darlington added, "The impact . . . may be impossible to assess, but the potential of their activism to challenge Thai Buddhists to rethink their religion, their society, and their place in both the political and the natural world cannot be denied."

We called such actions consciousness raising back in the '60s and '70s, and, twig by twig, we were able to eventually make a difference: reverse racist laws, end a war, trigger a sexual revolution. The Buddha said, "A jug fills drop by drop." I expected no less of this grassroots movement, with time.

seven

Wherever You Go, There You Are— Even in Hong Kong

The creative and imaginative efforts and actions of every one of us count, and
nothing less than the health of the world hangs in the balance. We could say
that the world is literally and metaphorically dying for us as a species to come to
our senses, and now is the time.

> —JON KABAT-ZINN, *Coming to Our Senses: Healing Ourselves and the
> World Through Mindfulness*

There is an orientalism in the most restless pioneer, and the farthest west is but
the farthest east.

> —HENRY DAVID THOREAU, *A Week on the Concord and Merrimack Rivers*

Molecular biologist Jon Kabat-Zinn, the founder of the Stress Reduction Clinic at the University of Massachusetts Medical School
in Worcester, had suggested I stop in Hong Kong to meet a Chinese clinical psychologist named Helen Ma. She had gone from her
home in Hong Kong to Worcester to take an eight-week intensive
training he led in Mindfulness-Based Stress Reduction (MBSR).
She then returned to Hong Kong to introduce it there in institutional settings. She was, he said, a good example of a trend I had
identified.

While it is generally, and rightly, assumed that the ideas of Buddhism came to the West from the East, it would seem counterintuitive, almost heretic and certainly disrespectful to the ancient Asian sages, to suggest the same wisdom, albeit repackaged, was being passed from the West back to the East. And, further, that in some cases these back winds sending seeds eastward were regerminating a Buddhist garden in Asia that had all but shriveled up. Yet my experiences and conversations corroborated my idea that this West-to-East migration of Buddhism existed—the Thai faculty, who brought back contemplative education from Boulder to Bangkok; Shantum Seth, who had to go to California to find the Buddhism that was under his nose in India; and now Helen Ma.

On the surface this immediately sounds jingoistic: the chauvinistic presumption of Westerners (and here I mean mostly Americans) to think they have something to tell Asians about a practice that has been in their culture for two millennia. Absurd, and insulting. This would be akin to that awkward moment when the son outruns his father, or when the disciple becomes the master's master. What if the Karate Kid turned to Mr. Miyagi and said, "No, it's wax on, *left* hand; wax off, *right* hand"?

In fact, were it not for several Westerners in the 18th and 19th centuries, Buddhist history might be languorously hiding under mounds of earth and shrubs, an idea whose time came and went.

In his terrific 2002 book, *The Buddha and the Sahibs,* the British historian Charles Allen describes 18th-century "Orientalists," a term now loaded with Western-centric arrogance that referred to Europeans versed in Oriental languages, literature and particularly archeology.

"The land which had nurtured the historical Buddha and given rise to the early Buddhist civilizations had been so thoroughly cleaned that the first Orientalists could see no trace of Buddhism on Indian soil," he writes. These Orientalists "initiated the recovery of South Asia's lost past. The European discovery of Buddhism and the subsequent resurgence of Buddhism in South Asia arose directly out of their activities." His book, he writes in his introduction, "tells how the person of Gautama Buddha, prince of the Sakya clan, and the faith he inspired was 'discovered' in the 19th century by a small group of Westerners and restored—not just to India, but to the wider world." Among the findings in India attributed to these Orientalists was the unearthing and repair of the Mahabodhi Temple in Bodh Gaya in the mid-1800s.

At just about the same time, there was also the case of the retired American Civil War Union officer named Henry Steel Olcott, now working for the government investigating fraud, corruption and graft at the New York Mustering and Disbursement Office. Investigating reports of "certain incredible phenomena" of an occult nature on a farm in Chittenden, Vermont, he there met an eccentric Russian living in New York named Madame Helena Petrovna Blavatsky, also said to have certain psychic powers and be privy to certain esoteric wisdom, of which she dropped "hints of the teachings of the Secret Doctrine of the oldest school of Occult philosophy in the world, a school of reform which the Lord Gautama was made to appear," as Rick Fields writes in *How the Swans Came to the Lake,* his exhaustive tracing of the Buddhist movement in the West. Together, with others, they founded the Theosophical Society in 1875 (which still has international headquarters in Chennai, India; and an American center in Wheaton, Illinois). To make short a long and fascinating chapter in 19th-century America's infatuation with occult-type spiritualism, the pair moved to India to establish their society there in 1879. Then, hearing that Sinhalese Buddhism was under attack and waning under the heavily Christian missionary influence of three successive waves of Portuguese, Dutch and British colonialism, they went south in 1880. In a ceremony before a Buddhist priest, they repeated the five Buddhist vows of abstinence (the five precepts to refrain from killing, lying, stealing, intoxicants and sexual misconduct) and recited the Three Refuges, becoming the first known Westerners to officially become lay Buddhists. Then they proceeded to energize the entire Buddhist community on the island, helping establish schools, defense committees and more. "To the Sinhalese, it seemed that the American Theosophists had single-handedly restored their religion and culture to them," Fields writes.

Among many others, they took a teenage boy from Colombo under their wing. This protégé, David Hewivitarne, later took the full vows of a bhikku, taking the name Anagarika Dharmapala, by which he is known to millions of Buddhists in Sri Lanka and beyond as South Asia's first modern Buddhist saint. Eventually Dharmapala read an article about the state of decay of certain Buddhist pilgrimage sites in India, written by yet another Westerner who awakened interest in Buddhism in the West. This was Sir Edwin Arnold, the author of *The Light of Asia,* a book first published in 1879 that's often credited with introducing the life of the Buddha to multitudes in the West. Inspired by the article, the Ceylonese monk founded the Bodh Gaya Maha Bodhi Society in Colombo in 1891 with "one paramount aim: to return Bodh Gaya to the world's Buddhists," Fields writes. The Maha Bodhi Society I visited in Bodh Gaya is a result of his efforts, and those efforts in turn are thanks to this vanguard group of Western Buddha-philes. Dharmapala also was at the vanguard of the engaged Buddhism movement, voicing his ideas in 1928 in the *Maha Bodhi Journal:*

> The aristocratic caste distinction which was organised by the Brahmans, He [the Buddha] repudiated as unjust. It was the ethic of spiritualised democracy that He enunciated. Happiness could be realised here not by sacrificing to the gods, and praying to get possessions, but in ceaseless activity in doing good in helping the sick, both animals and men, in giving pure water to drink, in distributing clothes, food, flowers, scents, perfumes, vehicles, to the poor and in building houses for their dwelling, and in teaching the law of righteousness.

Jingoistic or not, the relationship of Dr. Kabat-Zinn and Helen Ma was just the latest example of how Buddhist seeds blown from East to West to East again were part of a cross-pollination that has been creating hybrids for centuries, if not millennia.

Hong Kong itself was a country straddling east and west when Dr. Ma was born there in 1959. Hong Kong has absorbed several waves of immigration from Mainland China, as far back as the Stone Age, according to Neolithic artifacts collected by archaeologists in the 1920s. The territory was settled by Han Chinese during the 7th century CE, evidenced by the discovery of an ancient tomb at Lei Cheung Uk in Kowloon. More came during the Sung dynasty (960–1279). In the last 300 years, though, it was the British invasion that imprinted today's Hong Kong. Soon after the British East India Company's first successful sea venture to China in 1699, Hong Kong's trade with British merchants developed rapidly. After the Chinese defeat in the First Opium War (1839–1842), Hong Kong was ceded to Britain in 1842 under the Treaty of Nanjing. Britain was granted a perpetual lease on the Kowloon Peninsula under the 1860 Convention of Beijing, which formally ended hostilities in the Second Opium War (1856–1858). The United Kingdom, concerned that Hong Kong could not be defended unless surrounding areas also were under British control, executed a 99-year lease of the New Territories in 1898, significantly expanding the size of the Hong Kong colony.

In the late 19th century and early 20th centuries, Hong Kong developed as a warehousing and distribution center for U.K. trade with southern China. After the end of World War II and the Communist takeover of Mainland China in 1949, hundreds of thousands of people fled from China to Hong Kong. Hong Kong became an economic success and a manufacturing, commercial, finance and tourism center. In short, this group of 200 islands had become a gateway to the East. High life expectancy, literacy, per capita income and other socioeconomic measures attest to Hong Kong's achievements over the last five decades. Also among those socioeconomic indicators, however, were increases in stress, divorce, suicide—factors more reminiscent of the Western lifestyle. It came as no surprise to me that, therefore, tools for stress reduction might now be among the hottest new commodity imports in Hong Kong.

Helen's parents came to Hong Kong during the Japanese occupation of China in the late 1930s, but the tinge of British in her accent, her Western academic credentials and her leanings toward a more secular life suggested she had already made a shift in a Westerly direction. In terms of religious upbringing, she described her parents as secular Buddhists. "They queued up with others at the temples during the Guan Yin Festival, to burn incense and pray to the Buddha of Compassion, but otherwise it was a mix of folk, Confucianism and Taoism," she explained. "There was no Buddhist practice or reading or chanting whatsoever. The spirit of Buddhism is understood at a grassroots level here."

We were sitting in a faux Italian café in the seaside village of Stanley on Hong Kong Island, near where she lived. The meeting place, determined for her convenience, had an appropriateness I had not anticipated. The café was located in the Murray House, one of the oldest Victorian buildings in Hong Kong, built in 1844 by the British army. During World War II it was headquarters of the Japanese Army. Later it was moved brick by brick to this site and reopened in 1998 as the venue for several Western restaurants. Would Helen's parents have been offended their daughter even stepped foot in a building once occupied by the Japanese, who forced them from their homes in Mainland China? Did the historical irony even cross Helen's mind? It appeared not.

Having attended Catholic schools for 13 years, simply because the education was better than in Buddhist or nondenominational schools, it made sense that when she wanted to get away from it all, she took retreats at Catholic centers. She received her PhD in clinical psychology from the University of Cambridge in the United Kingdom. She moved to Sydney in 1990, where she worked in the psychiatric unit at the Royal Prince Alfred Hospital in Sydney. It was the appeal of the pristine setting of the Blue Mountains outside Sydney that attracted her to a retreat center, where, much to her surprise, the technique taught there was *vipassana* meditation.

"While psychotherapy was useful, there was still something I wanted to get to the bottom of—some ultimate answer," she said. "In *vipassana,* I experienced that. It was great for my own stress or depressive thoughts. But how could I integrate this spiritual aspect with my clients?" Intuitively, she sensed there was some overlap, but now, trained in the Western frame of mind, she was not willing to entertain another possibility without some empirical evidence. I don't know what dormant cell in my brain this line came from but I blurted out: "Faith is a fine invention for gentlemen, you see, but microscopes are prudent in an emergency." It was my Massachusetts compatriot Emily Dickinson, vintage high school poetry, memorized by rote, now regurgitated as Buddhist Dhamma. Dr. Ma didn't know my beloved Emily, but she nodded in agreement.

She returned to Hong Kong in 1996, and working now in hospice care made her "feel further that the psychological and spiritual were interlaced," she said. "Watching people in beds in pain, struggling both mentally and physically, it was hard to tease out where one ends and the other begins. 'Where am I going to?' they'd ask. How do you answer that?"

She found a possible clinical answer in a tape of the Bill Moyers *Healing and the Mind* PBS show that featured Dr. Kabat-Zinn and the MBSR program at U-Mass Worcester. She recalled one line from that tape that particularly moved her. Dr. Kabat-Zinn asked one woman struggling with chronic pain, "Do you want to move from existing to living?" She realized he held a key she had not yet found. Equally important, he had the published research to prove that key opened some doors she couldn't open. It seemed fitting to me that since the doors to Buddhist wisdom in Asia had been shut by Western empirical attitudes, it was now a Westerner, with empirical backup, who provided a Buddhist key to open them up again.

"Knock, knock."

"Who's there?"

"The Buddha."

"The Buddha who?"

"What, you didn't recognize me in my white lab coat?"

The Hong Kong Tourism Board gave me a brochure boasting of the city's superlatives: Asia's single largest foreign direct investment recipient, the world's 10th-largest banking and financial center, the region's major hub for foreign-owned multinational corporations, the world's 14th most popular and Asia's single most popular travel destination; home to three of the world's tallest buildings, the world's tallest soft drinks plant (Coca-Cola, of course), the world's longest covered escalator system (according to Guinness World Records). And, according to the United Nations Human Development Report of 2001, it had the world's highest capita ownership of cellular phones (64 per 100 people).

Obscured by all of the above was this factoid: Hong Kong boasted the world's tallest outdoor-seated bronze Buddha statue, at 26 meters, on Lantau Island, a 10-year project completed in 1993. This gave me an idea. If I could build a Buddha unique enough— define a niche so esoteric, such as "the only Silly Putty Buddha sitting on its head at Exit 145 of the Garden State Parkway—my Buddha and I could make it into the *Guinness Book of World Records*.

The hotel the tourism board had helped me find, the Miramar, in the heart of Hong Kong's crowded downtown, was huge, and, as evidence of the city's booming business, occupancy was at 100 percent. And every occupant, it seemed, smoked—and smoked everywhere. I don't mean "seemed" to smoke everywhere. This was a fact. On my floor, all the doors to the rooms were ajar; inside the rooms were groups of two, three, four people, sitting on beds, standing with drinks, laughing and, of course, smoking. I had asked ahead for a nonsmoking room. The reply e-mail practically laughed in my face; I might as well have requested hot and cold running vodka. Even my pillow reeked of cigarette smoke. For days after I left Hong Kong, the stench hung on the hairs of my nostrils. For relief, I retreated to a restaurant and bar below the Mi-ramar that reminded me of a Ruby Tuesday chain restaurant; of course, there was no escaping the smoke. But the restaurant of-fered a great deal; if you ordered two drinks, you could use its In-ternet station to check your e-mail. So I allowed the smoke to get in my eyes—as well as my nose, ears and throat—as I got shit-faced on boilermakers, scrambling still to make e-contact with a good fixer in China. I was reaching desperation mode. Was it an omen of bad things to come in the Land of the Sleeping Giant? My Zen journalism approach was in danger of backfiring on me. Where was the late Hunter Thompson when I needed him?

"People are getting richer but not happier here," Dr. Ma had said. "Hong Kong is becoming hungry for something spiritual."

This, she said, explained her impression that in the last two decades there are more meditation centers. That, plus the fact that now there is "evidence." She used that word "evidence" fre-quently.

"Intellectuals and young people who have been exposed to the West find that this repackaged Buddhism, which is no longer about superstition or just being a good guy, is appealing," she said. "There is scholarly evidence it works, and there are practical appli-cations."

Along with the growing body of research Dr. Kabat-Zinn and his American team have published in professional journals, Dr. Ma and her colleagues have added empirical proof. In a study reported in 2004 in the *Journal of Consulting and Clinical Psychology,* she and psychologist John Teasdale, of Cambridge, England, tested the ability of Mindfulness-Based Cognitive Therapy (MBCT) to re-duce the risk of recurrence of major depression in patients. MBCT, a variation of MBSR, reduced the rate from 78 percent to 36 percent in those with three or more episodes of relapse.

The Centre on Behavioral Health at the University of Hong Kong, where Dr. Ma is one of several psychologists leading 10-week MBSR sessions, has also conducted its own studies as well. "There is so much interest now," she said. "I think part of the appeal is that there are no religious trappings. I tell participants it comes from Buddhist tradition but that it's been *proven* in the West to be a very effective technique for reducing stress. 'Stress reduction' sounds so psychological."

She told me just the night before she had gotten an e-mail from the director of a palliative medicine committee at the Hospital Authority, Hong Kong's government health agency, asking her to conduct MBSR training for doctors. Another request had come in from a clinical psychologist at a community health center to lead a 10-week session for chronically ill patients. There was "evidence" this thing was taking root, or reroot.

The next day I had the opportunity to sit in on a session at the Centre on Behavioral Health. Psychologist Peta McAuley, an Australian transplant who has lived in Hong Kong for 25 years, led the one I attended. She, too, had undergone the MBSR training in Worcester. "I've got to hand it to those Yanks," she said. "When the Americans do something, they do it the best." She said it almost begrudgingly. She had enough American jingoism for the two of us.

Dr. McAuley and I talked before the session. She wanted me to know that *vipassana* was not her first Buddhist experience. For seven years she had been involved with Nichiren Shoshu, a Japanese Buddhism sect. Its founder, a 13th-century priest named Nichiren Daishonin, believed that anyone can achieve enlightenment by chanting a certain phrase from the Lotus Sutra, one of Buddhism's most influential sacred scriptures. I knew this sect; it happened to be a first brush with Buddhism my then wife, Iris, and I had when we lived in Boston. It was 1973, we hadn't been to India yet, and it was an absolute turn-off. People gathered in a Beacon Hill town house converted to a temple. They all sat on the floor of a long parlor room, facing a wall with a long vertical white piece of paper bearing some Japanese characters. They were chanting this one phrase over and over—*Nam-myoho-renge-kyo* ("praise to the wonderful Lotus Sutra"). The words blurred together in a low, almost sad sort of droll. The people seemed like robots; the whole scene felt cultlike to us. "Buddhism is not our bag" was how we probably put it. It was, after all, 1973.

I tried to put my "attitude" aside as Dr. McAuley explained a very interesting theory about the difference between Buddhism East and West. From her own cross-cultural studies, she said, "it's clear Americans are measurably more extroverted and achievement-oriented than Chinese, and Chinese are measurably more introverted and try to avoid conflict.

"Harmony is the name of the game here," she said. "Jung believed the psyche will seek its own balance." That's why Americans are more drawn to the internal practice of meditation, while Asians tend to do more chanting, incense burning and bowing. I had not heard this analysis before, and it struck me as accurate. Except that her theory fell apart with her: Aussies are generally very outgoing people. So why had she gravitated to a chanting practice? She didn't have an explanation and asked me, based on my travels, if I had one. This scared me: People were looking to *me* as a Buddhist authority? Well, anything is possible, as Master Eminem might say.

"Let me meditate on it," I joked, but she didn't seem to get it.

We then moved to what looked like a multipurpose room in the new wing of any American church: industrial gray fabric covering the walls, matching room dividers, no fresh air to speak of, metal chairs stacked in corners. It had as much personality as a dentist's waiting room—no, less. Cushions formed a circle in the middle of the floor. It was the end of the work day and people straggled in: the Chinese housewife, the female grad student, the Indian husband working in the HK office of some big multinational corporation with headquarters in New York. About eight people in all, we first sat in meditation for 15 minutes or so. It was probably the first time I got to sit for any length since India. It felt like being back in the saddle again. *Ahhh, the pain and the pleasure of it all.* What came up for me was this slowly growing sense that by sitting in this manner with any group, anywhere, of any origin, *there* was my Sangha. The breath, the moment, the shared knowledge that these people, too, were struggling with finding some way to harness the wild beast we conveniently call our mind, searching for some peace of mind—this is what the Sangha shares. This was such a simple understanding, attained in such an unlikely setting, that it stayed with me.

The women struggled with gender roles; several times I heard the phrase "the good Chinese _____" (fill in the blank here: wife, daughter, mother). The men struggled with their roles, mostly as breadwinners. The Indian gentleman's story got to me. I usually don't relate to anyone whose job title includes "multinational cor-poration," but this man suddenly was a foxhole buddy. We both suffered from the same malady, and, I suspect, we weren't alone. What seemed like such a pedestrian ailment, a petty little distrac-tion from the Much More Important Things in Life, was becom-ing epidemic in the shrinking global community. Let's call it e-mail-itis. Not that I suffered from severe panic attacks, as was my Indian friend's diagnosis, but we did share the cause of suffering—namely, ignorance. Of what? In my case, it was ignorance of the fact that it really doesn't matter how much I worry or plot or scheme or strategize over the e-mail messages I receive or send. Ig-norance of the fact that no matter how many times I read and reread an e-mail, the hidden message will remain indecipherable, the tone of voice and inflection inaudible. Ignorance of, or proba-bly just forgetting, the fact that for the majority of people typing words on a screen sounds ominously like Writing with a capital W, an endeavor that engenders deep-seated fear. Mostly, I was igno-rant of the fact that despite my best efforts and intentions, out-comes of e-mail interactions depend on some x-factor, x standing for everything out of my own control—which, it turns out, is everything.

In his case, as he explained it, it was simpler: ignorance of the mind-set of the executives sitting in cramped cubicles in midtown

Manhattan dashing off e-mails to him. "I just can't figure out what they want or what they must be thinking," he confessed, practically in tears. Yet he would stay up all night trying to decipher their meaning.

It sounded so innocuous at first, but when he described a day and night in his life, I cringed in recognition. Because of the time difference, his morning was his boss's evening. So he knew that an e-mail he sent to New York in the morning would not be opened for the rest of his own business day, while financial transactions were being conducted in Asian countries, transactions that could make him look bad. So all day he would have to sit on his anticipation. By evening, when he was ready to close up shop and retire for the night, he knew his boss would be opening his e-mails and firing off missives in response. Now the anticipation grew, sending the Indian into a tailspin of anxiety that triggered vertigo, nausea, headaches, indigestion, insomnia and a dangerous spike in his blood pressure. Unable to sleep, he would lie awake worrying. First he would try to calm himself down, as would his wife. "It can wait til the morning," she would try to console him. But inevitably, obsessively, he would get up at two in the morning and check his e-mail. It was a lose-lose situation. If he got bad news, he'd be up the rest of the night developing an action plan of response. If it was good news, the euphoria would keep him up. But the worst was no reaction, he said. In the void of knowledge, he realized, we create our worst nightmares. Was his boss so angry that he'd printed out the e-mail and passed it around the New York office as a laughable example of how *not* to do business? Was his boss fired? Had *he* been fired? Had the company gone belly up overnight, as could realistically happen in the volatile world of multinationals, or been eaten up in a merger-and-acquisition feeding frenzy? Had the e-mail not even arrived, still out there in virtual space? Then in the morning, it would start all over again, playing catch-up. The irony was that by being a day ahead in Asia, he was always a day behind the United States.

I could relate. I had discovered the same problem, but I was playing it from both ends: I was sending e-mails east and west, to time zones hours ahead and times zones hours behind. I was sending e-mails today to someone who would get them yesterday. *Was that even possible?* And the sad fact is that millions of people probably go through similar torture in jobs around the world. E-mail is the boon and bane of modern civilization. Most days I marveled at how journalists made their way around the world without e-mail. Some days I felt imprisoned by the Internet. Not only do we all suffer from information overload, but this expediting of information also creates urgency overload, increasing the expectation of an even more urgent response. Our heart rates speed up to keep up. Had the Buddha truly been omniscient, he would have given a whole sutra on the suffering that the Internet could cause if not approached with RightPatience.com.

The Indian shared that the MBSR program was helping. A Hindu, he had previously found solace in his daily chanting. But this emotional malaise had taken the benefit out of even that. Now, though, "the mindfulness is helping me do my prayers less mindlessly," he said.

After the session I surprised both him and myself by going up to him and giving him a good ol' American bear hug of commiseration. My ears heard my mouth actually say, "I feel your pain, friend." As we left, we exchanged business cards. "Send me an e-mail sometime," I said. We both smiled.

Recently, as I put the finishing touches on this section of the book, I sent Dr. Ma an e-mail to check some information. Her response seemed an appropriate way to end this chapter.

THIS IS AN AUTOMATIC REPLY:

Dear friend,

Thank you for your message. In an attempt to live a simpler and more balanced life, I now deal with my e-mails only occasionally. I hope that you'll understand. If your message is urgent, please kindly phone me.

If you'd like to be reminded to take a break during the long hours in front of a computer, you may like to download the "mindful clock" from the website http://www.mindfulnessdc.org/mindfulclock.html.

I pause and come back to my breathing for three breaths when the bell sounds—it is a nice way to refresh oneself. I hope that you'll enjoy it.

May every day bring you even more love, wisdom and peace!

Love,
Helen

eight

Awakening the Sleeping Giant

Buddhism Makes a Slow Comeback in China

*The softest things in the world overcome the hardest things in the world.
Through this I know the advantage of taking no action.*

—LAO-TZU

*They are not following dharma who resort to violence to achieve their purpose.
But those who lead others through nonviolent means, knowing right and
wrong, may be called guardians of the dharma.*

—THE BUDDHA

I knew about the human rights abuses. I knew about the 1.3 billion
people, though I could not fathom fitting four and a half times the
American population into an area approximately the same size as
the United States. (The United States has 78 persons per square
mile to China's 348.) I knew about the economic boom and I knew
about the resulting industrial pollution. While I was in China, in
fact, the *Geographic* came out with a story entitled "The Cost of
Growth in China," a devastating, hard-nosed look at the country's
rise in lung disease, filthy effluents and other detrimental environmental side effects of unbridled development. "The implications
of its gallop toward a Western-style consumer society are sobering,"

journalist Jasper Becker wrote. I was hoping that my very impressive letter of introduction would invite a warm embrace, but now my little blue-ribbon letter would be the kiss of death.

And I certainly knew about the horrific oppression and systematic repression of Buddhism—and not just since the days of the Cultural Revolution, but, as I soon learned, from much earlier.

You could say I really knew nothing about the China behind the headlines. And who could blame me? I was daunted by a history so long it makes American so-called history seem like an anthropological sneeze. Chinese kids can recite the Table of Chinese Dynasties, all 84 of them dating back to the 21st century BCE, with the same ease that guys in my old neighborhood used to rattle off the World Series champs since the first one in 1903.

Before I arrived, my China was a conglomeration of old clichés. I expected to see downtrodden people wearing gray uniforms, armed military everywhere and a pervasive gloom matched by a dark and heavy haze in the air. I expected not to be attracted to Chinese people. Except for the air, which reminded me of Gary, Indiana, but on a larger scale, my experiences proved me wrong on all counts.

For one thing, that worker-bee outfit has been replaced by more Western attire; it's hard to find a man *not* wearing a dark sports jacket or a suit, even just to hit the local teahouse. And Chinese people are fun and funny. What better indicator of a people's joie de vivre can you offer than to say they love to eat? In every town and city, no matter what size, I saw elaborate neon displays surrounding the entrances to what I assumed were movie theaters or nightclubs. They were restaurants. Eating is entertainment to the Chinese, and they go at it with a gusto unparalleled even in San Francisco, a city of foodies on a feeding frenzy since the 1980s.

In Chengdu, the capital of Sichuan, the first order of business upon my arrival, as far as my fixer Fu Ching was concerned, was dinner at one of the province's best restaurants. (Yes, through some 11th-hour miracle, I made contact with Beijing-based Jia Liming, longtime *Geographic* fixer, who in turn found Fu Ching for me.) This was my kind of fixer. The performance began as soon as we sat down. A waitress immediately appeared seemingly from out of nowhere. This already was not Western style. She and Fu Ching talked for quite a while. He seemed to interrogate the waitress over every item, which she adroitly explained with a well-rehearsed smile. She disappeared, and within a few short minutes, like a Chinese acrobat who switches masks so fast you cannot detect where the one went and other came from, she reappeared with what seemed like every item on the menu. Thick noodles, watercress with peanuts, chicken in a hot sauce, succulent sliced duck with a side of the skin, and sweet Tsingtao beer. The presentation and the tastes were worthy of applauds, but the showstopper came with the bill. My jaw dropped, and not from too much MSG. Dinner for two: about US $8.

The revelation that surprised—and inspired—me most also made me wonder about my commitment to cynical journalism, and cynicism in general. Slowly but surely, the weeks of travel had worn down my veneer; it's hard to remain a sinner among the saints. I was becoming a believer, or at least a wannabe believer. For, in small moments, I caught glimpses of a Buddhism renaissance in China. Perhaps it had never disappeared in the Chinese people's hearts and minds, or from the privacy of their homes. But now, in a country where freedom of religious expression had been suppressed and punished, people were slowly coming out of the Buddhist closet. There are an estimated 100 million–plus Buddhists, making it the country's fastest growing religion.

Like dogs that had been hit too often, they made tentative gestures. Perhaps emboldened by the showdown at Tiananmen Square in 1989, Chinese people were reconnecting with their Buddhism roots. To me it spoke of a resilience and irrepressibility of the tradition. Chinese Buddhism in the 21st century is the lotus flower emerging from the mud, an event as natural as nature itself.

For example, on my second day in China, Fu Ching took me to see the world's largest stone Buddha, in Leshan, west of Chengdu.

My very close buddy Cary Wolinsky, a photographer who had been shooting major features on China for the *Geographic* since the early 1980s, encouraged me to see it. He said I would not be disappointed. He was right.

Carved deep into the side of Lingyun Mountain in Leshan City, the 80-year project was completed in CE 803. Sitting with giant hands resting on its equally giant knees, this Maitreya Buddha, or the Future Buddha, overlooks the confluence of the Minjiang, Dadu and Qingyi Rivers. Though the site was an obvious strategic military lookout, the story I liked the best was that it stood guard over the turbulent tangle of strong currents, where there had been many reports of dragons and mysterious mishaps to seamen. This Buddha's steadfast and tranquil gaze would calm the most violent waters and declaw the meanest dragons.

From the parking lot full of tour buses, we followed a flow of visitors, mostly middle-class Chinese who seemed more like sightseers than spiritual pilgrims. A series of courtyards surrounded by ancient wooden temples led to a precipice, where hordes stood at the ledge overlooking the Buddha for the requisite photo op. They all repeated a ritual that went back a couple of dozen years at most, about the same time that cameras became required accoutrements for any self-respecting tourist. If you held out your arms a certain way, and the photographer framed it just right, you could swear the subject was caressing the Buddha's huge cheek—or, if the camera angle was slightly off, picking his nose. After the photo, everyone huddled around the shooter's digital to see if the moment was captured for posterity. I shot a profile of Fu Ching, a high-cheek-boned guy in his early 30s with a nearly shaved head, so that his face was side by side with the Buddha's. When I studied it later at home, I saw the striking resemblance between Fu Ching's bone structure and the Buddha's. I saw clearly that the blueprint for this Buddha was the classic Chinese face. I also saw clearly that this statue could have been a profile of Mickey Mouse, as far as some there were concerned. They were more enthralled with the engineering feat of building this monstrously large structure. This

Two views of the Leshan Buddha, the world's largest stone Maitreya Buddha, near Chengdu. Fu Ching, the Chengdu-based fixer, bore a striking resemblance to the Buddha.

was a piece of Chinese lore, a true tourist "attraction." The man who brought them a means to assuage their suffering was the last thing on their minds. Or so I thought.

From the ledge, people then walked single file down a steep stairwell carved into the mountainside that dates back to when the statue was built; the steps are now protected by guardrails that people hold on to for dear life. My hands ached by the time I got to the concrete base at the bottom, where people congregated and took more pictures. From there, I looked 71 meters up into the Buddha's nostrils. Mulling around the picture takers, I caught a glimpse of a pair of teenage women also looking up in awe, which suggested perhaps they saw something I, too, saw: an homage to a great man. At first I thought they were overwhelmed by the sheer size of it looming over our heads. But as I watched them, they appeared completely oblivious to their surroundings, transfixed, as if they were enveloped in an otherworldly bubble. They stared up for an inordinately, even inappropriately, long time, blissful smiles overcoming their wonderfully round faces. I realized the Chinese come to see historical and cultural sites such as this, wonders of construction, but they leave with a curiosity: *Who was that guy?* There is something universally compelling about the simple image of the Buddha, large or small; then it draws you into something deeper. Watching those women, I knew that here in what had been one of the most religiously repressed countries in the world, Buddhism would revive.

I had another such mini-epiphany in Shaanxi Province as I watched a group of about 20 women walking from Buddha statue to statue at Fa Men Temple, which houses what we're told is an authentic finger relic of the Buddha. The relic was found only in 1987 in a pagoda basement after the building had collapsed. Since then, tour buses bring more than 6,000 people a day to visit the cherished digit, which resides in an ornate golden box, protected by glass casement. The women, in their 50s and 60s, were following another woman around the temple halls, scrupulously copying her movements as she instructed them in the most basic of Buddhist rituals: where to place their feet, how to press their palms together, how to bow and light incense, what words to recite, and a little bit of why. Later, when I introduced myself, they told me they were neighbors who took frequent trips together to important Buddhist sites. Several months before they had taken a train to a sacred Buddhist mountain. They could have been my mother's mah-jongg group on a museum field trip.

"I remember these things from when I was a little girl," one of the women explained through my fixer. "But then . . ." Her voice trailed off, and I saw an apologetic sadness in her eyes. I knew she was referring to the period of the Cultural Revolution when the government closed monasteries and prohibited religious practice, and she knew that I knew. "We are happy to learn again these traditions of our ancestors."

❀

Erik Zürcher, a Dutch historian, put it best in the title of his 1959 book *The Buddhist Conquest of China: The Spread and Adaptation of Buddhism in Early Medieval China*. Was this title Dutch tongue-in-cheek humor? Buddhists as conquerors? What, wielding their incense like swords? Tripping over their robes, thrashing their enemies with lotus stems, breaking their vows of nonviolence? Surely not! But Buddhism "conquered" China the same way it "conquered" the countries I'd already visited. As he writes, "From the very beginning, the body of the foreign doctrine was reduced to those elements which, by their real or supposed congruence with preexisting Chinese notions and practices, were liable to adaptation and incorporation. The result of this intense and continuous process of selection and hybridization is widely divergent from the contents of the imported foreign scriptures which were so faithfully copied, memorized and recited by Chinese devotees."

Those "preexisting Chinese notions and practices" were Confucianism and Taoism, introduced by the other Axial Age heroes, Confucius and Lao-tzu. Today's "traditional Chinese religions" mixes those two, plus animism, totemism, local god worship and, now, Buddhism. (Traditional Chinese religion counts 405 million followers, ranking it the world's fourth-largest religion, behind Christianity with 2.1 billion, Islam with 1.3 billion, and Hinduism with 870 million.) In some Chinese circles, Buddhism is still considered a foreign import, 2,000 years after its arrival there.

This hybridization seemed to reach its apogee in China, creating a sturdy species, which may explain how Buddhism has survived so many attempts to kill it here. This analogy came to me as I stared out the window of a tour bus ascending one of the four Chinese mountains sacred to Buddhists, Mount Emei, not far from the Leshan Buddha. Through an increasingly dense fog, I studied thick stands of bamboo trees waving with the swirling winds, an undulating green dragon of many shades. Buddhism is like the bamboo, I thought. The most diverse group of plants in the grass family, the bamboo bends with the winds, rather than resist and break. It is one of the fastest-growing plants on the planet, some rising three feet a day, meanwhile developing miles of roots underground. The tree of the Judeo-Christian traditions would be the oak, held sacred by the Greeks, venerated by the Druids, dedicated to the god Jupiter by the Romans. Early Slavic and Norse cultures considered the oak the god of thunder, as it was more likely to be struck by lightning than other trees. It grows slowly and, though sturdy, its branches break off easily in a strong northeaster. The maples and chestnut trees I grew up with defined not just solid but stolid, impregnable and immovable, like the dogma of Christianity, Catholicism and Judaism.

When I got to the top, at Jinding Peak, 3,077 meters above sea level, from which I was told the most magnificent view in all China could be had, the fog was as thick as I had ever seen fog—and I had lived in San Francisco. From a ledge that, I cannot report, overviewed a breathtaking scene, I saw *zip* beyond three feet. "They were right about one thing," I told Fu Ching and my trusty tape recorder. "This *is* the ultimate Zen view: I can't see a thing."

Among the largest candles-cum-incense sticks the author saw in China, atop Mount Emei, one of four mountains in China sacred to Buddhists.

Exactly when Buddhism arrived is by now a familiar story: We're not sure.

"In actual fact, it is unknown when Buddhism entered China," confesses Dr. Zürcher. He speculates that it must have infiltrated from the Northwest into the rest of the country somewhere between the first half of the 1st century BCE and the middle of the 1st century CE. He reports the existence of a community of Buddhist monks and laymen in 65 CE in present-day Shandong Province, on China's eastern coast.

Where it entered is slightly better known. Along with trade and migration, the Silk Road, the world's oldest international highway, was the boulevard that spread Buddhism through Central Asia. The route started from northwestern India, arched eastward through modern Afghanistan, Pakistan, Central Asia and into

China. Basically following the northern passage across the top of the Himalaya range, Buddhism hitched a ride with the continuous stream of merchants, missionaries, mercenaries and nomads who had been bridging East with West since the Silk Road opened in the 2nd century BCE.

The more apocryphal version of Buddhism's arrival is that in about 65 CE Emperor Ming of the Eastern Han dynasty dreamed about a golden man 12 feet tall; the light from the man's head illuminated the whole hall. In the morning, Ming's advisers identified this figure as the Buddha, the god of the West. The emperor sent envoys to India to find out more about this Buddha. In 67 CE, the envoys loaded Sanskrit scriptures, a portrait of the Buddha and two Indian monks onto a white horse and returned to Luoyang. When living quarters for the monks were built in the temple the following year, the temple was renamed Baima (White Horse) Temple. The Baima Temple in Luoyang, in Henan Province, is traditionally regarded as the first Buddhist temple in China, though Dr. Zürcher notes that contemporary sources make no reference to White Horse Temple until the end of the 3rd century.

By the end of the 1st century, a religious community was established in Luoyang, then the capital. From then on, the Buddhist community grew continuously. By the end of the Han dynasty, an atmosphere of political unrest may have contributed to the receptivity of a new religion. Around 514, there were 2 million Buddhists in China. Buddhism reached the height of its popularity in China during the Sui and T'ang dynasties (581–907). However, in 845 CE Emperor Wuzong, under the influence of Taoist and Confucian advisers, began to persecute all foreign religions, including Buddhism. According to records of the time, some 4,600 Buddhist monasteries were annihilated, massive amounts of priceless artwork were destroyed and about 260,000 monks and nuns were forced to return to lay life. Buddhism never completely returned.

Late imperial China—covering the period from the Sung dynasty (960–1279) until the end of the Ch'ing dynasty (1644–1912)—continued the period of Buddhism's decline. Though its influence on Chinese culture was pervasive, as seen in art and literature, it was receding as an intellectual endeavor. "The shift of the Chinese elite's interest away from Buddhism and toward Confucianism, as formulated by its great systematizer Zhu Xi (1130–1200), was official state orthodoxy during the 14th century," writes Mario Poceski, assistant professor of Buddhist studies in the University of Florida's department of religion, in *The Encyclopedia of Buddhism*. "For the most part Buddhism after this point assumed a conservative stance, as there was no emergence of major new traditions or significant paradigm shifts."

One piece of Buddha trivia from that period. You know that big-bellied Buddha you usually see in the entranceway to Chinese restaurants? The same one you see lined up at souvenir shops in Chinatown, or as amulets? The very one that graces the cover of this book? That is not "the" Buddha. That is a Buddha, and, of course, there are factual and fictional versions that meld into one. Here's the story; its truth is for anyone to determine. After the wave of persecutions during the latter half of the T'ang dynasty, Buddhism declined as a state-protected religion demonstrating the ruler's greatness. Until then, some emperors had even claimed to be the Buddha incarnate. Buddhism became a religion of the common people. Among the monks who traveled the land, carrying all their worldly possessions in hemp bags, was an eccentric Ch'an monk who lived more than a thousand years ago and who went by the name of Hotai or Pu-tai. In Buddhist and Shinto culture he was best known as the Laughing Buddha. Because of this monk's benevolent nature, he came to be regarded as Maitreya, the Future Buddha. Hotei went around taking the sadness from people of this world.

The Laughing Buddha has become a deity of contentment and abundance and is considered the patron saint of restaurateurs, fortune-tellers and bartenders, as well as the weak, the poor and children. The cloth or linen sack (which never empties) is filled with many precious items, including rice plants (indicating wealth), candy for children, food or the woes of the world. His exposed potbellied stomach symbolizes happiness, good luck and plenitude. The begging bowl, also often seen with him, represents his Buddhist nature. In some scenes, the Laughing Buddha may be found sitting on a cart drawn by boys or wielding a fan called an *oogi,* said to be a "wish-giving" fan. Those who rub the great belly will gain wealth, good luck and prosperity.

So back to our history. As China entered the modern period and came more and more under Western influence, those aspects of superstition that had become part of Buddhism through earlier religious beliefs were seen as outdated. At the end of the late imperial era, Dr. Poceski notes, "China's inability to adequately respond to the challenges of modernity—rudely brought to its doorstep by the increasing encroachment of the colonial powers on Chinese territory in the 19th century—led to erosion and eventually disintegration of its age-old social and political institutions."

It was in such times of turmoil and hard self-examination that I had seen Buddhism reblossom in other cultures and other times, so I was not surprised to read that Buddhism staged a minor revival in the face of the new predicament. A movement more retro than reform emphasized Ch'an meditation and philosophical reflection; a progressive branch also established educational institutions that embraced modern thought.

And then, in 1949, came the People's Republic of China, under the rule of the Communist Party, ideologically opposed to traditional religious beliefs. The thrust through the 1950s was to control and restrict Buddhist activities, with the state in effect taking over Buddhist organizations. With the Cultural Revolution that began in the mid-1960s, violent suppression of Buddhism was the order of the day. Communist Party chairman Mao Zedong's Little Red Book, more officially entitled *Quotations from Chairman Mao Tsetung* (*Tsetung* was the English spelling at the time), became the country's Bible, Pali Canon and Koran all rolled up in one for Party loyalists. In the chapter on discipline, instead of the Four Noble Truths, he offered his own four less-than-noble nonnegotiable truths.

We must affirm anew the discipline
of the Party, namely:

(1) the individual is subordinate to the organization;

(2) the minority is subordinate to the majority;

(3) the lower level is subordinate to the higher level; and

(4) the entire membership is subordinate to the Central Committee.

Rather than the Buddha's Three Jewels we get . . .

Mao's Three Main Rules of Discipline

(1) Obey orders in all your actions.

(2) Do not take a single needle or piece of thread from the masses.

(3) Turn in everything captured.

And instead of the Eightfold Path, we have . . .

Mao's Eight Points for Attention

(1) Speak politely.

(2) Pay fairly for what you buy.

(3) Return everything you borrow.

(4) Pay for anything you damage.

(5) Do not hit or swear at people.

(6) Do not damage crops.

(7) Do not take liberties with women.

(8) Do not ill-treat captives.

"At the time it seemed that the twenty centuries of Buddhist history in China might be coming to an end," writes Dr. Poceski.

In 1979, things changed. Under Deng Xiaoping, chairman of the Party's Central Military Commission, which gave him control of the People's Liberation Army, a new policy opened foreign trade, and with it, the open exchange of ideas with the West, a dangerous influence as far as the ruling party was concerned. The "opening," as it's called, quite simply freed the Chinese to be more self-expressive. As mercantilism had brought Buddhism to China via the Silk Road, similarly it was free trade that may have compelled China's political leaders to loosen the religious restrictions, especially with the headlights of international human rights watchdog agencies glaring in their face. In 1989, the iconic image of one man standing at attention in front of a military tank galvanized the people of China.

This paradigm shift sent quakes throughout the People's Republic. With it came religious reforms, at least on paper. For example, a 1997 decree called "Freedom of Religious Belief in China," from the People's Republic of China's Information Office of the State Council, is a classic bit of New World Order doublespeak. Admitting that the Cultural Revolution "had a disastrous effect on all aspects of the society in China, including religion," it attempts to rectify matters. The document continues, "But in the course of correcting the errors of the 'cultural revolution,' governments at all levels made great efforts to revive and implement the policy of freedom of religious belief, redressed the unjust, false or wrong cases imposed on religious personages, and reopened sites for religious activities." And while it cites the 600 Protestant churches that have reopened each year since the 1980s, the 18 million copies of the Bible and the more than 8 million copies of a China Christian Council hymnal permitted to be printed, the 126 Catholic bishops ordained and the 900 young Catholic priests consecrated by the Chinese Catholic church, it cites nothing about Buddhist allowances. The purpose of such gestures of religious freedom is made clear: "The Chinese government supports and encourages the religious circles to unite the religious believers to actively participate in the construction of the country." In other words, insofar as religions can serve the goals of the People's Republic, they will be supported. This and other decrees make more than clear that each and every religious organization reports back to the Religion Bureau of the government.

I also had a hard time swallowing the following from that document as "truth": "In China all religions have equal status and coexist in tranquility. Religious disputes are unknown in China. Religious believers and non-believers respect each other, are united and have a harmonious relationship."

Had the writers of this document heard of Tibet and the systematic annihilation of Buddhism—and Buddhists—there? According to the Government of Tibet in Exile, since 1949 more than 6,000 Tibetan Buddhist monasteries and cultural centers have been destroyed and 1.2 million Tibetans have died from imprisonment, torture, famine and war. Speaking as a Buddhist, I would say this was clearly a matter of two people viewing the same circumstance from different perspectives. Speaking as chairman of the Reality Check Bureau, however, I would posit that one of the two was lying. Now, I ask you, would a Tibetan Buddhist lie? Would His Holiness the Dalai Lama lie?

The Chinese Buddhist Association, established in 1953 as a union of all branches of Chinese Buddhism ("a patriotic and educational organization," as the press release they gave me explained), provided me with this tally as of 2003: 8,400 Han Buddhism monasteries in Mainland China, and 50,000 monks and nuns; 3,000 Tibetan monasteries, and 120,000 monks and nuns; and 1,600 Southern Buddhism monasteries, with 8,000 monks. When I got back to the United States, I tried to check those figures with Human Rights Watch / Asia but was told there was no way to refute or corroborate the numbers, since getting reliable information from China's Religion Bureau, which oversees all religious organizations, is frustrating at best. When I asked one of the *Geographic*'s crack researchers for help, he forwarded an e-mail from a staff director with the Congressional-Executive Commission on China, in Washington, D.C., that further illustrated the elusiveness of Chinese authorities in this area: "Thank you for your inquiry . . . in which you inquired about how to contact Ye Xiaowen, the Director General of [China's] State Administration of Religious Affairs (SARA). Although we have met with Director

General Ye a number of times, we have conflicting information about where best to write or call him." (His business card showed a different address than a Web-based source.) "We don't have a current e-mail address for him. The one on his business card was crossed out . . ."

So much for open communication after the opening.

The government's subsidy of a number of archaeological projects and Buddhist cultural endeavors could easily be perceived as consistent with their statements in support of religious freedom. I took the earnest motivation behind these efforts with rock-sized grains of salt. For instance, why does the government refer to projects that uncover Buddhist archaeological sites or finds as "cultural relics," a spiritually benign naming, rather than "religious relics"? Nonetheless, it *is* investing in research advancing understanding of the history of Buddhism in China.

In Beijing, I was serenaded by a Buddhist temple band, an 800-year-old musical tradition that may be saved from extinction with support from the Chinese Technology Association of Cultural Relics Protection. At the 15th-century Zhihua Temple where they performed, the musicians told me afterward they were the last of a dying breed; there was only one young teenage student currently studying the ancient instruments to carry on the tradition. They were hopeful there might be more interest. Being a lifelong drummer, I asked to sit in, and played a three-foot-high red wooden drum that rested on the floor between my legs. All agreed that though I had fairly impressive chops, they would not be looking to me to save this tradition.

On another occasion, in Sichuan Province, I leaned like Spider-Man along a ledge in Guangyuan at the Thousand Buddha Cliff-side Statues, staring down at the muddy Jialing River. Beside me, archaeologist Lei Yu Hua explained how her findings now clarify this region's importance in the spread of Buddhism along the Silk Road into central China and beyond. She was quick to acknowledge her employer, the Cultural Relics and Archaeology Institute

Sitting in with a band that plays ancient Buddhist temple music, at the 15th-century Zhihua Temple in Beijing. The 800-year-old musical tradition may be saved from extinction with support from the Chinese Technology Association of Cultural Relics Protection.

of Chengdu City, an official part of and financial beneficiary of the Chinese government.

I had been told before I went to China that today Buddhist monasteries, under the Communist government's control, had become more like museums and tourist attractions. They are that—as much for Western visitors as for the Chinese—but as I watched local people lighting incense, bowing three times at each and every statue, I thought that sooner or later, by going through the motions, even if by rote at first, Chinese were watering the Buddhist garden.

Not that long ago the phrase "Chinese tourism development" would have read like an oxymoron. In 1978, a grand total of

10,000 tourists visited China. By 1988, the number had risen to 4.3 million. According to the World Tourism Organization, 41.8 million people visited China in 2003, ranking it fourth in the world. In 2004, the number grew by 48 percent.

Like any tourist, I was eager to visit what has been dubbed the Disneyland of Buddhist monasteries. So, too, for his own reasons, was Fu Ching.

Shaolin Monastery is a 5th-century temple (built in 497 CE) in the woods at the base of the sacred Mount Song ("shao" means mountain, "lin" means woods). There, an Indian monk named Ba Tuo began teaching a practice called Hinayana Buddhism, advocating self-extrication and study of the ancient scriptures of the Buddha's teachings. Later, in about 520, another Indian monk, Bodhidharma, arrived at the temple and began teaching Mahayana Buddhism, which the Chinese called Ch'an (when it migrated to Japan, it became Zen). This practice was more focused on meditation than on reading scriptures. When Bodhidharma saw that the monks were physically out of shape from sitting around with their noses buried in Sanskrit texts, he developed an exercise regime called the Eighteen Hands of Lohan to give them the stamina they would need to endure the long hours of meditation. He also wanted to arm them with a system to defend themselves against the ruthless marauders who swept through the region. These first moves evolved into today's kung fu.

Many Americans' first exposure to kung fu was the TV series *Kung Fu,* which first aired in 1972. The star, David Carradine, played a 19th-century Shaolin Monastery monk who, after avenging the death of his teacher, flees China to the American West, where he is pursued by bounty hunters. This led to a slew of early kung fu films, evolving into those graceful, if testosterone-driven, moves such as those Hong Kong action choreographer Yuen Wo Ping used in *Crouching Tiger, Hidden Dragon,* the *Matrix* franchise and the *Kill Bill* flicks. He, Quentin Tarantino, Uma Thurman, Jackie Chan, Jet Li and Carradine ought to make daily prostrations before a statue of Bodhidharma.

For the Chinese, interest in kung fu spiked with the 1982 film *Shaolin Monastery,* whose theme song almost every Chinese boy, and many girls, can recite from memory (by the way, Monastery and Temple are used interchangeably). Fu Ching sang the lyrics for me all the way from the airport to Dengfeng, the city in Henan Province about 10 kilometers from the monastery. He sang in Chinese, but months later sent me the translation (or his translation):

> *Shaolin, Shaolin, you are revered by so many heroes in the world.*
> *Shaolin, Shaolin, you are so wildly read by the supernatural stories.*
> *The exquisite martial arts—peerless!!! The world is overwhelmed*
> * by Shaolin.*
> *The long history, of long standing, the beautiful and resplendent*
> * Shaolin.*
> *A thousand-year-old monastery, a wizardly place: Mount Song*
> * Shan and deep and quiet valley. Everyone is yearning.*
> *The hometown of martial arts, attractive place, are well-known*
> * under the sun, leave a good name forever.*
> *Well-known under the sun, leave a good name forever.*
> *Well-known under the sun, leave a good name forever . . .*
> *Shaolin, Shaolin,*
> *Shao . . . lin, Shao . . . lin . . .*

"Every boy my age, his parents worried their son would run away to join the monastery after seeing that movie," he told me as we were driven to meet a real-live Shaolin monk. "Many did. It was my plan, too. But my parents were very strict, said they would punish me very badly if I did." He laughed.

I was not laughing, however, as I watched our driver careen through heavy traffic—heavy because new car sales had surged 82 percent in 2003 and 11 percent in 2004 in China. "Careen" must be in the Chinese driver manual because that was the style of everyone on the roads. That modus seemed to be based on this principle: "If I pretend not to see you careening ahead as I come careening around the corner without stopping or looking left and right, then you will have to stop or your car will come careening into mine." Based on what I witnessed over the dashboard, I was not surprised to read later that the number of people killed on Chinese roads had increased fivefold since 1985. In 2003, more than 104,000 Chinese died in traffic accidents, more than double the U.S. total, even though the United States has almost nine times as many vehicles on roads. I quickly dubbed this "kung fu driving." This approach seemed so contradictory to the Buddhist teachings of selflessness and compassion that I wondered if their driving teachers were non-Buddhists trained on America's meanest Machiavellian streets—in Boston. Sitting in the backseat tested my desire to control not just our car but all the others on the road. Despite watching my breath, I heard myself shouting obscenities. I probably left a hole in the backseat floor where I instinctively kept slamming on the brake pedal that wasn't there.

Somehow we arrived safely at Dengfeng. My own film about this city would be entitled *Crouching Tourism Boom, Hidden Agenda*. With more than 1.5 million people visiting the Shaolin Temple annually, Dengfeng has been the beneficiary of the kung fu boom, to the tune of more than US$66 million. Besides attracting the casual kung fu aficionado, however, the city has also become a magnet to a more serious student of the martial art. With an entrepreneurial spirit characteristic of the new China, many of the monks who were put out of the temple during the Cultural Revolution set up kung fu schools, now a veritable growth industry. There are more than 10,000 Chinese kung fu students in Dengfeng's 30 or more special schools and training centers, where they also study the three Rs of primary education. Dengfeng is the country's largest kung fu training base. At 4:30 in the morning, I drove around the city to watch up to a dozen bands of 40 to 100 boys from ages 8 to 18, in matching warm-up suits, running the city streets in formation, the modern version of Red Army soldiers who might have done the same run 40 years ago. By 6:00 a.m. they were doing warm-ups and practicing their forms in makeshift grounds behind buildings. Then it was classes in rustic rooms, back to kung fu practice and, finally, evenings studying in crowded dorm rooms lined with their bunk beds.

Families pay good money to send their kids to these schools; they get a mediocre academic education but are well trained. The carrot is film stardom (dreams of sword-wielding Jackie Chan or Bruce Lee dance in their heads) or jobs with the multitude of Shaolin touring groups, few of which can actually claim authentic Shaolin monks as members. In fact, the fight for the proprietary rights of the name is as tough as for a kung fu championship trophy. According to figures provided by the temple, 80 unauthorized kung fu schools in China have used the name Shaolin, and more than 100 businesses, including those selling cars, beer, tires and furniture, claim the Shaolin trademark, all without consulting the temple. The temple recently won a lawsuit against a company in a nearby town that used the Shaolin name to market its sausage. The temple has set up the Henan Shaolin Temple Industrial

Steve McCurry

Students of kung fu in Dengfeng, China, hope someday to either have their own martial arts school or star in a film.

Development Ltd. Co. to protect and administer the intangible assets of Shaolin Temple, and to investigate cases of unauthorized use of the temple's name.

The kung fu monk tradition at Shaolin Monastery is shrouded in mystery. At first I thought it was because trainings are so esoteric that only a precious few are deemed worthy enough for the transmission. Now I thought it was because they were all so protective of the copyrights. Making contact with anyone at the monastery had been impossible in the months beforehand. Finally, in an e-mail I got somewhere in Thailand, photographer Steve McCurry's able researcher Jennifer Warren found a man named Richard Russell, a doctor turned kung fu teacher based in Las Vegas, who in turn put us in touch with a monk who, he promised, was "the real deal," as Dr. Russell put it.

But the question still lingered: Was this man, Shi De Cheng, living at the monastery? Was he trained there? And the bigger question: is there still a tradition of Buddhist monks living and training behind the high red walls of the Shaolin Monastery? Behind all these questions, I hoped to prove that this seemingly aggressive violence-infested kung fu craze, as crazy as it seemed, was another factor that fed the rising popularity of Buddhism, both in China and in the West.

Some of those questions were answered when we got to the Shi De Cheng Wushu Centre of Song Shan Shaolin. I have shaken the hands of very strong men in my time, but there was something different about the handshake of Shi De Cheng. It wasn't just vise-like; it was both solid and gentle at the same time. And the way he stood, with his short legs slightly spread, made him seem like a tree deeply rooted in the ground over which he stood. He held my eye without a flicker. My well-trained shit-detecting antennae told me he could be trusted. It also told me that most likely he could take me in a fight, so I wasn't going to argue with anything he said. He told me his story.

When he entered Shaolin Monastery in 1980 at the age of about

15, his sole goal was to become an outstanding kung fu master. He had little to no interest in Buddhism but, as he found, the heart and soul of kung fu practice *is* Buddhist philosophy. As most young men and women discover, you cannot do kung fu without "doing" Buddhism. It demands a focus, a devotion to rigorous and repetitive practice and a control of one's emotions, he explained. "This is not a martial art of attack," he asserted. "The ability to subdue one's anger or to seek vengeance are among the first lessons one learns. As the ancient Shaolin saying goes, 'One who engages in combat has already lost the battle.' "

The deep understanding and practice of this philosophy probably rules out most kung fu movies as primers in Buddhism. For those who take it seriously, kung fu, I surprised myself to realize, is as legitimate a path to the Buddha's Truth as *vipassana*.

He told me he was sincerely grateful to the "opening" reforms in China. "If not for them, I would be a farmer toiling in the fields every day," he said, without the residual resentment I would have had in my voice had I said it.

Today, the 40-year-old devout Buddhist monk has some 200 students at a time, from all parts of China. He has also trained students from around the world, several of whom have started schools in Europe and the United States, to which he travels as the master. One young Frenchman I interviewed had been living and training here for six months. "I had no interest in Buddhism," he told me. "But now I want to learn more. When I see how tranquil my teacher is, I wonder, 'How did he get that way? It can't just be the kung fu.' "

After I watched some morning practice sessions, Shi De Cheng organized a short performance for me. I felt like a dignitary sitting in a row of folding chairs in the yard behind the school. A 30-yard-long colorful cloth had been laid on the ground, and some of Shi De Cheng's best students, dressed in long red robes or loose white pants and kung fu jackets, put on a spectacle of jumps and somersaults and running dives. After each form, they looked to me for approval. I clapped appreciatively, impressed with their precision and their dedication.

Eager to see the famed Shaolin temple, off we went in a van—Fu Ching, the French lad, Shi De Chung, me and several others close to the master—for the 10-kilometer drive along the base of Mount Song. When we got near it, I could see a big backup of traffic at the front gate. Shi De Chung directed the driver to pull the van out of line and go to the front. When the guards saw his smiling face, they waved him through. This was when I knew we'd met the "real deal."

The parking lot was a mob scene: indeed, more tour buses than I had seen at any other monastery in the People's Republic. Inside, it looked like every other Buddhist monastery in China. Various temple buildings surrounded a courtyard. There were the Bell Tower and the Drum Tower. There were the dark rooms housing various sacred scriptures, the statues of Buddhas on pedestals. The difference here, though, was that this temple was crowded. There were bands of schoolkids led by teachers with bullhorns and flags. There were Westerners with tour groups. There were teenage boys who looked like they'd just screened *Shaolin Monastery* for the 18th time. Walking from one temple to the next, they would break into some kung fu moves, a blur of criss-crossing arms and clenched fists and mean faces like their kung fu movie heroes. They reminded me of when I was a basketball-obsessed teenager, suddenly pulling up for a Bill Bradley jumper from the corner, leaving finger marks all over the living-room ceiling.

The French kid showed me the bark of a tree in the middle of the courtyard. It looked like someone had drilled about an inch-deep hole into the wood with a blunt edge. He told me this was where the monks of yore practiced; those holes were from their fingers repeatedly banging into the trees. He failed to add "according to legend," but he didn't need to for my sake. I worried that he would go back to France and impress his friends with attempts to do the same—and break his fingers trying.

Shi De Chung then took us to a corner of the main courtyard and through a gate into some private living quarters where he introduced us to his 80-year-old master, Shi Su Yuan. This was a very important gesture for Shi De Chung; he wanted to demonstrate his obeisance to his teacher. The Frenchman was so humbled by the meeting he barely lifted his eyes. Shi Su Yuan was feeble and less than mentally acute. But it didn't matter: I had met a real kung fu master inside the walls of the Shaolin Monastery.

Perry Garfinkel

Shi De Cheng, at right, with his master, Shi Su Yuan, in the private quarters of the Shaolin Monastery, outside Dengfeng, China, where both Ch'an Buddhism and kung fu are said to have originated. Shi De Chung now heads one of the dozens of kung fu schools in Dengfeng.

I asked to meet other kung fu monks who I assumed lived in residence. We walked into another private living area where several monks resided in very small, dark and cluttered rooms. The men looked out of shape, tired and not very vital—the opposite of Shi De Chung. Fu Ching and I caught each other's eyes. He looked shattered, and I knew why. From the brochures and films, we are led to believe young monks live monastic lives in the Shaolin Monastery, practicing their kung fu in the courtyards surrounded by red walls. This is not the case; it may have been, but is no longer. But perpetuating the illusion feeds a romantic vision that the Chinese desperately cling to, as it reinforces their connection to a time past. And, one might even believe, it inspires a fighting spirit that has helped the Chinese, especially the new generation, to challenge threats to their freedom, to stand in front of oncoming tanks.

More important, however, this well orchestrated smoke-and-mirrors act of the Shaolin monks has created a very lucrative industry. What exists today is a brand, one that people East and West fight over.

I left there—and the People's Republic—feeling strongly that the ism that will "conquer" China is not Buddhism or Communism, but capitalism.

From Shaolin I flew to Beijing, where I was met at the airport by the fixer who had found me Fu Ching. (He had flown back to Chengdu, and I just hoped he wouldn't leave his wife and family to become a kung fu monk.) If central casting had sent Zhang Ziji, the sword-wielding female star of *Crouching Tiger,* I would not have been more pleased. Her name was Jia Liming. She had dimples the size of Sichuan Province (that would be about five Texases), a chipped front tooth, which for no apparent reason I found captivatingly mysterious, and a robust laugh, unusual for Asian women, who usually cover their mouths when they laugh delicately. She was outspoken, hilariously cynical in a TriBeCa sort of way, and very, very smart. We got along famously, which was a great relief considering I thought I would be stranded before I got to China.

Something else interested me about Jia Liming. She was born in 1973, six years before the "opening." By the time she graduated from university in about 1994, the People's Republic she was born into had become a wholly different place—a wholly different planet, I imagined. Hers was a generation in transition. In a way, she was the Chinese equivalent of our American baby boomers. Most of her peers, she told me, were deeply committed to success in business. She, however, was rather like my generation of the late 1960s. Already fed up with China's relentless rush to consumerism, some well-educated people in her age group were dropping out of the urban rat race and taking to the hills, like our back-to-the-land movement. She told me she and lots of her friends disappeared to places like the northwest corner of Yunnan Province, to Zhongdian, which the Chinese government renamed Shangri-La in 2002, officially identifying it as James Hilton's *Lost Horizon*. In the shadow of Meili Snow Mountain, Yunnan's highest peak, in a region populated largely with people of Tibetan descent, they sat around rustic cafés, smoking cigarettes, drinking yak butter tea and beer, and drinking up the mystique of Tibetan lore and ritual. These were the "indigenous peoples" around whom young Chinese could rally, like our Native Americans, the gatekeepers to their own past—or the past they would have liked to claim. These tribespeople were the underdogs with whom they could identify.

She told me she had accepted the job to work for me because hanging out with the Tibetans has gotten her interested in Buddhism. While she knew Buddhist history and the various Buddhas, she recited them like a tour guide. I did not sense a spiritual connection—as yet. I took it upon myself to encourage her to try meditation, which she'd never done. One evening, seeing how scattered and frenetic she sometimes got, I suggested we try 10 to 15 minutes of *vipassana*. I talked her through my very rough version of one of those smooth-voiced guided meditation tapes. I opened my eyes after 10 minutes to see her staring wide-eyed at me, as if I was Woody Allen in *Take the Money and Run,* which was one of her favorite films. She could not take it—or me—seriously.

Among the people she lined up for me to interview was Chen Xiao Xu. She would appear to be a most unlikely poster child for socially engaged Buddhism, but in China the pickin's were slim. I decided that despite those government decrees, anyone here who publicly practices his or her faith makes a social statement that forces the government to live up to its freedom-of-worship promise.

Chen was an anomaly in any society. Celebrity, capitalist, woman, Buddhist—she was all of the above. Being Chinese made her all the more unique. At 39, she was president of one of Beijing's top advertising agencies, though she was more well known as one of Chinese television's most famous stars. In 1983, at the age of 18, she played the tragic heroine Lin Daiyu in the TV version of *A Dream of Red Mansions,* the classic 18th-century romance novel set against a backdrop of China's repressive, dying feudal system. Upon my arrival in China, the series happened to be celebrating its 20th anniversary of reruns. It had aired some 700 times on television since its first showing. It touches a nerve, I think, because the Chinese love tragic love stories; for them there is no other kind of love story. And in some ways, that time parallels this: the decline and fall of feudalism, the decline and fall of the Chairman Mao era. In preparation for the interview, Jia had offered to screen for me an episode of *A Dream* from her DVD collection. It's a multigenerational saga rife with incest, general lechery, political deception, marriages arranged to coalesce power, decadence and indulgence, murder, suicide, long-drawn-out illnesses, roller-coaster tales of rags to riches to rags. This family made *The Sopranos* seem like *The Waltons.* The take-away message: trust no one, every man for himself, every women for every man.

For Chen, the role meant financial success beyond her own wildest dreams. At a time when most Chinese were struggling to emerge from extreme economic deprivation, she was buying cars and apartments and homes for her family. Typecast as "the fragile lovelorn young woman," when she auditioned for other roles few offers followed.

"I started to wonder if I really was Lin Daiyu," she told me, as we sat in the conference room of her company, ShiPang Advertising in Beijing, in a modern high-rise building. Her long neck and delicate features were reminiscent of the regal but fragile-looking screen actress Audrey Hepburn, whose portrait in fact hung on the wall behind her. Chen's warm, empathic and expressive eyes reminded me of renderings of the biblical Madonna. She spoke no English; between her translator and mine, we communicated just fine, though. "I went through a lost time in my life. I had to struggle to find a new path."

Then in 1992, with her then boyfriend, a photographer, she helped start a small ad shop when advertising in China was in its infancy. At the time there were fewer than 100 agencies in the country; now there are more than 20,000. By 1999, she was back in the money.

"Once I got the taste, I always wanted more and more, bigger and bigger status symbols," she said. And then, almost illogically, it sank in: that feeling of emptiness so many people experience even when they have all the material possessions they desire. In Buddhism, this phenomenon has a name: the "hungry ghost" (*prēta* in Pali), referring to an appetite that can never be sated.

"I had it all—big car, beautiful house, travel wherever I wanted, with plenty of luxury to share with my family—but I was still somehow unhappy," she said. "I discovered the more I had, the less happy I was becoming."

Just around that time someone handed her a book about the life and teachings of Sakyamuni, the Buddha. "He was born to a wealthy family, but he, too, took less and less pleasure in the things of the world," she said. "I could relate to this part of what led him on a search for something more substantial, something that would bring me real happiness."

She became a sincere student of Buddhism, taking a teacher named Chin Kung, a Taiwanese monk based in Australia. Now her life revolves around Buddhism. "I start each day by reading from a Buddhist scripture called *Aparimitayur Sutra*," she said. "In the evening I read another. During lunch at work, I take a 30-minute meditation break." Her employees know to hold her calls during that time. One whole wall of her stark white office was dedicated to Buddhist statues and paintings, and pictures of her teacher. At the company's front desk were Buddhist-themed gifts free for the taking. ShiPang offers grants and financial support to a number of Buddhist-related media projects, such as assisting a young Beijing man producing animated cartoons for TV and DVDs, based on the life and teaching of Sakyamuni.

"A Buddhist in advertising, a professional whose whole goal is to whet the appetite of consumers' 'hungry ghost,' seems like an oxymoron, too, no?" I asked, though I knew translating that word would be a nightmare.

She got it immediately; whatever it translates to is quite familiar to the Chinese. Oxymoron is the Chinese way.

"Yes, some people ask me how to reconcile advertising, which feeds people's desire to acquire material possessions, with Buddhism, which promotes nonattachment to the very same things. I don't agree that Buddhism teaches people to lead a life of deprivation. The Buddha was simply encouraging people to create a happy world for themselves.

"If we collect 'things' or try to gain personal fortune for ourselves and our family, we may not find fulfillment, but we can use these same things to create greater benefit for others, and that is closer to what Buddhism is about for me."

I was not sure if she was bending Buddhist doctrine to justify her work. But I could imagine Madison Avenue knocking on her door once they put their own Zen spin on her theory of the difference between marketing East and West. Buddhist principles lay under her theory.

"China's general public still finds it difficult to understand the concept of individualism and personal creativity," she explained. "So American and European ads that sell the idea that you can gain personal enjoyment or satisfaction from a product wouldn't work here. We place more importance on generosity and tolerance; even the younger generation does not want to show their selfishness. So we design ads that show the product in light of how it can reinforce those values."

With Jia Liming, the Beijing fixer, in Tiananmen Square, straddling the line that divides the east and west sides of Beijing.

I was not clear how that worked with ads for one of her leading clients, the maker of a very popular brand of liquor. And I did not ask how she fit representing the brand into her Buddhist rationale; Buddhists are not supposed to drink liquor. Maybe she felt the need to play the role of Māra, the tempter, to challenge people's attainment of enlightenment. Maybe I was giving her the benefit of the doubt because I was becoming enamored with the beauty, charm and mercurial quality of Chinese women.

On my last day, since I didn't have time to see the Great Wall, the panda bears, the Chinese acrobats and other icons of China, I asked Jia to take me to Tiananmen Square. I didn't know that Chairman Mao's remains are enshrined in a massive granite mausoleum on the southern side of the square since his death in 1976. Past an entrance room where a marble Mao sculpture sits, in imitation of the Lincoln Memorial, the chairman's body lies inside a crystal sarcophagus, dressed in military regalia and draped in the red Communist Party flag. Side halls in the mausoleum contain relics of other "first generation revolutionary leaders, making this monument a true Ancestral Hall of the Revolution," the brochure tells us. The line to get in snaked around the building. They come still? After all he did to them and their country? Even when they are not required to, not ordered to? Jia explained that for some, this site might as well be the Leshan Buddha, a historic figure, a meaningful symbol. Meaning what? Symbolic of what? I had been used to seeing people circumambulate the relics of the Buddha. Were they making the parallel to Chairman Mao?

The square is in the geographic center of Beijing. Lines run through the square separating the city into four quadrants: north, south, east and west. I took Jia by the hand and maneuvered her so that we straddled the line.

"See, East meets West," I laughed. "And they lived in peaceful harmony . . ."

"Happily ever after," she finished with her signature tone of irony.

nine

Keeping the Heart Sutra of Buddhism Still Beating in Japan

You should not lose your self-sufficient state of mind. This does not mean a closed mind, but actually an empty mind and a ready mind. If your mind is empty, it is always ready for anything; it is open to everything. In the beginner's mind there are many possibilities; in the expert's mind there are few.

—SHUNRYU SUZUKI, *Zen Mind, Beginner's Mind*

Like a beautiful flower, full of colour, but without scent, are the fine but fruitless words of him who does not act accordingly. But, like a beautiful flower, full of colour and full of scent, are the fine and fruitful words of him who acts accordingly.

—THE BUDDHA, *The Dhammapada*

By the time I arrived in Japan, the cherry blossom season was at its height. It's a brief and bittersweet moment in the Land of the Rising Sun. Sweet because the explosion of pinks and whites is surreally saccharine. The parks make for such perfect scenic backdrops you expect to hear someone shout "Cut," and turn off the blue screen. Japan's amateur photographers—that is to say, the entire population of 127 million—are out in full force. But then, the floral display is gone all too quickly and fallen petals blanket the whole country like pink puddles of tears, leaving you missing what you hardly had time to enjoy. Oh well, another lesson in impermanence.

I had gone through several seasons—and a thousand years of Buddhist history and migration—in eight weeks. My time machine would have given Marty McFly travel sickness. I had accumulated a headful of ideas that indeed were driving me insane. While I was able to follow the simplicity with which Buddhism had begun, even comprehend how and why it slowly evolved and morphed as it traversed Asia, I found Japanese Buddhism complexing and confounding. By the time the Dhamma arrived in Japan, from China and Korea in approximately 550 CE, it would have been as unrecognizable to the Buddha as a cell phone. I could only begin to understand it, in a metaphor befitting the camera-crazed Japanese culture, through studying snapshots, frozen frames of meaningful moments laid out on a table. A few selects . . .

• KUNIO KADOWAKI, a seasoned Japanese fixer who had seen and done it all with *Geographic* writers and photogs, was hurrying me through the typical sights on my first full day in Kyoto. We visited the 700-year-old wooden Rengeo-in Temple, where 1,001 wooden statues of the many-armed Buddhist diety Kannon (the Buddha of Compassion: aka Avalokiteshvara in India and Kuan Yin in China) stand elbow to elbow for 390 feet along two hallways. Kannon literally means "watchful listening," and can be loosely translated as "the one who sees/hears all." I slipped off my shoes before entering the temple, as is the custom, ever careful to step onto the wooden platform in socks or bare feet only. Dashing to catch up to Kunio, however, I was somewhat careless and left my shoes askew from the other shoes, which I didn't have time to notice were in a neat row. I looked back to glimpse a nearby monk meticulously adjusting my footwear to be perfectly parallel with the others. Persnickety folks, I thought. It was the first sign of how

Japanese people can be fixed and calcified in their ways. But I realized, too, that I would need to see and hear all with a little more attention than was my habit. The Buddha is in the details here.

• THE WAY OF THE BOW is the martial art of Zen archery, known in Japan as Kyudo (pronounced cue-doe). I interviewed Kanjuro Shibata, a 21st-generation bow maker and archer whose father is well known in the United States as head of Zenko International in Boulder, Colorado. As we sat at a table in his dining room in Kyoto, I noticed a handsome wooden sign on the wall behind him, which he said was the Kyudo slogan. There were four beautifully painted Japanese characters. I asked Kunio to translate, thinking four characters would not be difficult to render in English. Half an hour later the two men were still going back and forth.

" 'Hand affect, mind obtain,' " Kunio suggested. Shibata-sensei, who spoke a little English, shook his head.

" 'Obtain mind, attain hand'?" Another head shake.

I tried. "How about 'Good mind, good hand'?"

"Not exactly."

" 'Clear mind, steady hand'?"

"Sort of" was the most Kunio would allow me.

The problem for a non-Japanese-speaking person is the language is so rich with metaphor, symbols and cultural references that it would take lifetimes to truly comprehend. A fan of haiku, the succinct 17-syllable Japanese poetry form, I realized how superficial English translations of them probably are, how lacking in the depth, breadth of meaning and texture compared to the original. How, then, I wondered, did we Westerners have the presumption to think we could comprehend the very esoteric and mercurial Zen Buddhism? With a clear mind and steady hand was the only answer.

• A 70-YEAR-OLD CALLIGRAPHY MASTER, Hakuju Kuiseko, was explaining where his inspiration comes from, what he feels, at the very moment he puts brush to paper. At least he was trying to explain. The problem this time wasn't in translating Japanese to English. It was in translating the nonverbal to the verbal. In a way, it reminded me of the difficulty explaining the experience of meditation to someone who has not had the experience. I would have preferred him to show me rather than tell me, but with my newfound deferential respect, especially for wise Asian elders, I did not want to seem presumptuous and so did not ask.

Sitting at my side, his wife, Ryokushu, herself a respected calligraphy teacher, pulled at my sleeve and whispered, "Ask him to demonstrate."

"No, I couldn't possibly," I said.

In a tone only understood between husband and wife, she said something to him and he jumped up excitedly. "He will demonstrate," she said.

Grabbing some brushes and ink, he stood over a long 15-inch-wide piece of paper on the floor. He closed his eyes, took several deep breaths, nearly hyperventilating, and virtually dived into the paper, making short, deft, decisive strokes. In a matter of seconds, he had drawn a simple circle that also had a lot of character.

"It means 'clear mind,' " Mrs. Kuiseko explained.

I did not need a better answer. This was not just the dilemma of getting a person whose medium is visual to express himself in words. This went deeper. The Japanese are not comfortable with the world of feelings, not comfortable with the words "I," "me" or "my." I had found that when I asked about their own relationship with Buddhism, they would recite the biography of their sect's founder, starting in 1173 or whenever, and continuing up to but not including their own lives. I wondered how much this had to do with Buddhism, with the idea that the Way, as it is called, is unspeakable and ineffable. And how much it had to do with how far the Japanese had taken the Buddhist concept of egolessness.

• **THEY ARE CALLED MARATHON MONKS.** Undergoing the most rigorous training in the Tendai Sect, founded in 805 by Saichō atop Mount Hiei outside Kyoto, where several other Japanese sect founders were trained, these monks walk some 18 miles on mountain footpaths. They walk from late at night until early morning, carrying lanterns and wearing strange white linen outfits with straw boots and matching hats that are supposed to be reminiscent of lotuses. If they came to your door at Halloween, you would think they were mocking a Lewis Carroll character. Offering prayers at 255 sacred sites along the way, they can accomplish their task either in 1,000 consecutive days or spread out over seven years. Kunio had succeeded in arranging an interview with Fujinami Genshin, a 45-year-old monk of this order. The practice, he

Perry Garfinkel

Fujinami Genshin is called a Marathon Monk. According to this Tendai tradition, monks walk hundreds of miles on mountain footpaths through the night, carrying lanterns and wearing white linen outfits, as part of their Buddhist training.

said, was supposed to help one attain enlightenment. To me, it sounded like the kind of austerities the Buddha had gone through—and rejected—as a way to attain enlightenment. Was Buddhism going backward here in Japan to pre-Buddha Vedic beliefs and rituals? Fujinami would not be engaged in such a debate. He said he was doing it because it meant he could attain a high position in some temple once he completed the training.

• REV. GENE SEKIYA, a Japanese American born in Fresno, California, heads the International Department of the Hongwanji denomination of Shin Buddhism, yet another sect, founded in the 12th century by Shinran Shonin. Rev. Sekiya, who now lives in Tokyo, is a handsome and highly intelligent man of 40. It was a great relief for me to speak about Japanese Buddhism with someone for whom English was his mother tongue. He asked me what I knew about Buddhism. I gave him the short-form answer that I had been practicing off and on for some 30 years.

"Practicing?" he asked in a pedantic style that immediately put me on the defensive, as it was intended to do. "I love it when I hear Americans say they 'practice' Buddhism. To a Japanese person that would be like saying, 'I practice being Japanese.' " The practice of which I spoke, meditation, is called *zäzen* in the Japanese Zen tradition. In the tradition called Pure Land Buddhism, it's the recitation of the name of Amida Buddha—in Japanese, *Namu Amida Butsu*. The nembutsu, as it's called, means "thinking on the Buddha."

I sensed an indignation that we Americans thought we could "practice" our way to the Way, when all the Japanese had to do was breathe it in. This was all well and good but it sounded like a cop-out, excusing Japanese from performing any kind of religious ritual connected with Buddhism, or a practice such as meditation. This was, after all, the country from which I learned of another sect of Buddhism called "funeral Buddhism." I had first heard the term from the editor of the Japanese edition of *National Geographic*. "Oh, you will see no signs of Buddhism in my country—except at funerals," he had said long before I arrived in Japan. It can't be, I thought then, not in the country many Americans associate with Buddhism. He must be an atheist, a nihilist or just oblivious to the traditions of his own people. Now, in Rev. Sekiya's comments, I realized it might be because Buddhism so penetrated the Japanese mind-set that they felt no need to observe it. I also considered the possibility that the form of their very rigorously performed rituals had overshadowed the substance for which those rituals stood.

The precise moment when God as I knew him/her/it ceased to exist for me was more than a snapshot. It was a full-blown wall poster, complete with a little wooden arched footbridge, snow-capped Mount Fuji in the background, a stand of bamboo trees off to the side and the half-concealed image of a woman in a kimono discreetly crossing the bridge.

The moment was so pedestrian, so innocuous, so ordinary, it would have gone by unnoticed had it not been for a little imaginary monk whispering in my ear, "Ahaaaaa." Students of Zen call it the "aha moment," when ideas align in such a way that you "get it," whatever the "it" of the moment is. This epiphany often occurs when one's rational mind gives up trying to decipher the indecipherable and goes tilt. Aha, Truth!

Mine came while visiting Hoitsu Suzuki, head priest of Rinso-in, a Zen Buddhist temple in the hills above the fishing town of Yaizu, population about 115,000, about 100 miles southwest of Tokyo. If it weren't for his father, Suzuki-roshi would be just another small-town Japan Zen priest. But his late father, Shunryu Suzuki, is a seminal figure in the history of American Buddhism. In 1959 the senior Suzuki moved to San Francisco and established a Zen center down the street from the Haight-Ashbury district, which was to become ground zero of the American hippie movement. Later he established the first Zen monastery in the United

States, at Tassajara, in the mountains south of the city. Shunryu's book, *Zen Mind, Beginner's Mind,* was the Zen primer for a whole generation. Now a small trail of Shunryu's followers make a pilgrimage to this modest temple to meet his son, whom they consider a lineage holder in American Zen Buddhism.

I had come to spend three days with a "typical" Zen priest and his family—the priest, who also was a calligrapher; the wife, who was a flower arranger; the son, who was also a priest and a skilled Kyudo practitioner; and the son's wife—all of whom were closely involved with running the temple and the other community responsibilities that any parish priest of any denomination would be required to handle. It was a rare opportunity to see life behind the rice-paper walls. Guest quarters were provided for Kunio and me on the other side of the temple. We took our meals with the family in the dining area of their private quarters.

Which is where my "aha" moment took place. Suzuki-roshi sat at the head of the long, low dining-room table. "Why do you call it low?" he had asked me. "To us, it is not low; it is just the right height. To us, your tables are too high." It was a simple teaching in relativity.

As a gesture of gratitude for accommodating us, on my last night there I had ordered a giant sushi tray, sake and beer (apparently, it's okay for Zen priests to drink). As his wife and daughter-in-law busied themselves in the kitchen, we sat and talked theology East and West while Suzuki-roshi kept one eye on the TV across from him. There was a New York Yankees game on; Yankees games are televised in Japan because the team's left-fielding slugger Hideki Matsui, born in Kanazawa, Japan, is something of a hero in this country of baseball lovers. Whenever he came to bat, it was understood the conversation would stop. Newspapers were strewn on the floor around Suzuki-roshi. It was such an entirely down-home atmosphere, like a Sunday of American football, pizza and beer. Who would have thought enlightenment could be had there and then?

In the previous days I had spent with him, I had seen him conduct several funeral services, rote affairs with drums and gongs and incense. He and the other participating priests wore gold robes and high hats with feathers; he carried a stick with long, white horse-hairs that looked like a duster. We attended one funeral held in a modern parlor, a building in a small industrial park where two other funeral parties waited in separate areas. Inside the entrance, there was a closed-circuit TV screen overhead for those who

Perry Garfinkel

Rev. Hoitsu Suzuki, head priest of Rinso-in, a Zen temple in Yaizu, Japan, leads a ceremony called the Consoling of the Fish on the port city's docks. This annual ritual absolves Buddhist fishermen of the sin of killing living things.

couldn't get into the crowded main hall. At the service, a teenage boy cried as he spoke about the death of his grandmother. I felt a collective shudder of embarrassment ripple through the audience of mourners, so unaccustomed are these people to public displays of emotion.

I had seen Suzuki-roshi conduct an annual event called the Consoling of the Fish. In this similarly formal ceremony performed right on the docks, with local media rolling tape and clicking away, he led a group of priests from several denominations—all dressed in elegant golden robes with feathery hats. Fishermen and others in the fishing industry sat in their work clothes in metal chairs facing a harbor full of boats coming and going. Since they are Buddhists, who by precept are not allowed to kill living things, these workers are absolved of their "sin" so that others may eat. I thought it should be called the Consoling of the Fishermen.

I had sat *zäzen* with him at 5:30 in the morning at a public sitting he holds every morning at his temple. Aside from me, his son and his daughter-in-law, only two people from the community attended as well. I had watched him practice calligraphy, which all Japanese priests are required to learn since they sign death certificates in the ornate style.

Now we debriefed as I tried to make sense of it all. Between Matsui's at-bats, I was asking questions to try to understand why there are so many sects in Japan, what distinguishes one from the other, why so few Japanese people seem to sit *zäzen* . . . In short, I was hoping this man would explain the history of Japanese Buddhism, as well as interpret Japanese psychosociology—and all between sips and strikes. Granted, it was a tall order, and it was clear I was wearing his patience. I was testing my own patience listening to my own questions, which were sounding more and more empty, but not in a Zen sense, except in one sense: The answers were contained in my questions. I was just having trouble hearing them.

He said he had recently come back from the United States and saw that "though Americans are rich materially and as a country, they are suffering." It was not a new point.

"Why do you think that is?" I asked. "Why don't the Judeo-Christian traditions fulfill that spiritual need?"

"Because they are looking for answers outside rather than inside," he replied. "The Buddha said the answers are not out there; they're within our selves."

Suzuki-roshi at his temple practicing calligraphy, which all Buddhist priests learn as part of their religious training, since they inscribe death certificates in this style.

"Yes, we look to God," I said. "God is there even in our casual language. We say, 'God bless you,' when you sneeze. We say, 'Thank God that truck didn't run me over.' We say 'God damn it' when we stub our toe or when Matsui strikes out."

He smiled wryly and looked over the top of his glasses at me. He did not want to play what he saw as a pointless game of intellectual masturbation. "Who is this God you keep talking about?"

The question was so simple that it cut through all the theological bullshit and suddenly—aha—I realized that belief in God perpetuated suffering. When the Buddha explained that the universe is not divided into self and non-self, me and not-me, that it is rather one interconnected entity, he essentially disavowed the existence of God, for God would be something or someone *else*. Without God, all the responsibility for the stubbed toe and everything else falls back on me. That in itself may be the reason we invent God, because it is easier to point the finger than to take the blame. But if we accept nondualism—that is, that there is no difference between subject and object, between knower and that which is known—there is no blamer, no blamee. God is also a means of explaining anything we cannot explain with our less-than-omniscient minds—even the good stuff. This whole theological conversation—of whether there is a God, or two gods, or even that we are God—becomes moot when tested against one of the Buddha's main theses: that we should accept only what we can experience directly or observe empirically with our five senses. What non-Buddhists do, see, feel or smell with their so-called sixth sense is up to them. Suzuki-roshi was giving me the Buddhist version of "I'm from Missouri." In other words, until I could point to something the two of us could "see" in that dining room, then the subject of God remained in the realm of hypothetical, and therefore as relevant as, say, the possibility of Suzuki-roshi pinch-hitting for Hideki Matsui.

At that moment I was trumped. It was as though, with one *whooosh* of a breath, Suzuki-roshi had toppled the delicate deck of cards I called God, demolished my God paradigm. Yet there was no panicky feeling, no desperate free-falling without a parachute, or a paradigm. And, for once, I let go. I was out of questions.

"Yes, the lotus of Buddhism sprouted many new branches by the time it came to Japan," Suzuki-roshi had said in that wonderfully poetic Japanese way. "But when the bell rings, they all return to the same place."

From reading about how so many sects appeared in Japan, it becomes clear that they all also come from the same place: China.

But it was the Korean prince of Kudara who made the first official presentation of the religion to the Japanese court in 538 CE, when a delegation of Buddhist priests sailed over, bearing gifts of sacred objects, sutras, banners and images of the Buddha. Until that time, the religious beliefs in Japan were strongly centered on the world of nature and spirits. Called Shintoism, or the Way of the Gods, it is, like traditional Chinese religion, an amorphous mix of nature worship, fertility cults, divination techniques, hero worship and shamanism, and remains a strong part of Japanese identity. In fact, almost every Buddhist temple ground that I visited provides an area for Shinto shrines. You also see such shrines— simple wooden A-frame temples about the size of a streetside newsstand—in the middle of downtown Tokyo, sandwiched between electronics stores and Salvatore Ferragamo retail outlets. Unlike most other religions, Shinto has no real founder, no written scriptures, no moral code, no body of religious law or fully developed theology, and only a very loosely organized priesthood. Its gods are called *kami* (divinities), but bear no resemblance to the gods of Buddhism, Islam or the Judeo-Christian religions. To Shintos, the Buddha was just another *kami*. In Shinto there are "Four Affirmations": to respect the tradition of family, with celebrations of birth and marriage; to honor the sacredness of nature; to practice physical cleanliness (followers take baths, wash their hands and rinse out their mouth often); and to give worship and honor to the *kami* and ancestral spirits.

Such a simplified practice was no match for the well-developed beliefs of Buddhism, already a thousand years old by the 6th century. But the area in which it especially added was in helping the Japanese face the darker side of life, for Shintoism offered little comfort in the face of sin, sickness and death. Through the Four Noble Truths, they saw a positive way to deal with them.

Prince Shotoku, who became regent to the emperor in 593, proclaimed Buddhism the state religion. Buddhism developed unabated for several centuries. However, during the 8th and 9th centuries, doctrines of what was called the Idealist School held that enlightenment was only accessible to aristocratic nobles and monastic officials, thus taking it away from the common people. In the meanwhile, this alliance between the ruling class and the prelates led to corruption within the monastic order. To end the reign of increasingly power-hungry Buddhist leaders, at the end of the 8th century the government moved the capital from Nara to Kyoto, thus ending the Nara period and beginning the Heian period, which lasted until 1200.

But then another fission occurred, this between and among the Buddhists themselves. It started in 788 when a monk named Saichō (767–822) ascended Mount Hiei, a peak outside Kyoto, and founded a small temple which eventually grew into Enryakuji, a complex of 3,000 temples dedicated to teaching what became a sect of Buddhism called Tendai. Tendai, which he had learned from the Chinese on a trip there in 804 (*T'ien-t'ai* in Chinese), emphasized the universality of Buddha-nature rather than enlightenment as the domain only of the rich and powerful. Another monk, named Kukai (774–835), also went to China at the same time. He, in turn, returned to Japan with the teachings of Tantric Buddhism, called in Japanese *Shingon,* or "the true word." Tantrism combines aspects of several religions, involving elaborate rituals consisting of body postures, hand movements and mystical utterances, all rigidly prescribed. The pageantry and mystery of these rituals must have impressed the Japanese, who had grown tired of the polemics of Tendai. Kukai founded his own monastery on the island of Koyasan. After the death of Saichō, Kukai became the presiding priest of the imperial palace. Then, at the peak of his fame, he had himself buried alive while immersed in deep meditation.

So Japanese Buddhism had divided into two distinct schools, but Shingon succeeded Tendai in popularity and in the eyes of the ruling class.

In the 12th century, yet another two sects emerged. Honen (1133–1212), a monk who studied at Mount Hiei and believed strongly that salvation came through the saving grace of the Buddha, proposed a simple, less mystical approach than Shingon. He founded a school called Jodo, or the Pure Land. By chanting *namu Amida Butsu* (homage to the Buddha Amitabha), one could overcome all sins and be redeemed unconditionally. This played well in a Japanese society now full of corruption, and Honen's popularity rose very quickly. But it did not go over so well with those in power, and his opponents banished him in 1207 at the age of 74.

Now, another monk, Shinran (1173–1263), also trained at Mount Hiei, had another interpretation of the teachings of Honen. Namely, he and his followers questioned whether faith is a free gift from the grace of the Buddha or whether it has something to do with one's own intention—similar to the free will versus destiny debate. This group became known as Jodo Shinshu, or the True Doctrine of the Pure Land. After the exile of Honen, Shinran, who would have been about 30 at the time, gave up his monastic robes, worked as a common preacher in the country, married and raised a family. This secularization of the Buddhist monk, which forever changed the religion in Japan, contributed to the popularization of Jodo Shinshu in Japan. It remains the largest sect in terms of numbers.

Yet two other sects emerged. One was started by a monk named Nichiren (1222–1282). He reduced all the teachings to a simple formula, the adoration of the Lotus Sutra, which he believed embodied the wisdom of the sutras. But he did not stop there, attacking Honen and all the other sects as hypocrites and traitors. This did not endear him to these people, and he was banished to a remote peninsula. When he was released after three years, he found his ideas had caught on and that he had more followers than before. Banished again, he was about to be murdered when a ball of fire flashed across the sky. This so unnerved his executioners that they instead banished him as planned. Once freed, he passed the last years of his life less fiery but no less adamant, claiming to be a prophet sent by the Buddha. The chauvinism and militarism that characterized Japanese policy during the 19th and 20th centuries could be traced, to some extent, to the aggressive attitude and ideas of Nichiren.

Eisai (1141−1215), a monk dissatisfied with the scholastic tendencies at Mount Hiei, went to China and brought back one more piece, Ch'an, or Zen in Japanese. The monk credited with making Zen popular in Japan, however, was Dōgen (1200−1253), who also traveled to China. There he found a teacher who taught him *zäzen,* a tradition directly descended from India through Bodhidharma, the monk who had brought it to the Shaolin Monastery. Bodhidharma was said to sit *zäzen* so long in one place at the Shaolin temple that his shadow, cast against the wall where he sat, is now permanently visible in that place. I saw that darkened spot on the wall when I was at Shaolin, though I can neither confirm nor refute the claim by tour guides there of its origin.

In reading the history of Buddhism in Japan, I saw for the first time two words side by side that I never would have thought possible: "warrior monks." Yet through its 1,500 years in Japan, Buddhism had taken a turn to violence, ego struggles and other unsavory human traits for which even my studies in Thailand and China had not prepared me. I guess I had assumed that if Buddhism had indeed reached its peak in Japan, absorbed and assimilated and learned from the mistakes of the past, it would be the most evolved, the least corrupted or corruptible.

Though I thought I was out of questions, I had one more for Suzuki-roshi. "How did this happen?"

His typically succinct reply: "A dog can only be a dog."

Man can only be man, he meant. Even if we naturally have Buddha-nature—the inner wisdom that enables us to love, forgive, find tranquillity—we also have human nature, flaws and all. This enigmatic truth of Buddhism was the bone I was left to chew on.

Rev. Yoshiharu Tomatsu is a Japanese priest who straddles the worlds of Buddhism old and Buddhism new, Buddhism East and

Buddhism West. It's a precarious, frustrating and at times conflicting position for him.

"I struggle with some of the hypocrisies of the old traditions and with the gap between what the Buddha taught and what Buddhism has been turned into here," said Tomatsu-san, "san" being the more casual term of friendship he asked me to use.

A third-generation priest in the 800-year-old Jodo Shu Japanese Pure Land Buddhist sect, the boyish 50-year-old is the head of the Shinko-in Temple, which has been serving the community for 50 generations. The small 17th-century wooden temple where we sipped green tea is situated, almost too symbolically, at the base of the Tokyo Tower, Japan's iconic image of technological modernity. A club DJ in college, Tomatsu-san once harbored dreams of becoming a music industry executive. But he pursued the path of his father, eventually spending three years in Cambridge, Massachusetts, while obtaining a master's degree in divinity from Harvard University. Now he lectures at two prestigious Tokyo universities and is senior research fellow at the Jodo Shu Research Institute of Buddhism. When he's not in suits or black robes, he wears khakis and pastel-colored crewneck sweaters draped around his neck and tied at the sleeves, Ivy League style. When he wasn't introducing me to Japan's slowly emerging engaged Buddhist movement, he was indulging me in his hobby as a gourmand, sharing tastes of Japan's finest culinary traditions. Through him I learned the esoteric secrets of the perfectly boiled pearl-colored thick and velvety udon noodle, and I shall never be satisfied with American imitations again—my culinary "aha."

He is, he said, a "funeral Buddhism priest," and his tone made it clear he thought of it as a pejorative term. He's also an aggressive and outspoken advocate of a Buddhism in Japan that should be much more socially relevant.

His spiritual moment of truth—the turning point that started him questioning the traditional rituals of his Buddhist sect—came in the mid-1970s as a priest volunteering in an AIDS clinic.

"We walked around giving massages, holding people's hands,

just literally keeping these victims in 'touch' with humanity," he said, as he drove me around the crowded city of Tokyo one afternoon. "You wear gloves. It's just common sense. But the chief abbot didn't wear them when he touched patients. I didn't have gloves on that day and I tried to reach out and touch one dying man, too, but I couldn't. I froze. At that moment my kids' and wife's faces flashed in front of me. *What if I got AIDS?* I just couldn't extend my hand, and I cried for myself. I understood my limitations, and I blamed it on the fact that I am a secularized priest."

To him "secularized" meant something more than priests marrying, serving in the military, eating meat, not having to shave their heads or wear their robes all the time. It implied a dilution of the sacred esoteric Buddhist traditions. I could imagine the Buddha wondering the same thing upon hearing that two nuclear power plants near Kyoto are named after Buddhist gods: Monju (for Manjushri) and Fugen (Samantabadhra).

This secularization process can be traced back to the founder of his own sect, the 12th-century monk Honen. However, it has intensified with the speed of Japan's famous bullet trains since World War II—some say even earlier, since the arrival of Commodore Perry in the mid-19th century.

"But it's ironic," Tomastu-san said as we reached our destination. "As much as Japan has looked to the West for its cultural cues, it has not so wholeheartedly embraced this western style of engaged Buddhism. And if it doesn't meet the changing needs of modern society, Japanese Buddhism will die."

Now it was my turn to see the irony: many in the West first heard of Buddhism through Zen, which originated in Japan. Popularized in the West by the Beat literati of the 1950s and '60s, Zen became known through art forms like calligraphy and ikebana, in rituals such as the Way of Tea ceremony, or a gourmet dining tradition called *kaiseki* that came out of Japanese monasteries or swordsmanship. Once Madison Avenue took hold of it, dozen of products were named Zen. So it came as a shock to hear Japanese

Buddhism, considered the wellspring of Buddhism to many Westerners, had turned into a dry institution devoid of spiritual meaning and social currency.

Perry Garfinkel

Rev. Yoshiharu Tomatsu, head of the 17th-century Shinko-in Temple in Tokyo and senior research fellow at the Jodo Shu Research Institute, is spearheading a small engaged Buddhism movement in Japan.

Tomatsu-san was taking me to see some signs that the heart of Buddhism was still beating. I came to see him as Japanese Buddhism's human pacemaker and social engagement as his defibrillator.

The first stop was a nongovernmental organization (NGO) he had helped establish with other Buddhist priests. Called Ayus, which translates to "life," it was created in 1993 to help channel funds to other NGOs working in such areas as urban poverty, HIV and AIDS programs, education and emergency needs such as in Iraq and the beleaguered Chittagong Hill Tracts tribes of Bangladesh.

It's a small program, distributing about $300,000 among 10 NGOs each year. Of the 300 contributing Japanese donors, two-thirds are Buddhist priests. Eleven of the 13 board members are Buddhist priests. "If we want these ideas to trickle down to the people, we spiritual leaders have to be role models," Tomatsu-san explained in the small cluttered office with the one staff member who serves as administrator. "But we're having difficulty. The priests all say, 'Oh, it's a great idea but I don't have time to get involved because I have so many other responsibilities to my temple members.' In other words, they can't take time away from officiating funerals or leading memorial services. But at least they are giving some money and now they aware of this need."

Next, we met with a hospital administrator from whom Tomatsu-san had heard that a hospice program was started under the auspices of a Buddhist temple. From the conversation with the administrator it became clear that this "model program" was still a premodel; visits had been made to two or three patients in the last year throughout the city, nothing more. The administrator told us, "To my understanding, as such, there is no hospice in Japan." When I told the executive about the Zen Hospice Project I had visited in San Francisco, he had more questions for me than I had for him. I'd become one of the cross-pollinating seeds blowing in the East/West winds.

Outside in the parking lot, Tomatsu-san could not contain his frustration. "I thought this was more developed," he confessed. "It's sad, but I'm not surprised. It's a reflection of the medical system in Japan—and about our people's avoidance of the reality of death. They take cadavers away in the middle of the night on employee elevators. Do you know a priest is not allowed to wear a Buddhist robe when he goes in to see a patient? That would mean a patient is dying, and the hospital is afraid patients would get upset."

Our next visit was to the world headquarters of the Rissho Kosei-kai, a new Buddhism that the more traditional sects call a "new religious organization." Founded in 1938 on the Buddha's teachings and Buddhism's Lotus Sutra, it claims 1.8 million households in Japan. One difference is that it's a lay organization, in an attempt to avoid the institutional hierarchy that flawed the traditional sects, according to its founder. Another is it addresses the world's problems. Members abstain from eating two meals a month and instead donate that money to the Rissho Kosei-kai Peace Fund, which in turn supports some 900 peace, economic development, refugee, hunger and other social-service programs worldwide. The organization pushes campaigns to send blankets to Africa and a kids-oriented campaign that sends homemade bags of toys and personal message cards. Rissho Kosei-kai has given about $60 million to UNICEF in 25 years.

Upon arrival, I was toured through the extensive compound. This new Japanese Buddhism draws its inspiration from the West, it was clear to me. The "temple" is now called a "church." The church has a giant pipe organ; the Buddha's name in Sanskrit is inscribed above colorful stained-glass windows. My hosts explained the founder had drawn architectural inspiration from Catholic churches in Brazil.

Then we sat in on a program called *hoza* that directly addresses crippling domestic social problems that now beset Japanese people—problems such as divorce, suicide, drug addiction and depression that are conversational taboos in a country whose national character practically glorifies emotional inexpressiveness.

Led by a facilitator from the ranks of the Rissho Kosei-kai movement, a group of people sat in a circle openly sharing personal dilemmas, mostly revolving around family strife. As Tomatsu-san and I sat on the outside of a circle listening to women ranging in age from mid-20s to late 70s talk about marital problems, about their kids disrespect for their elders, about self-doubts over the direction and meaning of their lives, it struck me as similar to what Western psychologists call "talk therapy."

Tomatsu-san later said he was taken aback by "how ordinary the issues were" but also "touched by how relieved people seemed to feel just talking and getting consoled." People everywhere are so starved of attention and solace that the simple experience of being listened to—and being heard—is an elixir for whatever ails them. Socially relevant Buddhism doesn't have to address the big global issues, the environment, prison reform. The kitchen table can be a war zone, too.

On our final stop—my last interview before flying east to California—we met a Buddhist priest I had seen at a protest rally several days earlier in front of the National Diet building, Japan's parliament. Hundreds of demonstrators had gathered in opposition to the Japanese Self-Defense Forces' involvement in the war in Iraq, demanding the release of Japanese hostages there. In the building's lobby, people crowded elbow to elbow listening to politicians' speeches. Camera crews were everywhere. Fringe groups, with their own agenda, jostled for media exposure. Amid the chaos, conspicuously positioned at curbside in front of the building, Takeda Takao led several priests wielding bullhorns, drums and a banner. Their presence lent a certain calm to the whole charged scene.

Tomatsu-san had also heard of Takeda and wanted to meet him, too. In his very modest office that also appeared to be his bedroom and his dining room, Takeda told us he was part of Nipponzan Myohoji, an international Buddhist organization founded in the early 20th century. Throughout the world, the monks and nuns of this sect conduct long walks, chanting and beating their drums in a call for peace, a tactic inspired by Mahatma Gandhi. Once a year, Takeda leads an 800-mile three-month memorial peace vigil from Tokyo to Hiroshima honoring the lives lost there in the 1945 bombing.

I asked him what had turned him into a radical.

"Not radical." He stopped me. "This is logical and practical. Violent action always loses. Bureaucratic channels are an endless maze. Peaceful protest is the only way to make change. Anger creates more anger in the world. Peaceful people make a peaceful planet."

The mid-1970s protests against the construction of Narita International Airport 40 miles outside Tokyo led him to this conclusion. He had participated in riots defending the rights of vegetable farmers to keep lands the government had taken over. In 1978 the airport opened nonetheless, costing farmland and human lives. In a field just outside the runway fences, the Nipponzan Myohoji order had erected a peace pagoda that still stands, Takeda told me.

A couple of hours later, as my plane ascended from Narita, I happened to peer out the window just in time to catch a glimpse of that same tiny, white peace pagoda. It stood out, starkly juxtaposed against the gray urban sprawl and industrial development, a bright memorial to the Buddha's timeless message. Tomatsu-san need not worry, I thought. Contrary to his prediction, Buddhism is not dying in Japan; it's just going through some long-postponed growing pains.

ten

Back in the Om of the Free and the Brave

American Buddhism Is the Latest Wrinkle in a Perpetually Smiling Face

Believe nothing, no matter where you read it, or who said it, no matter if I have said it, unless it agrees with your own reason and your own common sense.

—THE BUDDHA

"Mahatma," Gandhi was once asked by a reporter, "what do you think of Western Civilization?"
"I think it would be a good idea," he said.

I like too many things and get all confused and hung-up running from one falling star to another till I drop. This is the night, what it does to you. I had nothing to offer anybody except my own confusion.

—JACK KEROUAC, *On the Road*

I landed back in San Francisco, where I had garaged my car before I took off. The plan was to spend a week or so in the Bay Area, then drive cross-country back to the East Coast with a stopover in Boulder. In Colorado, I would revisit Naropa University, the country's only four-year accredited college whose curriculum is based entirely on Buddhist principles.

I had left the United States months before (or was it years?) with a certain perception (or was it perspective?) of American Buddhism. Having watched, covered and participated in the American fascination with Eastern wisdom for some 30 years, I was of the opinion that our interpretation and practice of it was a dilution of the Asian original. I guess, as it turns, I'm a purist after all.

Often, it seemed to me, American Buddhism was a mishmash: a little Tibetan mandala meditation here, a touch of Zen tea ceremony there, a tad of Theravada Buddhist breath awareness somewhere else, with perhaps a bit of homegrown Native American ritual and Jewish kabbalistic mysticism thrown in for good measure. Not only did we want our spirituality served smorgasbord style, but also, like our fast-food diets and our one-minute management style, we wanted our enlightenment instantly, preferably on our coffee break. Flitting from one esoteric practice to another—to get deeper? It seemed an intrinsically self-defeating exercise. And yet, isn't that the American way? We're ethnic mutts grazing at the cultural smorgasbord.

This dabbler's approach to Buddhism was graphically typified at Tao, a trendy Manhattan restaurant I'd visited before I had left the United States. Co-owner Rich Wolf sat with me in the private balcony-level dining area at a long rustic wooden table where Leo and Uma and other celebs often partied. We were eyeball to eyeball with a two-story 16-foot statue against the opposite wall that he nicknamed his "Mr. Potato Head Buddha." He came up with the concept of this Buddha to complement the restaurant's Pan Asian cuisine that blended Thai, Japanese and Chinese tastes. Rich, who knew next to nothing about Buddhism, was nonetheless mesmerized by the visual image of the Enlightened One, though he couldn't exactly explain why. His obsession led him to travel throughout Asia collecting a thousand Buddha pictures en route. Not satisfied with any one style in particular, he picked the elements that most appealed to him—the braided hair of Thai Buddhas, the high cheekbones of those from China—and designed his own. There seemed nothing wrong with it to him; in fact, he boasted about his inventiveness. I found it repugnant, disrespectful of each culture's individuality.

Dining there one night with my daughter Ariana and future son-in-law Ryan, we slurped down paper-thin slices of Kobe beef—at $12 an ounce, thank you—that we grilled ourselves on hot stones at the table while gawdy Mr. Potato Head loomed over us. It's very disconcerting to be in the throes of gustatory self-indulgence and have this figure staring down his nose at you, as though to say, "Do you know how many cows were killed so that you may stuff your face?"

This mix-and-match approach to Buddhism, of which many other American examples abound, had put me off at the time. But now I saw it with new eyes and a new appreciation. The American strand was exhibiting the same cultural adaptive behavior I'd now seen Buddhism undergo since around 250 BCE when it left India. Our polyglot culture was just putting a modern American-centric spin on it, the same way the Thais had added tattooing and the Chinese Confucian ideas and the Japanese Shinto. Why not Mr. Potato Head Buddhism? Or "enchilada nirvana"? Or *Buddhism for Dummies*?

Nowhere better could this new species of Buddhism be observed than in San Francisco, where Hoitsu Suzuki's father, Shunryu Suzuki, had established a Zen center and, later, America's first Zen monastery, Tassajara, in the rugged Los Padres National Forest near Carmel, California.

Historically, San Francisco was where people went to reinvent themselves. It became a creative environment where cultures collided and fed off each other, a perfect breeding ground for Buddhism, as I had seen elsewhere.

It already had a head start during the gold rush of the 1840s with the influx of Chinese immigrants, who established one of the largest Chinese communities in America. They opened a Buddhist temple in San Francisco in 1853, believed to be the first such temple in the United States. In the small bustling city, immigrants from throughout the world, looking for gold in them thar hills, would have had at least a tangential introduction to Buddhism through Chinese merchants with whom they did business. Later in the century, the Japanese came, too. Pure Land Japanese Buddhists had established the Buddhist Mission of North America in San Francisco by about 1898. Now called the Buddhist Churches of America, it remains an active organization. They, too, would have exposed the locals to their practices.

In the middle of the 20th century, San Francisco played host to another wave, this time of Americans themselves. In the late 1950s, the Beat Generation set up its unofficial headquarters at Lawrence Ferlinghetti's City Lights Books in North Beach. Around their lit'ry scene swirled progressive jazz musicians, topical folksingers, controversial comedians. The Beats drew their spiritual sustenance from Zen Buddhism, which is why Shunryu Suzuki saw this garden by the Golden Gate as rich mulch in which the ever-ready-to-adapt Buddhism could easily take root and grow a distinctly American strain.

I had moved to San Francisco on December 8, 1980. The date is etched in my mind because it happened to be the night John Lennon was murdered. I myself was escaping the East Coast, ready to reinvent myself in the wake of the marriage I had let die. By the time I got there, the Bay Area was even more of a hotbed of spiritual exploration. There were many other names and guises by which it was recognized: the human potential movement, the self-help movement, the New Age movement, the Age of Aquarius. Beats had become hippies, hippies had become yippies and yippies had become yuppies. The Me Decade had become the What About Me Decade. The running joke in the Bay Area was that half the population was seeing a therapist and the other half were therapists. In the country that had adopted General Electric's slogan—"Progress is our most important product"—as its national anthem, now "process" was our most important product. This searching and this splintering—in the wake of my country's disillusionment after suffering the assassinations of two Kennedys and one King, after the self-destruction of rock icons like Janis and Jimmy and

Jim, after the travesty of Vietnam, the embarrassment of Watergate, the collective disgrace of Nixon's demise—was what reminded me of the Axial Age of thousands of years ago. As some compensation, all of this sent Americans of conscience to search their souls, or in some cases to search for their souls.

I was in that spiritual dabbler group, by then having sampled Hinduism, Sufism, Buddhism and such offshoots as Arica and EST. Several years after my arrival in San Francisco, I also dipped into my Jewish roots, working as a media liaison for the regional Jewish Community Federation, which raises funds for a wide assortment of social-welfare agencies and institutions, and promotes Jewish identity as well. Ambivalent about my own Jewish identity, I recall telling people it was the "Community" part of the group's title that attracted me more than the "Jewish." As you know, though, there was some debate in my own head as to my interest in being part of any community (read Sangha). Despite my initial resistance, though, hanging out with mostly assimilated West Coast Jews—who have an altogether different DNA than the arm-waving, loud-talking, emotionally intense and intellectual East Coast Jews of my upbringing—turned out to reinforce my own Jewish identity. Eventually, predictable of me, I defected from that job and the local Jewish community as well—though, as the saying goes, some of my best friends were Jewish.

There was, then, fitting symmetry to my now returning to San Francisco the day before Yom HaShoah, the Jewish Day of Remembrance set aside annually to memorialize the Holocaust and to warn against its repetition. The first stop on my global journey had been to bear witness to the Holocaust at the Auschwitz-Birkenau compound in Poland with Zen Peacemakers. Now, to honor Yom HaShoah, an observance I previously would have ignored, I attended a daylong retreat that combined Buddhism and Judaism. A program of Congregation Beth Sholom, in San Francisco's Richmond District (where many middle-class Chinese now live), it was led by a Jewish rabbi with a longtime Zen-sitting background and a Zen priest who had been abbot of the San Francisco Zen Center and also is Jewish. Rabbi Alan Lew and Rev. Norman Fischer interspersed Buddhist chanting and meditation with Torah readings, Jewish prayer and contemplation, along with some yogic breathing and stretching exercises. The participants were all Jewish, though many seemed conversant in Buddhist philosophy and practice.

The whole thing would have smacked of gimmickry before I left. Now—whatever! The participants took it all in stride, as natural as ordering Chinese takeout and matzo ball soup—together. I, however, still struggled to integrate these two belief systems into one small head: the religion that invented the One God Theory versus the religion that invented the No God Theory. As my mouth chanted the Hebrew kaddish prayer for the dead, my ears heard Buddhist chanting . . .

> . . . *Yeet'barakh, v' yeesh'tabach, v' yeetpa'ar, v' yeetrohmam, v'*
> *yeet'nasei, v' yeet'hadar, v' yeet'aleh, v' yeet'halal sh'mey*
> *d'kudshah b'reekh hoo.*
> (CONGREGATION: B'REEKH HOO.)
>
> *L'eylah meen kohl beerkhatah v'sheeratah, toosh'b'chatah*
> *v'nechematah, da'ameeran b'al'mah, v'eemru: Amein.*
> (CONGREGATION: AMEIN.)
>
> *Aleynu v'al kohl yisrael, v'eemru: Amein.*
> *Y'hei shlamah rabbah meen sh'mahyah, v'chahyeem.*
> (CONGREGATION: AMEIN.)
>
> *Oseh shalom beem'roh'mahv, hoo ya'aseh shalom, aleynu v'al kohl*
> *yisrael v'eemru: Amein.*
> (CONGREGATION: AMEIN.)

Blessed, praised, glorified, exalted, extolled, mighty, upraised, and lauded be the Name of the Holy One, Blessed is He.
(CONGREGATION: BLESSED IS HE.)

Beyond any blessing and song, praise and consolation that are uttered in the world. Now respond: Amen.

(CONGREGATION: AMEN.)

May there be abundant peace from Heaven, and life upon us and upon all Israel. Now respond: Amen.

(CONGREGATION: AMEN.)

He Who makes peace in His heights, may He make peace, upon us and upon all Israel. Now respond: Amen.

(CONGREGATION: AMEN.)

Gate, gate, paragate, parasamgate, Bodhi Svaha!

Gone, gone, gone beyond, gone completely beyond. Awake, so be it!

I had heard the Buddha referred to as the Blessed One, Lord Buddha, or simply Lord. I could imagine devout monks assuming those lines from the kaddish—"Holy One, Blessed is He/Beyond any blessing and song, praise and consolation that are uttered in the world"—pertained to *their* Blessed One. By the same token, "gone beyond" might have had intonations of kabbalah, the more mystical end of Judaism, in which "the unattainable can have no name," as kabbalists put it.

Another Hebrew phrase, *tikkun olam,* which translates to "repairing the world," resonated with the socially engaged Buddhism I had tracked.

"Jews feel they have to seek truth, and to save the world," Rev. Fischer told me on a break. "The Torah says fix the world. *Tikkun olam.* And 'You are to be a nation of priests.' " Now he maintains his meditation and teaching practice through the Everyday Zen Foundation in Mill Valley, California, whose mission is "dedicated to listening to the world, to changing it and being changed by it." In his book *Jerusalem Moonlight,* he addresses his work on the Jewish-Buddhist dialogue.

"Buddhism and Judaism are both mindfulness practices," added

Rabbi Lew, author of *One God Clapping: The Spiritual Path of a Zen Rabbi*. Prior to becoming engaged in Judaism, he spent 10 years as a serious student of Zen Buddhism and was the director of the Berkeley Zen Center. Since then he had founded a Jewish meditation center, called Makor Or ("source of light"). "They are both based on the direct experience of this world. And I think this makes them different from other religions. Judaism is a deep, profound, rich spiritual path. But you would hardly know that from what you see in the American synagogue."

"The religious impulse in my generation of Jews had atrophied," agreed Rev. Fischer.

I could not agree more. I recall attending services on the Jewish High Holy Days—Rosh Hashanah, celebrating the Jewish New Year, and Yom Kippur, the Day of Atonement—at my suburban New Jersey synagogue in the late 1950s, thinking it seemed more like a mink-coat fashion show than a religious service. My disillusionment only grew as I got older. The last straw came at my bar mitzvah, in 1961. When the rabbi leaned forward to deliver the speech to me that would signal my arrival into manhood, the smell of alcohol on his breath repulsed me and repelled me from my own faith.

These two San Francisco men, the majority of my American Buddhist friends and I belong to a uniquely American sect. We are called Bu-Jews. The observation has been made quite often that a fairly significant percentage of American Buddhists—I have read as many as 30 percent—are of Jewish background (Jews comprise about 2.5 percent of the American population). The founders of the first *vipassana* retreat center, Insight Meditation Society, in Barre, Massachusetts, sound more like a Jewish law firm than hardcore Buddhists: Goldstein, Schwartz, Salzberg & Kornfield. The question that is either unanswerable or has too many answers is, why? Both Jews and Buddhists, who share a tendency toward answering a question with another question, would inquire, why not?

Jews are intellectual. Buddhism is the philosophy of mind. Jews have been subjected to persecution since the founding of the religion. Buddhism acknowledges that suffering is a part of life and offers a system of alleviating the pains associated with it. Buddhists chant "Om." Jews chant "Oy." Jews are analytical. Talmudic study requires the most detailed scrutiny of Jewish scriptures, right down to a numerological interpretation of each letter of each word. Freud, a Jew, developed a system of studying the mind called psychoanalysis. Buddhism is nothing if not analytical. As I wrote earlier, the Buddha's minute study of how one's own mind leads to unhappiness was a breakthrough in self-understanding that predicted Descartes and Freud. Furthermore, Jews of the mid- to late-20th century had moved to the forefront of the middle class, meaning they actually had attained a level of comfort on the material plane. This, in turn, meant that they might also be at the forefront of the "hungry ghost" brigade—when having everything they'd striven for still wasn't enough. As I'd seen, those who have either too much or too little seek solace in the Middle Way.

> Life is full of misery, loneliness, and suffering—and it's all over much too soon.
> —WOODY ALLEN

Jewish humor is born of necessity: to laugh in the face of thousands of years of persecution has been an expedient coping mechanism. It also proved to be substantiated as good medicine when Norman Cousins, a Jew, literally laughed his way out of ankylosing spondylitis, a painful disease causing the disintegration of the spinal connective tissue. He published his findings in the *New England Journal of Medicine* in 1976, and three years later in his book *Anatomy of an Illness*.

Jews do not have an exclusive on humor and laughter, nor on its applicability to human suffering. But when you read the film and sitcom television credit rolls and the comedy club lineups, you have to admit they may be a majority shareholder.

So it stood to reason—given that this was San Francisco—that the man who billed himself as the world's first Buddhist stand-up comic would be of Jewish upbringing. It also stood to reason that the guy would be one of my closest friends.

On a stark stage at the Marsh, an off-off-off-Broadway theater in the city's predominantly Latino Mission District, I watched Wes Nisker work the crowd.

"Before I became a Buddhist, I worried about my life." Pause. "Now I worry about my next life."

Nisker is a lanky 60-year-old with a rubbery face, prominent ears and an omniscient grin that evokes the iconic face of his first wisdom teacher, Alfred E. Neuman, the "What-me-worry" mascot of *Mad* magazine.

He delivers Zen zingers with borscht-belt timing.

"The disciple comes to the master and asks the time-honored question, 'Knock, knock?' The master replies with the number one spiritual question: 'Who's there?' " Another pause. "If you don't get the joke, you will reincarnate over and over until you do."

The audience, a mix of former hippies, yippies and yuppies sprinkled with a younger generation drawn to things Eastern, giggled knowingly and self-deprecatingly. They got his humor as though it was an inside joke. I heard the sound of many hands clapping.

I should insert here Nisker's credentials aside from being my friend. He also happens to be the co-editor of *Inquiring Mind*, a biannual international magazine for practitioners of *vipassana*; author of several books on Buddhism, including *Essential Crazy Wisdom* and *The Big Bang, the Buddha, and the Baby Boom*; and longtime meditation teacher and retreat speaker. However, he is best known in the Bay Area as "Scoop" Nisker, an FM-radio newscaster and commentator who since the late 1960s has taken acerbic aim on right-wing zealots, war hawks, corporate Amerika, and environmental polluters.

He is also Exhibit A in answer to the inquiry, "What's a nice Jewish boy doing in a monastery like this?" His story began in alienation, surrounded by cornfields, in the 1940s as one of the only Jewish families in Norfolk, Nebraska. He identified with alienated '50s celluloid antiheroes like Brando and James Dean.

The theme continued in college while he was absorbing the existentialists—Sartre, Camus. Having read the transcendentalists—Emerson's "Self Reliance" ("Nothing at last is sacred but the integrity of your own mind") and Whitman's *Leaves of Grass* ("I celebrate myself . . .")—Nisker took in the Buddha's suggestion to "be a lamp unto yourself." By the time he got to Kerouac, Ginsberg, Gary Snyder and the other Beats, he was primed for a philosophy that refuted God and any other authority, that admitted to suffering, but that also offered a nondogmatic way out. In 1970, he ended up in Bodh Gaya, India, doing Goenka's retreat, meeting John Bush, Ram Dass, Daniel Goleman and others at the forefront of the East-West synthesis.

Recently, he put together a comic monologue, based on *The Big Bang, the Buddha, and the Baby Boom,* mixing one-liners with his personal odyssey and thoughts on Buddhist cosmology, the big bang theory, quantum physics and the much maligned boomer generation, along with wisdom from assorted sages from his own readings. Had he grown up in another era, he might have been a regular on the borscht belt in New York's Catskill Mountains. Instead, he travels the American Buddha belt, doing his one-man show at Esalen Institute in Big Sur, California, Spirit Rock in Sonoma County, California, Insight Meditation Society in Barre, Massachusetts, Omega Institute in Rhinebeck, New York, the Asia Society in Manhattan and retreat centers elsewhere.

His performance, laced with self-penned songs, manages to make suffering a knee-slapper. He is Woody Allen meets the Dalai Lama. Though he confesses to an ambivalent relationship with his Jewish roots, on stage the *schtick* rolls out naturally:

"Have you noticed how many Jews become Buddhists? In tribute to this spiritual cross-pollination, I'm starting a whole new sect. We'd call ourselves the Bu-ish people. Our mantra would be 'Om, shalom.'

"I've already started channeling the Bu-ish guru, the Swami from Miami, who reads astrology charts by day and at night does rope tricks in the lobby of the Fontainebleau."

"I am a cynic in recovery," he told me later, keeping up the repartee even with his friends. We were sitting in a redwood hot tub behind the cottage he rented in Oakland, California, with his wife, Terry Vandiver, a landscaper and yoga teacher. His bouncy gait and thick black hair belie his age, as do impish eyes that hint at a pun in the making. We'd met 20 years ago through the extended dharma circle that bridged both American coasts. Along with cynical self-effacing Jewish humor and a nonetheless optimistic view of life, we both were single dads with daughters the same age. We did father-daughter weekends; we, and our daughters giggled for 48 hours. With my new Buddhist lens, I recognized him now as my Sangha.

When he does get serious, he is well versed in Buddhist philosophy, and it informs his underlying message. "My hope," he said, "is that my show reminds us to be at ease with life and its conditions, that we remain in awe of its essential mystery and learn how to take better care of it."

He attributes his Zen sense of humor to his Jewish upbringing. Being the only Jewish kid in small-town Nebraska, when it came time for his bar mitzvah he had to take lessons from a circuit rabbi who would arrive by Greyhound bus, he said, "preparing me for a ritual to join a community that in my hometown did not exist. How Zen is that?"

Still a political activist, he proposes a new movement he believes will solve many of America's problems. He calls it Zen socialism: "Zen, as in letting go," he explained, "socialism, as in together— letting go together."

Now he slid right back into his stand-up routine, as though he were a guest on Jay Leno: "The first step would be for the United States to resign as a superpower. As an ordinary nation, we could redirect our $500 billion-a-year defense budget to build the greatest education and health systems in the world. To ease the transition, I'd introduce a plan, not unlike the New Deal, called the New Age Deal, or the Great Leap Backward.

"I would establish a U.S. Department of Meditation and Therapy, with deprogramming centers to teach hyperactive people to become less-productive members of a less-productive society. Then we'd put them to work on disassembling lines, shoveling metal back into the ground and deconstructing highways. We'd invite Third World countries to send volunteers to teach us how to live with less and how to take siestas.

"Then we would do what we do best: entertain. We'd invite everyone to witness the world's first intentional decline and fall at a theme park called Formerly Great America. The downhill rides would be spectacular," he said, an omniscient grin overtaking his face. Before my very eyes—perhaps due to the heat of the hot tub, perhaps to the jet lag catching up to me, perhaps to seeing way too many Buddha images in the last two months—I saw his expressive face fading in and out between Alfred E. Neuman and Sakyamuni.

Wes's levity is a welcome addition to the generally sober Buddhist scene, and a uniquely American spin. Maybe it's because we are such a stressed-out society that we need the salve of humor more than other countries. It is not, however, that Americans take Buddhism less seriously. In fact, compared to other countries, I now realized American lay Buddhist practitioners often put a more earnest emphasis on meditation practice, on reading books about Buddhism, attending lectures and participating in intellectual conversation about Buddhist philosophy than Asian counterparts. Where we probably fail is that once we get off the cushion, put down the books and leave the lecture hall, we then shout at some tailgating SUV. It's in the day-to-day practice that Wes's humor becomes an excellent made-in-America new tool of the Dhamma. For example, I used to resent those omnipresent yellow smiley faces that pop up on my IM. Now they remind me of Scoop, and they, too, become the smiling face of the Buddha.

✿

Wes Nisker is the latest in a lineage of American Buddhist innovators who can trace their formal origins on this continent to 1893. That year, in conjunction with the Chicago World's Fair, the

World Parliament of Religions played host to representatives from India, Japan, China, Siam and Ceylon—in turn speaking on behalf of Hindus, Parsis, Sihks, Jains, Confucians and practitioners of Zen and other Buddhist sects—showcasing a new field called comparative religion. The majority of the delegates and audience, however, were Christians "who still argued that the highest development of the religious impulse could be found only in Christianity," as Rick Fields reports in *How the Swans Came to the Lake*. (Fields, also Jewish, found this fun fact: The *Journal of the Mahabodhi Society* reported that at the end of the parliament, a gentleman named Charles T. Strauss, a 30-year-old businessman from New York City, pronounced the vows of the Three Refuges and became the first person admitted to Buddhism on American soil. Strauss, Fields notes, happened to be Jewish.)

Among the speakers was Anagarika Dharmapala, from Ceylon, who, you will recall, had been initiated by the Westerners Olcott and Blavatsky. A fiery speaker, Dharmapala at one point asked how many in attendance had read a life of the Buddha. When five hands went up, he chastised the gathering: "Five only! Four hundred and seventy-five millions of people accept our religion of love and hope. You call yourselves a nation—a great nation—and yet you do not know the history of this great teacher. How dare you judge us!"

Despite the potential for creating more schisms among the isms, the event went off relatively ecumenically and did spread seeds of Asian religious ideas on the fertile American landscape. Another speaker was a Japanese roshi named Soyen Shaku, representing the Rinzai sect of Zen and the first Zen master to visit these shores. He returned in 1905 to lecture throughout the United States; in fact, I found a speech entitled "What Is Buddhism?" that he delivered in Washington, D.C., to the National Geographic Society in April 1906. It was Soyen Shaku's student, Daisetz Teitaro Suzuki, who further cultivated the Zen tradition in the United States when Soyen assigned him to translate Asian writings for Dr. Paul Carus, editor of a small Illinois publisher, Open Court Press.

Carus, writes Fields, "believed that Buddhism was more fitted than Christianity to heal the breach that had opened between science and religion, since it did not depend on miracles or faith." The plethora of current American-based magazines—*Turning Wheel, Shambhala Sun, Inquiring Mind, Tricycle*—owe a debt to this pioneer in the frontier of Buddhist publishing in America.

D. T. Suzuki himself came to write in English on his own, including what became the must-read for many Beat Buddhist wannabes. *An Introduction to Zen Buddhism,* first published in 1934, included a foreword by the esteemed psychiatrist C. J. Jung, which I found both illuminating and confounding; illuminating in that even this brilliant man flounders when it comes to putting into words the basics of Zen; confounding in trying to interpret his attempt, even watered down for the Western mind. In offering a definition for satori, a state that is neither enlightenment or transcendence, he first tries by the time-honored tradition of the parable. He writes of the monk who went to his master and wanted to learn where the entrance to the path of truth was. The master asked him, "Do you hear the murmuring of the brook?" "Yes, I hear it," answered the monk. "There is the entrance," the master instructed him.

Herr Jung should have stopped there, but he struggles on: "It is far better to allow oneself to become deeply imbued beforehand with the exotic obscurity of the Zen anecdotes, and to bear in mind the whole time that satori is the *mysterium ineffabile,* as indeed the Zen masters wish it to be. Between the anecdotes and the mystical enlightenment there is, for our understanding, a gulf, the possibility of bridging, which can at best be indicated but never in practice achieved." So frustrated is he by his own failure to offer clarity that he does what a Western intellectual always does: add more words. In a footnote to that comment, he adds: "If in spite of this I attempt 'explanations' in what follows, I am still fully aware that in the sense of satori what I say can only be useless. I could not resist, however, the attempt to maneuver our Western understanding at least into the proximity of an understanding—a task so difficult that in so doing one must take upon oneself certain crimes against the spirit of Zen."

In the end, he throws up his hands in surrender: "For these and many other reasons a direct transmission of Zen to Western conditions is neither commendable nor even possible." Yet he opens the door to a dialogue that many in the field of body-mind research, East-West psychology and holistic medicine have joined in recent years. He writes, "The psychotherapist, however, who is seriously concerned with the question of the aims of his therapy cannot be unmoved when he sees what ultimate result an oriental method of spiritual 'healing'—i.e. 'making whole'—is striving for." These comments led to further explorations in bridging the gap between Eastern thought and Western psychology. Today, the conversation has continued, led by psychiatrist Mark Epstein *(Thoughts Without a Thinker)*, psychologist/journalist Daniel Goleman *(Emotional Intelligence)*, psychologist Paul Ekman *(Emotions Revealed)* and the dialogues between His Holiness the Dalai Lama and forward-thinking Westerners, sponsored by the Mind & Life Institute.

Had Buddhism landed in the United States before Native Americans were relegated to reservations and reduced to Injun clichés and sports team mascots, it would have mixed with an indigenous religion more like that it encountered in, for example, Thailand and China. Though each tribe has its own specific practices, the majority of Native Americans follow a nature-based belief system of animism. Their mythic figures were inspired by the coyotes, eagles, turtles, horses and other animals that surrounded them. They pray to the spirits of these entities for good health, good fortune, good fertility and good weather. The earth itself and every living thing on it are part of a totality they worship as the Great Spirit. The elders and their ancestral lineage are held in the highest regard. Shamans, spirit guides, medicine men, sacred sites and rituals all play in Native American spirituality.

Instead, however, there was a Christianity that had already splintered into many factions. The Separatist Puritans and the mainstream Puritans had merged into Congregationalists. Members of the Anglican Church later became Episcopalians. Presbyterians, Baptists, Methodists, Quakers, Shakers, Lutherans—so many that it made Japanese Buddhist sects seem cohesive. Thus, the religious landscape here was similar to the past of countries I had visited over the last two months, in which spiritual chaos and dissatisfaction with existing institutions sent people looking for answers out of their ordinary theological paradigms.

In late-Victorian-era America, "there was a growing dissatisfaction with the answers provided by the traditional religions of the time," writes Charles Prebish, associate professor of religion at Penn State University, in his introduction to *The Faces of Buddhism in America*. But "while Buddhist sympathizers resonated favorably with the mid-Victorian period's emphasis on optimism and activism as important cultural values, on the whole, Buddhism's presumed characterization as pessimistic and passive made a much more compelling argument for its detractors."

On the heels of a Civil War that left the country bloodstained and divided, the post–Industrial Revolution Victorian era marked the fast ascent of American opulence. The Rockefellers and Carnegies set the pace for a consumerism unrivaled here and abroad. Could decadence and descent be far behind? As I had seen, it was in such times, when individuals and/or countries had fed their hungry ghost but were still not satisfied, that they turned to Buddhism. The United States was entering such a point.

Then, as suggested above, came the timely arrival of several waves of Asians. The most recent form—and one of the most popular—to join the American Buddhist melting pot is from Tibet. The sheer charisma and tireless touring of His Holiness the Dalai Lama have something to do with its appeal, as does the inherently magical attraction to the land of its origin, "the roof of the world." The political urgency of an oppressed people, and the resulting Free Tibet movement, add to making Tibetan Buddhism something more than just a religion—it's become a cause célèbre. Celebrity and a cause—now that's American!

Tibetan Buddhism is as confusing to me as Christianity, with its four schools—Nyingma, also called Red Hats; Kagyü, also called Red Hats but sometimes Black Hats; Geluk, called Yellow Hats (the Dalai Lama's sect); and Sakya, whose ceremonial turban hats, though red, are not called Red Hats—and its *tülkus* and *karmapas* and *rinpoches* and *lamas*.

This complexity was recognized by a Tibetan who was instrumental in repackaging Tibetan Buddhism, and Buddhism in general, for a Western audience. Chögyam Trungpa (1939–1987), born in Tibet, was the 11th descendent in the line of Trungpa *tülkus,* important teachers of the Kagyü lineage, the Tibetan school renowned for its strong emphasis on meditation practice. Already installed as the head of several monasteries in eastern Tibet, Chögyam Trungpa was forced to flee the country to India in 1959, at the age of 20. In India, the Dalai Lama appointed him as spiritual adviser to young lamas. In 1963, Chögyam Trungpa moved to England to study comparative religion, philosophy and fine arts at Oxford University. In 1967, he moved to Scotland, where he founded the Samye Ling Meditation Center, the first Tibetan Buddhist practice center in the West. Shortly after a car accident that left him partially paralyzed, he give up his monastic vows to work as a lay teacher. In 1969, he published the first of 14 books he would write in his lifetime. The next year, he married a young Englishwoman and moved to the United States, where he established his first North American meditation center, Tail of the Tiger (now known as Karmê Chöling) in Barnet, Vermont.

His approach was innovative and controversial. On a personal level, he was not exactly the purest of monks. The rumors spread of his drinking and womanizing. He hung out with the poet Allen Ginsberg and the Harvard psychologist-turned-LSD-advocate-turned-Hindu Ram Dass. He knew it would take someone who spoke their language to shake young Americans out of their psychedelic somnambulant state. In his 1973 book, *Cutting Through*

Spiritual Materialism, he shows an understanding of the particular dilemma faced by American spiritual seekers used to the more-is-better principle:

> We may have studied Western philosophy or Oriental philosophy, practiced yoga or perhaps have studied under dozens of great masters. We believe that we have accumulated a hoard of knowledge. And yet, having gone through all this, there is still something to give up. It is extremely mysterious! How could this happen? Impossible! But unfortunately it is so. Our vast collections of knowledge and experience are just parts of ego's display, part of the grandiose quality of ego. . . . But we have simply created a shop, an antique shop . . . We searched the world over for beautiful objects—India, Japan, many different countries. And each time we found an antique . . . we saw it as beautiful and thought it would be beautiful in our shop . . . But when we brought the object home and put it there, it became just another addition to our junky collection. . . . Proper shopping does not entail collecting a lot of information or beauty, but it involves fully appreciating each individual object.

In 1974, he brought together a group of his outrageous friends in Boulder and put on a summer session of spiritual dialogues, workshops and panels that he called Naropa Institute. It included the Jack Kerouac School of Disembodied Poetics, under the direction of Ginsberg and the poet Anne Waldman. Those sessions continued for several summers, eventually leading to a year-round schedule of classes. Naropa was accredited in 1986 as a four-year college, and in 2000 changed its name to Naropa University. Today, it has about 1,100 students, of which two-thirds are graduate and one-third undergraduate students. The university itself consists of a cluster of trailers and several small buildings behind a back parking lot in the shadow of the sprawling campus of the University of Colorado.

The curriculum is "Buddhist-inspired," as the university catalog explains, offering a "contemplative liberal arts education . . . that integrates the best of Eastern and Western educational traditions, creating and implementing a new paradigm in higher education.

With Carrie Mattison, the author's niece, in front of the Great Stupa of Dharmakaya, at the Rocky Mountain Shambala Center outside Boulder. Built to last a thousand years, it is in memory of Chögyam Trungpa Rinpoche, the Tibetan who founded Naropa University.

This model seeks to help students know themselves deeply so that they can engage constructively and effectively in a world of individuals who are not like themselves." Most classes begin with a short meditation. Meditation and Buddhist philosophy courses are offered as part of the core curriculum. Faculty often sit together; many sit alone. Almost all have a long background in Buddhist practice, but it is not required.

It is the only fully accredited four-year college in North American and Europe whose defining mission is Buddhist-based. And, as such, it the best example of educationally engaged Buddhism in both the West and the East. As you already know, it inspired some Thai academicians.

The real roots of Naropa go back to the Buddha himself, who emphasized education as an important cornerstone of Buddhist practice. "Know well what leads you forward and what holds you back, and choose the path that leads to wisdom," he said. He dedicated his life to teaching, rather than simply luxuriating in nirvana. His first lectures were at Sarnath, where the so-called Turning of the Wheel of Dharma took place, not far from Bodh Gaya. He continued teaching until his death and, his followers say, beyond. The sutras describe how his teachings unfolded as the Buddha moved from village to village with his small but growing Sangha. One time he stopped in a particularly tranquil setting by a mango grove and stayed for three months. Eventually, 500 merchants bought the grove and donated it to the Buddha. Several hundred years later the great Indian King Ashoka visited this site on his own Buddhist pilgrimage and erected a pillar, as was his custom.

At that site, about two hours by car from Sarnath, north of the ancient city of Rajagriha, some 1,000 years after the Buddha's death the world's first tuition-free residential international university was founded. Some 2,000 teachers and 10,000 students from all over the Buddhist world lived and studied at Nalanda University. Here the world's best and brightest studied and debated the Mahayana and Hinayana schools of Buddhism, the Brahminical and Vedic texts, philosophy, logic, theology, grammar, astronomy, mathematics and medicine. Seen today, the ruins of red brick, the remains of stupas, temples, monasteries and monks' cells with thick intact walls barely suggest the intense academic community that once thrived there.

Joshua Mulder, who oversaw the construction of the Dharmakaya stupa, touches up the Buddha inside the stupa.

Steve McCurry

One of the best-known students to have ever studied at Nalanda was a young prince named Naropa, who lived from 1016 to 1100. A giant portrait of Naropa hangs in the two-story lobby of Naropa University's main building, a century-old converted schoolhouse on the bonsai-like Boulder campus.

I stood in the lobby, staring up at the princely Naropa. I had been to the ruins of Nalanda University in India. I had met the Thai people who journeyed here to learn from these teachers. I was now in Boulder. The dots of my journey were connecting themselves—from West to East to West and back again. I imagined in several hundred years some journalist standing where I stood, in front of what would be ruins here, equally awed that the Wheel had rolled this far and for this long.

I am kneeling in a sort of doggy position, butt thrust up in the air, chin cupped between my palms, in the middle of a seven-by-seven-foot windowless room that's painted vomit green, with matching fluorescent lighting of an equally nauseating hue. It is perhaps the most awkward position I have ever allowed my body to assume.

I've been instructed to maintain this position for 45 minutes while contemplating the states of jealousy and wisdom, flip sides of the emotional coin that this color is meant to evoke, according to Tibetan Buddhist theory. "I'd like to see the Buddha attain enlightenment in this position," I'm mumbling to myself. Then I remember those Tendai Marathon Monks and don't feel so bad. At least this is soft shag.

There are four other rooms surrounding this one, each painted and lit in a different color, each color evoking another set of emotions, the whole thing designed to replicate a traditional Tibetan mandala.

These colorful cubicles, called Maitri rooms, are in the basement of Naropa's administrative building, down the hall from the computer center. They are part of the transpersonal psychology graduate training program, and they integrate millennia-old Buddhist wisdom with modern psychology and the magic of fluorescent lighting. The idea is based on the philosophy, or more accurately psychology, of the Five Buddha Families. Each room correlates to one of five human psychological traits (anger, pride, passion, jealousy and ignorance) and their opposites (wisdom, equanimity, discrimination, accomplishment and all-pervading awareness). Each trait has its own corresponding element, color and geographic direction. Tibetans stare in meditation at mandalas—huge circular paintings, richly colored, minutely detailing stories of the Buddha's life—and these colors and stories evoke associations that connect them to their culture and their history, to their lineage holders all the way back to the Buddha himself. And, finally, to their very essence. This does not happen to the rest of us, no matter how long we stare at it, no matter how many cups of yak butter tea we drink. Generally, we marvel at them in museums or see them in friend's living rooms and ask, "Where'd you get it? How much did you pay for it?"

Trungpa knew this. Yet he also knew that if he could get Westerners to somehow experience what Tibetans already knew on an intuitive level, he could teach us two lessons for the price of one. One: we would come to terms personally with our own demons and saints—acknowledge, own and embrace them. The other: in case we were among the very few in our species who had not felt any of the above emotions, we would develop empathy for those who had felt them. This, in turn, would be beneficial for all mankind. It would be an especially valuable asset for those in the helping professions.

So Trungpa and, as the story goes, a wild-eyed Japanese priest friend concocted this system, designed the rooms, came up with original positions vaguely like yoga asanas, and a methodology of immersion. As explained in the course outline, the Maitri Space Awareness practicum requires students to lie in the rooms—five hours a week, 45 minutes in each room followed immediately by 15 minutes of "aimless wandering." Students I met at Naropa told me the experience can be more than unnerving, releasing long-pent-up feelings that draw out neurotic thoughts they'd rather not have to face within themselves. The key is to take the time to marinate. I asked if I could do the whole Maitri process, usually spread out over the course of a semester, in three days. That might not have been a good idea. It was like standing under a magnifying glass in the Sahara Desert. I had a headache and an upset stomach after each session, as though I had swallowed sour milk. And the back that had been doing so well by me was suddenly aching. Was it the 12-hour drive from San Francisco to Boulder? Or was it from carrying my own emotional baggage way too long? Or was it just the awkward position Trungpa randomly selected?

Long or short, it was a powerful experience. Yet there was something about it that bothered me. Once again, the word "gimmicky" came to mind. It seemed like the work of an overactive and complex mind. Had Trungpa gone too far? Stretched the bounds of one tradition to make it appealing to another tradition? In repackaging an internal Eastern experience into an external Westernized experience, had he sabotaged his own best intentions? Had the medium spoken louder than the message? I came out of the Maitri rooms fascinated by the effect fluorescent lighting and truly inspired marketing genius could have on one's self-understanding. I know I didn't give the experience enough time. I am sure I would eventually break through the weird sense that I was on the set of some kinky postmodern sci-fi movie. But I found that the environmental bells and whistles distracted me from deeper exploration of my self.

Meanwhile, I had been told, now they've developed 3-D plastic glasses with colored lenses matching those of the five Buddha Families so you can have the same visual experience of the Maitri rooms anywhere. I heard Tibetans living in Boulder were taking them back to Tibetans living in India. Now the western interpretation of Buddhism would be introduced to Tibetans, who would interpret that in yet another way. The permutations of this cross-pollination could get dizzying.

I wondered if Tibetans who practiced with the Maitri glasses would lose the very thing to which we Westerners aspired: the ability to internalize the wisdom? This line of thinking recalled the insight of Peta McAuley, the Aussie psychologist I'd met in Hong Kong who led groups based on the Mindfulness-Based Stress Reduction methodology of Jon Kabat-Zinn. She noted that

Asians are introverts and Americans are extroverts; therefore, drawing on Jungian thought, the former are drawn to more external Buddhist practices and the latter to more internal practices. So, according to her theory, Tibetans naturally would be more inclined to this external practice. Mandala meditation itself is just such an external practice.

The inconsistencies of her analysis aside, my own experiences in the Maitri rooms at Naropa University combined with her theory suggested a possible answer to a question that still perplexed me: Why had the socially engaged Buddhist movement become more popular in the United States than in Asia?

One answer may be found in the difference between what cultures of the East and West value. In the East the emphasis is on "being." In the West, it's on "doing." In the East we internalize: we be. In the West, we externalize: we do. In the Buddhist countries of the East, being a good person is considered a remarkable and enviable accomplishment. In the Judeo-Christian countries of the West, it's not enough to be good—you have to do good. Deeply embedded in the values of Jews and Christians is the idea that "good deeds" or "good works" earn the merit points Buddhists earn by walking in the Buddha's footsteps. Some may argue that in the West doing has become a convenient way to avoid being. Yet without that do-good ethos, many of the programs and initiatives I encountered—not only in the United States and Europe but also throughout Asia—might not exist. And without them, I can guarantee there would be more suffering in the world.

In this way, socially engaged Buddhism blends the best of East and West, of the Buddhist desire to end suffering and the Judeo-Christian impulse to do something proactively about it. As such, the movement is the logical continuation of Buddhism's historic pattern to adopt and adapt to local cultural cues. My hope is that while the East may be taking clues from the West about how to reinvigorate the grand traditions of Buddhism in their own countries, this application of Buddhist practices in socially relevant areas of contemporary life finds fuller expression in Asia.

eleven

Gautama Goes to Gaul

Buddhism with a French Twist

My path is the path of stopping, the path of enjoying the present moment. It is a path where every step brings me back to my true home. It is a path that leads nowhere. I am on my way home. I arrive at every step.

—Thich Nhat Hanh, "I Have Arrived, I Am Home."

Holding on to anger is like grasping a hot coal with the intent of throwing it at someone else; you are the one getting burned.

—The Buddha

True greatness consists in the use of a powerful understanding to enlighten oneself and others.

—Voltaire

From Boulder, I drove nonstop to the East Coast. I felt like a horse with the scent of the stable in his nostrils; I couldn't wait to get home. Still officially homeless, however, "home" was just a concept and a loose one at that. Ariana and Ryan were getting married on Martha's Vineyard; then I planned to settle down on the island and "just sit," albeit in front of a laptop.

Sitting in "driving meditation," speeding at 75 miles an hour across the conveyor belt of American highways, I had a lot of time to think. But mostly I savored the Kerouacian thrill of being on the road, in a familiar element, behind the wheel and whizzing by the lush green landscape that lulls you into a drone state.

Travel is a contagious disease. It has its own cause-and-effect syndrome: movement begets movement, speed begets speed, restlessness begets restlessness. I had been in motion for so long now that my momentum seemed to be running away with me, and sometimes even without me. As nervous as I was about taking off on this journey, I was getting equally nervous about the prospect of its end. Not only did it mean I would have to write the article, but it also meant the magic dust would wear off, that I would be drowning in receipts and financial problems, back problems and relationship problems. Once the trip was over, I worried that I would fall into the same old rut I'd been in before I left.

Daniel Goleman points out in *Emotional Intelligence* that the word "emotion" derives from *movere,* to move. It is a brilliant observation, and I interpret it in several ways. Movement implies change. Change, as students of the fight-or-flight hormonal syndrome will tell you, causes stress. Movement therefore causes emotions. Emotions also "move" you from one feeling to another. Your reaction to an event, conversation, memory or even a smell can shift—move—you from happy to sad, from hopeful to pessimistic, from anger to laughter, from alienation to love. As we now know, emotional shifts also trigger biological and chemical shifts within your body. Then, too, to express the emotion caused by the motion—to emote—is to move these feelings from inside yourself to outside yourself.

The Vietnamese monk Thich Nhat Hanh has noted that when he sees a person always on the move, someone who has difficulty settling down and setting down roots, he knows this person is suffering from the hungry ghost syndrome. No matter what excuses I made—things would be better *if* I lived somewhere else, *if* I had a different job, *if* I had a different girlfriend, *if* I had a different *life*—I knew he was right. I knew my motivation to move was dissatisfaction. I also knew stopping would mean sitting with my stuff, marinating in my *mishigas*. I just wanted to postpone the inevitable.

My temporary reprieve from the mirror of reality came in the form of the e-mail I had been waiting for since January. With it, I knew there was one more leg of my expedition to complete before I could rest my weary body/mind/spirit.

This would not be just one more interview; this would be the Interview of a Lifetime, the jewel in the crown of interviews on my worldwide inquisition. After many months of waiting, the Office of His Holiness the 14th Dalai Lama had finally offered a date for a 45-minute interview. The *Geographic* had promised to fly me to India for the interview if I got it. Once I got the confirmation, I then planned to add a stopover in France to interview Rev. Hanh at his Plum Village retreat center in the south of France. Quite savvy to media manipulation, Rev. Hahn—or Thây, Vietnamese for "teacher"—sets one requirement for interviews: that you join at least five days of a retreat. Very smart move. He understood that by participating, a journalist would have a personal experience of meditation, the better to write about it. Sitting would also put the journalist in a more calm and tranquil demeanor, thus undermining the very quality of antagonism that drives us to ask hard questions.

For me, it was the briar's patch. I was looking forward to—almost craving, if there can be a good type of craving—a retreat to collect my thoughts, to counterbalance this "motion sickness" I suffered and to prepare me for the long writing meditation I was about to begin. I also thought it would help me get more centered for the Big Interview with His Holiness.

Thây's people were enthusiastic for me to attend the retreat and then interview him. There was just one problem. To keep on my schedule, I would have to miss a retreat for Israelis and Palestinians, which promised to be highly charged and particularly interesting for me personally. Jewish Israelis and Muslim Palestinians would attend discussion groups, workshops and, of course, dharma talks and sitting and walking meditations—all side by side. Thây and his close associate Sister Chân Không would mediate between the meditating. These ancient antagonists would learn to apply mindfulness in the toughest circumstance. How do you make peace with your enemy? Thây's simple and elegant prescription: First make peace with yourself.

Instead, I would join the retreat that followed, with some 200 Vietnamese people from throughout the world, most from Europe and some from the United States. As much as it is a meditation retreat, this summer retreat is a cultural communion and familial reunion for Vietnamese emigrants and expats. Many had left Vietnam in the mid-1970s after the Communists took over the country. Like the Chinese and others before them, this next great Asian wave of emigrants to the West brought their Buddhist practice, traditions and temples. Now their children and grandchildren, raised in the West, were cultural hybrids, speaking with their peers in German or French but with their families in their joyfully melodic mother tongue. While they may live and work in Paris or Frankfurt or elsewhere and maintain friendships with and even marry European-born people, in their homes close-knit Vietnamese families maintain their style of eating, their language and culture. And they fill their shelves with statues of the Buddha.

Sainte-Foy-la-Grande, 85 kilometers east of Bordeaux in one of the world's most fertile grape-growing regions, is the train station stop for Plum Village. It's drop-dead gorgeous south of France, the way they show it on the Travel Channel. Fields of sunflowers in full bloom form yellow borders around just-ripening vineyards in valley after rolling green valley. I fully expected to see the ghost of van Gogh painting at a canvas in the middle of one row. On my way to the retreat center, nose glued to a shuttle van window, I laughed to myself. What a waste of great scenery, I thought, knowing most of the time I was going to be sitting in a meditation hall, eyes closed.

Plum Village is a complex of converted old wooden and stone farmhouses, with several new meditation halls. The compounds, which they call hamlets, are spread out in a 5- to 10-kilometer district. The original two are Upper Hamlet, which sits on 23 acres in the village of Thénac; and Lower Hamlet, on 50 acres, in Loubes-Bernac. Now, because of Thây's growing popularity, there are newer New Hamlets being added.

When I asked Thây later how he chose this location, he said cryptically, "We didn't choose it; it chose us."

Thich Nhat Hahn (pronounced "Tick Knot Han," his name means "one action") speaks this way. As a longtime poet, he enjoys the play of words. There was little playfulness in the Vietnam of his youth. Born in 1926 in the central part of the country, he ordained as a monk at the age of 16. By then, Vietnam, having already endured a thousand years of harsh Chinese rule, was the pawn in a three-way political chess match among the French, who had colonized Vietnam in the mid-1800s; the Japanese, who had occupied it since 1940; and the Communists, who hoped to seize power amid the chaos. Meanwhile, the United States waited in the wings, and in 1954, when the Communists forced the French out, it entered the fray. By 1964, the United States was fully committed to the war in Vietnam.

That same year Thây was working hard to get the Unified Buddhist Church of Vietnam (UBCV) to call for an end to the war. He had already studied at Princeton and taught at Columbia from 1961 to 1963. In June of 1963, Thây returned to Vietnam after a Buddhist monk poured petrol over his body, took up his lotus position and set himself on fire in a plaza in Saigon to protest the war. Newspapers around the world printed the image, burning it into our brains.

In 1965, Thây established the School of Youth for Social Service, a Peace Corps of sorts for Buddhist peace workers, a grassroots relief organization that rebuilt bombed villages, set up schools and medical centers, resettled homeless families and organized agricultural cooperatives. He also set up the Order of Interbeing, the Tiep Hien Order. *Tiep* means "being in touch with" and "continuing." *Hien* means "realizing" and "making it here and now." It's his way to express the Buddhist concept of interdependence. He suggests we learn not only how to "be," but also how to "be" with others.

These are the origins of the modern socially engaged Buddhism movement. As Patricia Hunt-Perry and Lyn Fine write in a chapter of *Engaged Buddhism in the West,* "Despite the presence in Vietnamese history of earlier roots of engaged Buddhist practices, the approach of Thich Nhat Hanh and the UBC was a departure from the 20th-century traditional monastic Vietnamese Buddhism. A Buddhist collective action emerged which was aimed at directly influencing public policy and establishing new institutional forms. One form of collective action was noncooperation with government, such as strikes, mass resignations, the return of government licenses, and boycotts of classes by students. Another was the use of cultural forms such as fiction and nonfiction writing, and anti-war songs."

His nonviolent activism evoked Gandhi and Martin Luther King, Jr. In 1966, at the age of 40, Thây accepted an invitation to participate in a forum in New York, sponsored by Cornell University, examining the American policy in Vietnam. He planned to be away from Vietnam for three weeks. But, marked by the Communist government as a troublemaker, he was exiled and, until his three-month return to Vietnam in the winter of 2004, had not set foot on his native country for 30 years. To mount the journey and go in itself was an act of engagement, as I saw it. It forced people in power to sit around tables and discuss Buddhism. In 1967, Martin Luther King, Jr. nominated Thây for the Nobel Peace Prize.

He settled in France, since he had friends there and spoke the language. In Paris, he continued antiwar work with the Buddhist Peace Delegation until the war's end, in 1975. The Plum Village lands were acquired in 1982 and annual retreats began immediately. The summer program draws thousands now; he has written more than 75 books of prose, poetry and prayers; he has monastic centers in Vermont and outside San Diego, California, and leads retreats throughout North America and Europe.

Though I have attended close to 20 retreats over the years, I had not participated in one of Thich Nhat Hanh's. That was not why I felt like a fish out of water. It was because I felt little in common with Vietnamese people. I had never been to Vietnam. I knew little to nothing about their culture, except that I loved their spring rolls. I obviously didn't speak Vietnamese. Though I had protested the war in Vietnam, had taken tear gas at Dupont Circle in Washington in 1969, had seen them on television through the '60s and early '70s, their faces speaking the international language of grief and terror, I had never actually met a Vietnamese person.

Over several days, however, these people won my heart with their warmth and compassion, with their good humor, curiosity and intelligence, with their friendliness (after some initial shyness), and with their delicious spring rolls. There was something else we shared, as I found out shortly.

Knowing Thây's influential role in spearheading socially and politically relevant Buddhism, I was surprised that his talks were about relationships—about open communication between parents and children, about keeping love fresh between husband and wife, about the importance of nondiscrimination and mutual understanding in the increasing number of relationships between couples of different religious and cultural backgrounds.

"Aren't there enough relationship gurus?" I asked when we met. I was thinking of all the American TV talk show experts and best-selling relationship book authors. "Aren't there more important issues to discuss?"

"Such as war, violence, death, economic problems, terrorism?"

he asked rhetorically. He spoke so softly I knew my tape recorder's mike would have trouble picking up his voice. Tall and thin, he walks delicately. You really sense "peace in every step," as one of his book titles says. I had seen children follow him around the grounds as though he were the Pied Piper. Picturing this gentle man as a hard-core activist was difficult for me, but his commanding ambience told me he would stand firm in tough negotiations. "The conflict in the Middle East, tension between religious groups—these are about relationships. The Buddha identified ignorance as the second noble truth. We create ignorance through poor communication. Misunderstanding begins in the microcosm, between two people. It creates fear, and fear creates violence. When you act with violence and anger, you create more violence and anger. The majority of the people who come here suffer from relationship, health and work problems. But if your relationship is good, then you are happy, your health improves and you'll be more successful in your enterprise."

The key is communicating before misunderstandings occur, he said. But for Vietnamese that presents a problem. "They are not like Westerners," he explained. "They do not have the habit of sharing what's inside very easily. Only when the atmosphere is very intimate and there's a lot of trust do they dare to slowly open up."

I'd become aware of this myself in the days before my interview with him. After a morning of meditation, dharma talks, walking meditation and meals, groups gathered in the afternoon under the trees surrounding the dining halls. A monk presented an idea and asked people to respond personally. Many people, I noticed, offered predictable clichés that revealed nothing personal about their own experiences. Others were forthcoming but, I could see, their candor made others feel awkward. After several days with the same Sangha, people slowly revealed more of themselves, or maybe I just got better at reading their body language and interpreting the interpreter who was whispering translations in my ear. Among my group were a couple about 65 years of age, Quang Trung Tran and his wife, Thi Tram Nguyen, whose daughter and son-in-law, I soon figured out, were also in our circle. The young couple, Kim Le Viet and Chau Nguyen, were about 32 and 28. Born in Vietnam, they had grown up in Germany, and seemed more European than Vietnamese. I had chatted with Kim Le Viet, and with his father and his uncle, well-educated and convivial men also on the retreat.

On the fourth day, rain forced our group to meet in the dining hall. It was August, and muggy. While daily meditation brings you more into moment-to-moment awareness, which is often a *good* thing, sometimes that awareness zooms in on painful experiences and things about yourself you'd rather remain fuzzy. Sometimes people get a little edgy before they get mellow on retreats.

Thi Tram was talking about how the teachings of Thây had helped her husband work through his intermittent bouts with anger, during which he'd lashed out at his loved ones. As she talked, I could see her wiping tears from her eyes, while her face and torso stayed quite rigid. Meanwhile, her husband, Quang Trung, two seats away, stared down at his shoes, blinking and almost convulsing. Then he erupted, barking something and repeating the same words several times. At this point the translator was having great difficulty keeping up with what they were saying. "Tell me later," I said. I watched the family drama play out like a silent movie. Then, his voice lowered, he told a long story. By now the wife had a hankie in her hand, the daughter was dabbing her eyes, too, and Kim Le Viet was staring at his shoes, his face stony and ashen. Immediately after the session, I went up to Kim Le Viet and asked if I could talk with him and his father-in-law.

We found a spot to sit. Quang Trung sat across from me, a thin, unprepossessing man in his mid-60s. Kim Le Viet sat between us.

He recounted the scene I had just witnessed. When his wife told people that he used to have anger fits, he said to the group, "Do you want to know why? Do you? Do you want to know why I got angry?" He went on to tell them, and now me, that when the Communists took over in 1975, "we lost everything."

He was taken prisoner by the North Vietnamese and tortured. Before becoming a financial accountant, he had served as a soldier for the South Vietnamese. An American major in the military, for whom Quang Trung had worked, came to his family home to visit one evening. Neighbors saw the major come and go and must have reported to authorities that Quang Trung was in cahoots with the American CIA. At least that's what he thinks. They threw him in prison and for one month did terrible things to him. He described being dangled upside down, copper wiring wrapped around his big toes.

"No," I shouted in disbelief. Quang Trung said his toe turned completely black. I was surprised it didn't fall off.

Repeatedly, they asked him about his involvement with the CIA, which he continued to deny, which made them beat and punish him more. He offered to show me the scars and pulled off his sandal. I didn't want to see, but I looked. There was where one bullet went right through his leg; there one bullet got lodged. The toe still hurts, he said; when it's cold his ribs still ache from the beatings. He spent another 44 months in retention camps, treated harshly and beat up from time to time.

"Since that time, I got angry," he said. He did not have to explain further. It brought me right back to Auschwitz. What I could not understand was why he wasn't still in a rage; I knew I would be.

"What got you through?" I asked. I wanted him to say he kept a little statue of the Buddha locked away and surreptitiously meditated in the predawn hours.

No, it was family. "Sometimes I wanted to kill myself," he said. "Then I thought of my wife and children; they need me."

Years later, living in Germany, he was introduced to the writings of Thây by Kim Le Viet. Kim Le Viet beamed modestly when he translated that. And yes, the practice has helped him deal with the anger.

"I hated the Communists," he said. I could tell he repeated the Vietnamese word for *hated*. "*Hated* my torturers. And now I can forgive them for what they did to me."

"Seriously?" I asked, making sure I got the translation right, perhaps thinking back to my encounters in Auschwitz. "You can forgive them?"

"Well, not that I forgive," he qualified. "But I hope to forgive, I *want* to forgive."

"But is that possible?"

"I just will try hard."

That alone seemed like a fairly enlightened perspective considering what he'd been put through. I know Americans who scrupulously avoided the draft and marched on Washington and, while never having been tortured, still harbor harsh hostility for the Vietcong. To ask Quang Trung to forgive and forget was asking more than should be expected of a person. He confessed it was a struggle, that he can cry just thinking about what he endured. But, he added with a laugh, his dreams are full of the Buddha's face, not his torturers' faces. He considered that alone a kind of Buddhist triumph over his own psyche.

Earlier, I had asked Thây a question that the American rabbi Harold Kushner many years before had tried to answer in a book: "Why do bad things happen to good people?" This was the Jewish koan, the lingering quandary of a people who try to live ethically but have been persecuted endlessly. "Why us?" "Why me?"

"Bad things happen to all of us," he stated. "That is karma."

As unsatisfying as that answer was, it was less frustrating than the response I got when I asked the same question of the American Zen priest Eido Shimano. In response, he had asked, "What is good? What is bad?"

When the most brilliant minds in the world cannot answer a question or do a theological tap dance around it, I have concluded, the fault lies not with the answer but with the question. In this regard, I was happier with the Zen "don't know" approach. There are some things not meant to be comprehended. Some questions have no answers. This was a tough pill for a journalist to swallow. I gulped as hard as I could.

These thoughts did lead me to one conclusion. I realized what the Vietnamese and we Jews have in common. We have suffered. And we have hope. We have sadness, and we have enduring love.

These emotionally wrenching interviews made me feel particularly open and receptive. Then, at the end of one of Thây's talks, something unexpected happened—something that hit home in the personal relationship department. Before getting up from my cushion on the floor, as I twisted to stretch my back, thinking how proud I was of my spine for not once collapsing on me, I scanned a sea of faces: mysterious dark eyes, thick black hair and beautiful caramel-colored skin. My eyes landed on one woman who radiated serenity, grace and beauty. I almost gave myself whiplash doing a double take. I was immediately drawn in. "Whatever," I said to myself. "She's probably married. She's probably got a boyfriend. She's probably with her parents or about to become a nun. She probably doesn't speak English. Anyway, this is a spiritual retreat, no place for romance."

In the West, we call them "*vipassana* romances." At retreats conducted in silence, where people are not even allowed to make eye contact, it's quite easy to fall in love with the projection of a person based simply on the way she walks, smiles, or washes her plate in front of you in line. We imbue these people we never meet with the highest ideals. *Vipassana* romances never—and probably never should—develop into actual romances.

I put her out of my mind, collected my tape recorder and headset and stood up. When I turned, there she happened to be, standing four feet away, oblivious to me. Grasping for an opening line, I made some inane comment about the weather. She replied with an incandescent smile and, in somewhat halting English, spoke with me for 10 minutes. Her name was Anh Thuy Nguyen. She was born in Saigon, but at the age of 12 she left with her family to live in Paris for the next 25 years. Her family had known Rev. Hanh in Vietnam; she first came to Plum Village when she was a teenager. A cousin had taken ordination with Thây's monastic community, and her best friend had left a cardiology practice to also don the robes of a monk there. About three years ago, for reasons she promised to explain another time, she started coming again to Plum Village. In short order, she wrote her e-mail and home address in my notebook. I was taken aback by her forthrightness. Entranced, I made up some excuse to interview her for my story and asked if we could meet the next day for a little while.

That same day we bumped into each other twice more—leaving off our dishes at the same time, entering the meditation hall side by side. On the third encounter, she said, "That's a third time." Her expression was of neither delight nor disappointment, but more of simply observing phenomena rising. She was just noting, as *vipassana* junkies would say. "Hmm, this is interesting," she seemed to be thinking—or so I projected. Was it kismet? Yes, kismet, karma, coincidence or whatever else you want to call carefully orchestrated coincidental bumpings into each other.

Suddenly, the entire focus of my retreat shifted. My "awareness" revolved around her. Without speaking or making eye contact with her, I nonetheless followed her. I tried to keep track of where she was at all times, and when I didn't, I went into a bit of a tailspin. When I saw her wielding her camcorder, I was a happy camper, wondering perchance if she was slyly filming me. Once Thây led a walking meditation around a lotus pond and through aisles of plum trees. I kept looking back and around for her; then I saw her right behind me, hand in hand with a girlfriend of hers, and was completely flustered.

I had it bad. But it was nothing, illusion, all my projection. I had no idea what she thought or felt about me—if she thought or felt anything about me. I thought, "You have gotten nowhere, Perry. After 10 weeks in the footsteps of the Buddha, you see one pretty face and you run helter-skelter down the path of desire and passion." I had roamed the globe in search of truth, meaning and happiness, but as soon as an attractive woman crossed my path, I could care less about enlightenment.

I managed to talk twice more with her. I felt quite comfortable with her. We had very good "flow," as she put it. On the day before I left, knowing it might be my last chance to share my interest in her, I wrote her a schmaltzy but sincere note suggesting that if she, too, had some interest, if she was not married or had a boyfriend, if she was not planning to ordain as a nun anytime in the immediate future, perhaps we could arrange to meet again. I left her a phone number in Paris where I could be reached before I was to leave for India and my interview with the Dalai Lama. All the time I was thinking, "Bad, Perry, bad. Is this what you plan to do with your Buddha dust, hit on beautiful women?"

But if . . . if . . . if . . . The possibility of a love built on Buddhist foundations and on Thây's teachings, auspiciously begun at a retreat at Plum Village, seemed like more than magic Buddha dust. It seemed like an entirely good idea. And, if nothing else, something to strive for.

I brought the note to our last meeting, along with a little present of a jade turtle, which represents longevity in Asian cultures. I planned to give both to her only if I got some sign. ("Show me a sign, dear Buddha, show me a sign." This was my mantra the night before.) So I was pleasantly surprised when, before I could say anything, she said, "Perry"—rolling the double r with a French accent that sent shivers behind my ears—"I have something for you." She took out a tiny vial of Vietnamese oil that smelled like Ben-Gay, but stronger. "This is good for travel and headaches and any other sickness. You rub it on your forehead and under your nose." I had my sign. I handed her my note and gift. She smiled so broadly that I knew something was possible.

When I got to the Four Seasons George V in Paris two days later, a message was waiting for me from her. She *was* interested. We spoke twice before I left. I would meet her in Paris on my way back to the States. I almost did not need to board a plane for India—I already was floating so high.

twelve

☙On Interviewing the Dalai Lama

He Had Me at Hello

The hope of all men, in the last analysis, is simply for peace of mind.
— His Holiness the Dalai Lama, *My Land and My People*

It's hard to find a noble person; such a person is not born everywhere. When such a wise one is born, the family flourishes in happiness.

— The Buddha, *The Dhammapada*

It took nearly a year to nail down an interview with His Holiness, the 14th Dalai Lama. This despite sending my best clips, a book I wrote, and, of course, my official *National Geographic* letter of introduction, impressive blue ribbon attached. I guess he's a busy man who just doesn't need the publicity. In the confirmation e-mail, his appointment secretary, Tenzin Taklha, who is also a nephew, requested that I send a list of questions I would ask.

> This is not to censor your questions, but rather to ensure that if an interview is scheduled, then it is successful and we are able to avoid unnecessary questions. In the past, we have had interviewers ask questions which His Holiness has explained in detail and are easily available in published works or on topics that His Holiness has

explained many times in recent years. Through years of experience, we have found that interviews work out better when there are not many of these questions. We hope you understand. At the same time, I think it is important to mention here that if an interview is granted it will be scheduled for around 45 minutes at the most. As a result, we would recommend that you prepare about 8 to 10 questions and prioritize them as you may not even have enough time to ask all ten. Let me warn you that His Holiness tends to give lengthy answers to questions. This often results in interviewers not being able to ask all their intended questions within the allotted interview time.

> Best wishes.
> Yours sincerely, Tenzin Taklha
> Deputy Secretary
> Office of H. H. the Dalai Lama

It seemed reasonable and delicately put, if a bit controlling. But I was so thrilled I responded like a trained puppy dog, not the dogged tough-hitting journalist I don't even pretend to be, dutifully suggesting some softball questions that also might be different from others. Like:

- There are now more than 3 million Americans who in the last census registered as Buddhists, three times as many as 10 years ago. To what do you attribute this rising popularity of Buddhism among Westerners?

- Do you think the Buddha would appreciate how Buddhism is being interpreted in the West?

- There is a skin-care line called Zen, a trendy restaurant in New York called Tao and another in Paris called the Buddha Bar. Taco Bell (a Mexican fast-food chain in the United States) now runs a TV commercial promoting "enchilada nirvana," with a man levitating in lotus position. How do you feel about what I call the Madison Avenue–ization of Buddhism? Does this dilute the message of Buddhism? Is it a good thing?

- I understand your interest now is to spread the philosophy of Buddhism around the world, and that that is even more important than spreading "Buddhism" itself, as a religious movement. Is that your hope? Can you elaborate? Could that also lead to a dilution of Buddha's message?

- I have been reading about the Axial Age, the time in which the Buddha was born, along with Zoroaster, Confucius, Socrates, Plato and Aristotle. Do you think perhaps there will be another so-called Axial Age? Is it possible we are in it right now?

They weren't the best questions I had ever made up, partly because by this point I was dubious the interview would take place, partly because it's impossible to come up with new questions for a man who has been interviewed billions of times, perhaps over billions of lifetimes, so why try? The whole idea of interviewing the Dalai Lama was intimidating. It's also quite impressive. Try saying it out loud in front of a mirror as though you were telling friends at a dinner party: "I'm going to do a one-on-one interview with the Dalai Lama next month." Right there alone in the bathroom, you will impress even yourself. I did. And then think about actually conducting an interview that will keep him interested and a paralyzing intimidation quickly sets in. I did and it did.

In preparation, I started reading one of the Dalai Lama's autobiographies, *My Land and My People*. But I didn't get past the opening paragraph:

> I was born in a small village called Taktser, in the northeast of Tibet, on the fifth day of the fifth month of the Wood Hog Year of the Tibetan calendar—that is, in 1935. Taktser is in the district called Dokham, and that name is descriptive, for *Do* means the lower part of a valley that merges into the plains, and *Kham* is the eastern part of Tibet where the distinctive race of Ti-

betans called Khampa lives. Thus Dohkam is the part of Tibet where our mountains begin to descend to the plains of the East, towards China. Taktser itself is about 9,000 feet above sea level.

There was my hook: I would find that place and go to it, a sort of sidebar "in the footsteps of the Dalai Lama," if only to use the experience as a great conversation starter. But I seriously thought it would inform my understanding of him. He himself had not seen that village since he was recognized as the next Dalai Lama and taken from it in 1939, at the age of 4.

I had no idea what to expect there, or even where it was, but that only added to the appeal. Once I had secured the interview with His Holiness, I convinced the magazine that this journey to Tibet was essential, thereby subsidizing perhaps the most expensive icebreaker in the history of journalism. To find the village and escort me to it, I commissioned Jia Liming, the Beijing-based translator I had already worked with on my first trip in China, who spoke some Tibetan and adored all things Tibetan. She would also take care of obtaining the appropriate paperwork to gain entrance to Tibet. That is not an easy task, harder still for journalists. Through her various contacts (and I did not press her on the who's and how's of her methodology), she secured the necessary papers.

I flew from the West Coast to Beijing, where I picked up Jia. We then flew from Beijing to Lhasa, the capital of Tibet, where we spent four or five days doing the things one does in Lhasa: Potala Palace, Jokhang Temple, the longest *tankha* in the world at the Tibet Museum, adjusting to the elevation (Lhasa is at 3,600 meters, or 11,200 feet), learning how to drink the oddly bittersweet, almost rancid tasting yak butter tea, and then learning how to politely refuse a refill despite the host's insistence.

From there we flew northeast about 780 miles to the city of Xining, the capital of the Chinese Province of Qinghai, half of which rests atop Sichuan, the other half north of Xizang (aka the Tibet Autonomous Region). Now a disputed region, it was called Amdo and was considered part of Tibet when His Holiness was born; it remains culturally Tibetan. Part of the difficulty and confusion in even finding it on a map, at least to me, was that it goes by its Chinese name to the Chinese and its Tibetan names to Tibetans.

We took off with a driver from Xining early in the morning. As we left the city, where the population is roughly 1 million, the Tibetan highlands took over the landscape. Verdant farmlands and rolling green meadows rising to hillsides and then ascending to the skies, this was easily the most gorgeous part of China I'd seen, the China of ancient dreams and New Jersey Chinese restaurant murals. I could care less whether this was Tibet or China: I was in the province of landscape euphoria.

At a nondescript turnoff, a billboard pronounced, "We should develop a spiritual civilization and a material civilization," as Jia Liming translated it. She said the local government's emblem was at the bottom.

We took that turn. There were no other identifying road signs, but the driver apparently knew this was the way to the Dalai Lama's village. The road got narrower, the bends got more treacherous, and within minutes we were switchbacking up a steep incline. With each turn, the view became more and more incredible. And more and more remote. Across the next valley I could see spots of villages, nothing that might have looked like the sort of settlement where a man of the Dalai Lama's stature would have been born. The paved road gave way to a dirt road, and then a mud road. Now we were on a single lane that seemed wide enough for a cow. Indeed, as I started losing hope that this would lead to our destination, around the next turn we came to a sudden halt, face-to-face with a family of five riding in a small tractor.

"We are so lost, Liming," I said. "This can't be it. Please ask these people if they know how to find it."

She obliged. Without hesitation, they pointed directly behind us to a small muddy foot path that ascended into a cluster of mud and brick houses built into the side of the cliff. "Up there," the young father told her.

"Up there *what*?" I doubted he understood the question. "Tell him we are looking for the village the Dalai Lama was born in."

"I did." Liming tried to reply patiently, but I could see her eyes roll. "He says that"—and here she pointed up the path—"*is* His Holiness's village of birth."

"Can't be. Ask him again. No, ask her; she looks brighter."

Liming did not even honor the question. She started grabbing our bags, more excited than me and certainly more sure this must be the place. I had no choice but to follow her. I instructed the driver to wait for us there and we went off on foot.

It was as humble a village as I had seen in China, or in many other parts of the world. No town center. No storefronts. No cars. Very little color except for brown. 'This is *it?*" I kept muttering. "The man who billions of people think of as the most spiritual man in the world today, the man who Tibetans hope will lead them back to the country from which they were exiled, the 1989 Nobel Peace Prize winner, the author of some seventy books and recorded 30 audiotapes, the icon who travels tirelessly meeting with international dignitaries, giving lectures to full football stadiums in the United States—this is where the Dalai Lama was born?" If true, it made his life that much more astounding.

But it was true. Here, on July 6, 1935, Lhamo Dhondrub was born to a poor potato-farming family. He was recognized as the Dalai Lama (Mongolian for "Ocean of Wisdom") at the age of 2 after identifying the previous Dalai Lama's rosary. In Tibetan Buddhism, the Dalai Lama is believed to be an incarnation of Avalokiteshvara, the Buddha of Compassion. When the Dalai Lama dies, his essence is believed to pass into the body of an infant. Upon recognition, Lhama Dhondrub was renamed Jetsun Jamphel Ngawang Lobsang Yeshe Tenzin Gyatso, and is referred to as Yeshe Norbu, the Wish-Fulfilling Gem, or Kundun. In 1939, at the age of 4, he was taken from his home and began his training as a monk at Kumbum. When the Dalai Lama was a teenager he became the head of the Tibetan government as it fought against the occupying forces of the People's Republic of China. Since 1959, the Dalai Lama has been the leader of the government in exile. Once in his lifetime he returned to visit the village of his birth, but only for two hours.

We got to the top of the path and saw a building that appeared to be a monastery—*the* monastery. Entering tentatively, we were met by a woman who Liming established was married to a nephew of His Holiness. Her name is Tsekutze. Yes, this was the place of his birth, she confirmed. She was trailed by her cute 10-year-old grandson, Tezin Sonan who, she told us, was named by His Holiness.

Once inside, it looked like many other temples, with small rooms off a center courtyard and colorful tattered prayer flags on flimsy cloth, defiantly fluttering against the elements. Waiting for the Dalai Lama's nephew, we were ushered into "the room," the room where he was born. It is a relatively stark room with linoleum flooring. In the center is a wooden prayer wheel, which we gave a spin. The walls are covered with photos of His Holiness, *tankhas* and white silk scarves, the traditional gift of exchange between His Holiness and guests. The ceiling is a canopy of Tibetan tapestry. On a table that serves as the altar, against the wall behind the wheel, were offerings of cookies and apples and several American dollar bills. What could they possibly buy here with U.S. currency? I wondered. Then I realized I brought no gift. My gift, I rationalized, would be to bring these sights and sounds to His Holiness in person.

On the altar is a photo of the exiled spiritual leader, some ritual brass bowls that he sent from India and a letter written in his own hand. "I was born here with the name of Lhamo Dhondrub," it reads. "I was discovered to be the reincarnation of the previous Dalai Lama and went away. I have never forgotten my home village. I pray for its people and hope they are safe."

When the nephew arrived, we sat in what appeared to be the family living room, with pictures of their own family. Much to my stomach's dismay, they served us yak butter tea. I drank it very slowly.

The nephew, Gongbu Tashi, a man of 58 who was born and grew up here, had been a teacher and head of the local elementary school. Now he was vice president of a county association that holds conferences, which purpose I was not able to ascertain. There are about 50 families, maybe 300 people, living in the village; most are still simple farmers, as in the days when the Dalai Lama was born. Electricity and running water came to Taktser in the late 1970s; hot water came in 1989. The village is called Hong Ai, or Dang Cai; the county is Ping An.

Gongbu Tashi explained that the government of Tibet had built the house in 1943 for the family of the Dalai Lama. With the Cultural Revolution, it was all destroyed. But in 1986, the government rebuilt it. Although we had been told that the room we just visited was where His Holiness was born, that wasn't exactly correct, he said. He was born in a room that would have been on that spot, he assured us.

I maneuvered the conversation to stickier issues. I asked how tolerant he thought the Chinese government was to Buddhist practice and worship.

"Now it's quite free," he told me. "It's not just a religious issue; it's a political issue, too. Our country does a pretty good job for the freedom of religion." Was he kidding? Was he saying this just for me? Had he been brainwashed? Did he know about the human rights violations regularly lodged by various groups, not just the Tibetan government in exile? Had he heard of the Free Tibet movement? Was he on the dole and concealing the truth? I asked none of these questions and respectfully remained silent.

Gongbu then took us outside. Standing in front of the monastery, we looked across valleys that rose and fell like green waves. In the distance, he pointed out, was a range that is part of the Kunlun Range.

"That mountain with the clouds is the highest of the whole area and holy to Tibetans," he said. It was Mount Tsongkhapa, whose peak, he said, resembles a lotus. "The whole place looks like lotuses and this village is in the path of the lotuses. Very good feng shui to this village."

Off to the right at the crest of one small rise we could see a lone white stupa with a little spire reaching up to the endless neon blue sky. "That stupa," he said, "is the center of the lotuses.

"There are magical things, you can never tell why they happen," he went on, and then proceeded to tell us a story of the 13th Dalai Lama, Thupten Gyatso (1876–1933), who also had to flee Tibet, first in 1904 when it was invaded by British troops from India, another time to India to elude a Chinese plot to depose him. He, unlike the 14th Dalai Lama, prevailed, and in 1911 Chinese military influence in Tibet virtually disappeared. Like the present Dalai Lama, Thupten Gyatso had great foresight and helped Tibet enter the modern era, instituting a postal system, paper currency, roads and the country's first power station. He is credited with revitalizing the institution of the Dalai Lama through his forceful character and political insight, and with trying to end Tibet's centuries of isolation.

Once, traveling with his entourage from Kumbum to a monastery in Gansu Province to the north, Thupten Gyatso spent a while resting at that little stupa across from us. As the story goes, he said he thought the village across the way was so tranquil that one day he would like to be reborn there.

And so it came to pass. Apocryphal or not, it was the stuff of Chamber of Commerce dreams. But here in Tibet, on the roof of the world, tourism development proceeds along wholly different promotional sensibilities.

"What would you say to your uncle if he were standing here right now?" I asked Gongbu spontaneously. "In fact, tell him now," I said, shoving the tape recorder close to his mouth. "And I'll play this tape for him when I meet him next month."

He smiled and immediately started in Tibetan, which Liming later translated for me: "Every day we are waiting and hoping and expecting you. You are my uncle and you are getting older and it's time for you to come back. The statues of Buddha and pictures you gave me in India, we put up, and every day a lot people come to this place to worship. Not a few—a lot. Here especially we are free to believe in Buddhism or whatever religion. It's pretty good now. This is from the bottom of my heart. Now the government is doing really good job and gave us all freedoms."

I was so moved by his sincerity that I forgot those hardball questions from earlier. It didn't matter if he was brainwashed or in fear or on the take. The man felt free. Who was I to argue?

Now it was six weeks later, and, tapes and photos from Taktser in hand, I was standing in Tenzin Taklha's office, staring at several shelves full of binders with such identifying tabs as "Interview Requests 2002–2003." "Media Requests for Interviews: Accepted," "Media Requests for Interviews: Rejected." It went back several years and continued right up to me.

I had already passed through security at Tsuglag Khang, the complex in McLeod Ganj that includes the temples, worship rooms, monastery, monk's dorms and sanctum sanctorum that comprises the Office of His Holiness the Dalai Lama (OHHDL). It's up the windy road from Dharamsala, where the Government of Tibet in Exile has its own complex of buildings, with various ministry headquarters and the parliament hall. Before the Tibetan government came here in 1960, Dharamsala was just another sleepy village in the northern Indian state of Himachal Pradesh, hugging the ledge of the Outer Himalayas with the mighty Dhauladhar Range above, at heights of 5,200 meters (17,000 feet). Now they call it Little Lhasa. The streets are lined with shops selling local fabrics, jewelry and other indigenous items. Walls along the streets are plastered with cries for justice in the Tibetan struggle for independence from the Chinese government.

On my way to the interview, I stopped to read one or two posters, reflecting on Gongbu's heartfelt expression. I contemplated "Free Tibet"—the phrase, the T-shirt, the bumper sticker,

Jia Liming

In the birthplace of His Holiness the 14th Dalai Lama, teaching the Tibetan leader's great-grandnephew Tezin Sonan the ways of the West: how to high five.

the movement—and now had to ask, "Free it from what?" Sure, free it from the well-documented Chinese Communist oppressive control. Free it from an even more devastating and systematic decimation of their cultural heritage. But several thousand years of living independently, in geographic isolation, in political separation, in a cultural vacuum, and in religious self-expression had already set them free. If you have met a Tibetan person in Boulder or Seattle or Boston, you are often struck by how easily they laugh, how radiant their faces are, how their eyes seem to dance and how, in the older ones, they exude some knowledge for which you and I will never find the Web site. They seem unburdened of, and not bothered by, the incessant white noise Westerners call their minds. If Gongbu thought he was free, he was free. Freedom is a state of mind.

Tourists, pilgrims, Tibetans, Indians, Westerners, Easterners wander through the temples that surround the courtyard outside the Office of His Holiness. They turn the wheel one more time for good luck. They watch student monks engaged in their age-old theological debates. Small groups of maroon-robed bald-headed young men cluster around one monk. Exuberantly slapping one palm against the other, they challenge each other's position on Buddhist doctrine. The slap signifies a question mark, punctuating some inquiry like "What is emptiness?"

Tenzin led me to yet another waiting area. In this room, every available inch of wall space was filled with citations and awards and photographs with presidents and stars; bronze plaques of gratitude, handsomely framed and laminated letters of adulation, metals, medallions, honorary citizenships from places like the Orange County, California, Board of Supervisors. I was sitting with the man who would be my translator, Lhakdur, who explained that my interview was delayed by a pair of filmmakers from the BBC making a documentary about His Holiness.

I'm in pretty heady company, I thought. My next thought: tough act to follow.

I wondered if they might ask to film my interview with His Holiness. I toyed with the idea: I'd have it for posterity and as a clip for my own PR. Mostly I was concerned that their time was cutting into mine; Tenzin had been clear that I would have only 45 minutes to complete my interview.

The pair from the BBC finally came out and walked directly to me. "Are you from *National Geographic*?" asked Jonathan, the tall one, who bore a likeness to Hugh Grant. Yes, I nodded meekly.

"We heard you were here," he nearly shouted. "Good show! Honored to meet you. My dad used to get the magazine for years."

"You read it lately?" I asked.

"Buggers, no. Who's got time? Except when you're in the dentist's office."

Jonathan was not your shy retiring type of Englishman, but I was surprised at how quickly he cut to the chase. "Say, could we film your interview? You know"—and here he made a bracket with his thumbs and first fingers and swept it across an imaginary TV screen to show where the following would go—" '*National Geographic* Interviews His Holiness.' "

This guy was good. Was I that transparent? Now I had to do battle with my own ego. Do I let them film me and forthwith gain so much attention the BBC offers me a job roaming the world interviewing fascinating people? Or do I protect the privacy of the interview I waited so long to get and maintain my integrity? I know: the choice would seem obvious. Nonetheless, I was dying to say yes. Wouldn't you? Even the Buddha had to face down temptation under the Bodhi Tree, struggling to resist the seductive powers of Māra who taunted the young Siddhartha, "You are not pure, you fancy you are pure. The path of purity is far from you."

Then I heard the lyrics to "Lose Yourself" playing in my ear. Would I seize my one opportunity? Or blow it?

Lhakdur wouldn't have known Eminem from an enema, but he studied me as if he could read my inner turmoil. "So what will you do about the BBC?" he asked.

"I think I will decline the offer," I said.

"It's a wise decision," he replied, nodding his approval. He probably thought this was a sign of my integrity, but I knew the truth: I wanted the Dalai Lama all to myself. I did not want him distracted from *me*.

"His Holiness is ready for you now," an assistant announced.

I have done thousands of interviews in 35 years as a journalist. This one was scaring the shit out of me. The night before I had reviewed my questions and my strategy. I cued up the tape to the section with his nephew's comments and practiced how I would suggest the Dalai Lama attach the headset to his ears. I meditated and tried to think only pure thoughts, knowing full well if I had one impure thought he would be able to see right through me and terminate the interview then and there. I nibbled on fruits and nuts and I went to bed early.

Now, as I stood and gathered up my paraphernalia, I went into a panic. I had not studied—or even bothered to ask anyone about—the protocols involved when meeting a Tibetan lama, much less the highest-ranking lama. The one rule, which seems to be appropriate upon meeting any Buddhist priest of any rank throughout Asia, is "Look but don't touch." I decided I would bow with palms together, but not extend my hand, as is the almost involuntary gesture Western men make with each other.

We walked out the door of the waiting room that leads to a veranda overlooking a garden and lawns. I was expecting a long walk to yet another holding area and then, perhaps, to be ushered into His Holiness's interview area. As we turned the corner, I was looking down because when I am nervous I have a tendency to be klutzy. When I looked up, I almost walked into His Holiness. I stepped back quickly, placed my palms together and modestly dipped my body from the waist up. As I began to bow again (I remembered you are supposed to bow three times, one for each of the Three Jewels of Buddhist wisdom, the Buddha, the Dhamma and the Sangha), I saw him stepping toward me, hand extended presumably to shake mine, Western style. I looked to Mr. Lhakdur inquisitively. Again he read my mind, smiling and nodding ahead, which I took to mean it was okay to make physical contact.

The Dalai Lama—the 14th reincarnation of the Buddha of Compassion, winner of the Nobel Prize winner, revered as an enlightened being—took my hand and shook it robustly. Awkwardly at first and then enthusiastically, I returned the shake—and added a bit of my own robustness. Still trying to maintain decorum and out of great respect (and the fear that my sweaty palms would belie my exterior cool), I tried to withdraw my hand, working on the assumption that there must also be some protocol that defines the length of time it is appropriate to shake a Dalai Lama's hand. But much to my surprise and delight, he tightened his grip.

Sure, I thought, keep my hand—forever. His grip softened slightly but he did not let go. Rather, he led me like that—his right hand holding my right hand, walking side by side—from the veranda all the way into and across the length of a large room until we came to a stop in front of his seat. Finally, he let go, at this point to my relief. If he did not let go—and halfway across the room I decided I would hold on until he let go, and no sooner—I was already strategizing how I would maneuver the tape recorder with one hand.

We must have held hands for close to a minute. I have never shared an experience like that with another man, and I have hugged more men than the average guy. It completely disarmed me—as a man, as a journalist, as a human being—and at the same time it made me feel completely embraced. It was asexual but very sensual. His gentleness was palpable. And somehow his calm made me feel calm. It was like he was gave me a tranquillity transfusion from his hand through mine.

The man had me at hello.

So much for your journalistic objectivity, I thought. I was putty in his hands, and any idea of a no-holds-barred interview vanished. He took his seat, a high-backed stiff-looking wooden chair, covered with the thick tapestries characteristic of Tibetan furniture. I sat beside him on a high, oversized couch that made me feel about 9 years old, my legs dangling over the sides.

Seeing him so close up, about two feet from me, I was riveted. He has a huge face, dominated by his glasses, and it is an expressive face. He shifts from earnest man to wise man to jokester in the same sentence. He has very few age wrinkles, just laugh wrinkles.

I immediately went into the *shpiel* I had been rehearsing for about six weeks.

"Holiness, I know I sent some questions and I'll get to as many as you let me ask. But I want to depart from that and ask your indulgence first."

I briefly explained about my journey to Taktser. "So I brought you back something from where you were born," I said, and with that I brought out the photos I'd had printed up back in D.C. and showed them to him. Among them was a shot of the white stupa in the next rise from Taktser. He stopped at that one and said, "Has anyone told you or not . . . ?" he started. I knew the story I thought he was going to launch into, but I shook my head. I wanted to hear his version, already prepared to ask a question about it.

"It was in this place that 13th Dalai Lama . . . I don't know exactly, but I was told the 13th Dalai Lama was passing through this way. Then here he stopped and took some rest, and looked toward my village. Then he exclaims, 'Ah, this village is very beautiful.' People said the 13th Dalai Lama determined his next reincarnation will come in that place."

He told it simply, careful to add those qualifiers of "I was told" and "people said." I waited a second to see if he would go on, ready to ask my first potentially upsetting question, which would have been "Do you believe that story?" Before I could, however, he paused with perfect comic timing and added, "Who knows?" Then he let out his signature laugh, a rippling giggle that went on so long it seemed to have a life of its own. Though obviously a believer in reincarnation, he looked at such divinations with a certain realism.

I pulled out his nephew's cassette. "Now I have a message for you from someone you know in Taktser," I said and handed him the earphones, which he took and adjusted on his head without hesitation, apparently happy to play along. For no particular reason, it was an odd sight: the Dalai Lama wearing a headset. Very un–Dalai Lama–like.

I put on the tape of his nephew; the segment lasted about three minutes. During that time he listened intently, his face softening, his brows furrowing at one point. He smiled, and nodded.

"Every day they are thinking that way," he said. Then he went silent.

"Walking up to that village," I said, "I thought, 'How amazing that from such humble beginnings a man could rise to such world renown.' Does it ever amaze you, too?"

"Yes, if you look back, a person from very small village eventually reaches Lhasa with the name of Dalai Lama. So then in the last few decades the Tibetan nation's interest is somehow very connected with that village boy." He laughed, as though the implausibility of it just struck him.

It made me think of Abraham Lincoln, who every American kid knows was born in a one-room log cabin to poor Kentucky farmers and from whom every American kid of humble roots takes hope that he or she also could rise to be president of the United States. I mentioned this to His Holiness, then recalled Lincoln's nickname, the Great Emancipator, a champion of freedom for American slaves of African descent. Now I was sitting with a man of similar humble background who may someday be recognized as his nation's emancipator. Of course, I did not forget the major difference between the two: Lincoln was elected by the American people, and the Dalai Lama was elected thousands of lifetimes ago.

"We believe we have not one but many lives," he continued, "so we can explain something as very certain or as coincidence . . . Of course, generally speaking, all human beings have same potential, each individual, no matter where that person or little boy was born. I don't know if it's facility or opportunity or circumstance. From Buddhist viewpoint, we have limitless past lives. So then during last, say, hundred or several thousand years or lifetimes we make different karmas, or links, so that eventually creates different destinations . . . Something like that."

Something like what? It sounded like Buddha-babble to me. I tried to interpolate it to something I could understand: "So maybe humans start out headed for one destination but then, like Ping-Pong balls, they are hit and move in other directions? Something like *that*?"

"That's right," he confirmed. "Also, from Buddhism viewpoint, from those thousand lifetimes or years certain shapes eventually develop, but until last moment other factors are possible and can make changes. Many factors. Like from a seed growing into a flower, until the last moment anything is possible."

"Like the wind takes it in another direction and you could be a farmer in Taktser?" I asked.

"Ohhh, that's right." His Holiness laughed.

"Though somehow I don't think you'd still be a farmer in that village," I proposed. He laughed more loudly. "Well, I'm glad to bring you these things from Taktser."

"Thank you, thank you," he said.

Now I was ready to launch into the questions I had prepared. But, as his front men had predicted, he took so long to answer the first question I barely got to the rest. The Dalai Lama is a systematic thinker. I had recalled that one of his hobbies was taking apart and putting together watches. It was evident in the way he organized his answers. When I asked why he thought Buddhism was growing in popularity in the West, the $64,000 question I'd been asking around the world, he began creating "categories," as he called them. They came fast and furious.

"In the West, people have a view that Tibet is a mysterious land. And then also I think there is a generation who enter the establishment now, so they want something new. During the happies . . ."

Here Lhakdur corrected him, "That's hippies." We all laughed.

"I like your pronunciation," I said. " 'Happies,' better than hippies."

"Ha, ha, ha." His Holiness got it. "I think they are quite free, quite happy. So that's one category. Another factor, another category maybe, genuine Buddhism concept is self-reliance, and self-transformation. Why do I put 'genuine'? On a popular level many people worship something like prayer flags or . . . these people are usually satisfied with these things but that's not genuine Buddhism concept. 'Genuine' means he looks inward to self-transformation.

Not only true prayer or recitation but meditation, analyze, thinking. I believe genuine Buddhist technique is just increased awareness: What's the reality on the basis of the law of causality?

"Another category: Then some describe Buddhism as a kind of humanism, just emphasis on the human good quality.

"Next: Some people not much concerned about next life or nirvana. They want some kind of transformation on an emotional level. Result: more happier, more calm.

"Then another category: thinking, reality. Buddhism's explanation about mind is quite sophisticated. Now some scientists are carrying on some experiments."

"Yes," I interrupted, dying to impress him with my contacts and knowledge. "You might be talking about some of my friends, Richie Davidson and Dan Goleman, old friends of mine." Luckily, he did not call me on my egotism.

"Yes," he went on, "they found some effect, new findings, new fact. So, including some scientists, it appeals to intellectuals and philosophers who are showing deeper and more and more interest in Buddhist explanation.

"Another category: Buddhism has different gods and goddesses, of wealth and long life and curing illness. Something like that. Protection cords. Pray to gods to cure illness or for more successful business. [Here he let out a chuckle.] That's superficial. Not the main thing."

Now I offered my own theory: "In my interviews around the world, I've noticed people and even countries historically find Buddhism when they are fed up with money, success, political power. Even fed up with religion: They question the faith-based religions. Buddhism does not ask you to take a 'leap of faith,' as we say. It's all empirical, as you said. Do you think there is validity to this idea? That people shift to Buddhism when they are full but still not satisfied? And now, the West is at that same point—full, but empty."

"Yes," he said. "This is a new category. Firstly, the material. There are limits. At the beginning we felt, 'Ah, once we have prosperity, then all problems can be solved.' We put every hope in money or power. Then when you have these things, through your own experience you notice their limitations. You could be billionaire, then still something missing."

"We call this diminishing returns," I suggested.

"So, through deeper awareness, through one's own experience, they turn to inner value. Inner value is not necessarily Buddhism's alone but other traditions too. Then I have Christian friends who adopt Buddhist techniques for meditation or to reduce anger and increase patience. Perfectly fine, without losing one's own main faith, to increase some of the basic human values. This should be allright for an open-minded Christian.

"This leads to another category: kind of people curiosity. Once people get to deeper levels, they ask: 'What's reality? What is I? What's God? What's the beginning? What is the ultimate reality of nature?' "

"You describe me," I said.

"So, finally, I usually describe Buddhism as a combination of science, philosophy and religion. Combined. As a science, we look for external signs of mind or emotions. From Buddhist viewpoint, I think this is a science. What is reality? It's a subtle energy. We call it wind. Wind means movement, energy. In scripture it mentions wind, means energy. The description of reality is a science. On that basis, the reality itself should change. By nature there are contradictions. So first things always changing, then second contradictory movement. Therefore transformation is possible. That is basis of Buddha Dharma. We take the values of good and bad out of the opposites. Now I can take action. Karma. But we cannot make distinction on the action itself—the demarcation of right action or wrong action or positive action or negative action—but on the motivation. Motivation is so important. So motivation means hatred, jealousy, compassion, forgiveness, fear, all those emotions. Some action comes from serving without self-interest, genuine service and helping, not due to money or fame but genuine altruistic motivation. That really brings positive, useful, beneficial actions.

Therefore when we realize that, then try to transform or reduce negative and try to increase positive. How? Understanding the contradiction of forces."

"And wrestling with those contradictions," I said, but what I thought was, "Whew, that was a mouthful."

He tried to reduce it back to simple terms: "Like once you recognize anger is bad—for myself, my body, my peace of mind, for my friend and the whole world on a global level—then you consider what is the opposite force? Compassion, love. Try to increase love and compassion. And why do I need loving-kindness toward others? Because it brings increased benefit to me. Not for next life but even in the moment. The more compassionate mind becomes something fuller: self-confidence, fearless determination."

This was something I could grasp. Though he talked in circles and fragmented sentences, with imperfect grammar, he nonetheless conveyed his meaning. The man is brilliant, there is no doubt. Part of his brilliance is that he explains Buddhist concepts, and the complexities of Tibetan Buddhism in particular, in a way that Westerners can comprehend. It was hard not to idolize him.

"How do you keep people from hero-worshipping you?" I finally asked.

"In the realistic way," he replied and explained by small example: "Yesterday I met one sick girl. They brought her to me with some expectation. I said, 'I can't help you, but I can give some advice.' That is my limitation. I just share their worry, same worry. I can't do anything, I accept the reality. So when I describe myself as a simple Buddhist monk, that is reality. I don't care what other people say or feel. Important is mindfulness myself. I should not exaggerate from reality. I am human being, I am Buddhist. But in the name of humility, you can belittle yourself too much, and then that is also not realistic. One of the important purposes of education is to try to reduce the gap between appearance and reality."

I got to witness his skillfullness with this "reality" after my interview ended when some dozen Westerners, fresh from a three-month retreat nearby, filed in, bowing in adulation. Their leader pulled out a sheet of questions each had composed for His Holiness. Their questions were preceded by elaborate intros, such as "Holiness, in your infinite wisdom and with greatest respect for your thousands of lifetimes and bowing to the gods of compassion and . . ." Though I'm sure the questions were causing each of them great suffering, they seemed mostly inane and selfish, or of such a personal nature that there would be no way for His Holiness to offer guidance without spending hours (in some of their cases, years) in personal psychoanalysis with them. One woman wanted to know what Buddhist tradition of retreat she should do next? Another was struggling with his relationship with his stepfather, with whom he did not get along. It went on. With each question, the Dalai Lama listened patiently, scratched his jaw, even asked a question or two. Then, with great delicateness and discretion, he made simple recommendations. Mostly his suggestions could be reduced to two words: Keep sitting. But I saw how these people, vulnerable in that way people are when they come out of long retreats, hung on his every word. I knew they would do whatever he said. They would go home and for months his off-the-cuff suggestion would be their guiding mantra, their compass in life. What a burden. What a responsibility. But he, too, knew that they would do whatever he said, so he was careful and conservative in his responses. It only made me respect him more.

In sum, I would like to report, first, that the 45-minute interview turned into 90 minutes. Later, I was told that that was quite exceptional. "He really warmed up to you," Lhakdur said. He liked me; he *really* liked me. For months afterward, when people asked about our interview I joked, "We really bonded."

I would also like to report on all the details of the encounter, but in truth the whole thing went by like a blur. Later, when I transcribed the taped conversation—and I waited six months to do so, like a kid who saves the cherry on the sundae until the end—I discovered that much of what he said was just barely interpretable. Sometimes in interviews people express what they mean more through inflection and pauses and meaningful looks, or even through physical gestures and mannerisms, or through the trappings of their clothes or the room furnishings. But this was in the extreme. I pieced together fragmented sentences to make it all make sense.

In an attempt to glean deeper meaning from it all, I noticed how many times he used certain words, thinking that he might have been talking cryptically. Indeed, the words he used most frequently— reality, realistic, reason, intelligence, intellectual—spoke volumes about the deeper point he was making about the essential nature of Buddhism.

I came away believing His Holiness the Dalai Lama is a man of science, a man of intellect, a man of reason, a man of ethics, who himself is part of the reason Buddhism has grown in popularity. Had he not become the 14th Dalai Lama, I think he would have still become a valued citizen of the planet. He is a man of deep compassion, embedded in all the best religions. And, finally, he is a religious man. He is the leader of a nation not through instinct or desire, but because history required it of him. He had told me that he does not proselytize Buddhism, that he rather promotes "human values." Nonetheless, without ever intending it, he is Buddhism's best advertising agency.

thirteen

Breathing In, Breathing Out

The Search Continues

Before enlightenment, chop wood, carry water. After enlightenment, chop wood, carry water.

—ZEN BUDDHIST PROVERB

For someone at the journey's end, freed from sorrow, liberated in all ways, released from all bonds, no fever exists.

—THE BUDDHA, *The Dhammapada*

In my end is my beginning.

—T. S. ELIOT, *Four Quartets*

Between the interview with His Holiness and my romantic hopes, I was in such euphoria that now I absolutely could have flown to Paris flapping my arms.

I will save you the suspense: Anh Thuy and I met in Paris and within days fell madly in love. There were, however, complications. She was breaking up with a boyfriend. She read English better than she spoke it; I spoke no French and less Vietnamese. I had a massive writing project ahead of me that would distract me for the next year; unemployed, she was waiting for a wrongful termination suit to come through. She wanted kids; I wasn't sure. There were 18 years between us. It was, in short, your typical international modern romance. But we thought the Buddhist Force was with us; we rode on the belief that through Thây's relationship manual, we could overcome any obstacle. The talk he had given, in fact, on the day she and I first met at Plum Village was about the keys to successful relationships—understanding and communication. We chose to ignore the intrinsic language, cultural, generational and geographic gaps in our mutual understanding and communication.

I will save you further suspense. We dated long distance for eight months. She was wonderful to and for me. She called me her "ideal." Then, eight months later, on the same day I found out my story had been accepted by *National Geographic* she called from Paris and out of the blue broke up with me. She said she "had to take reason." I suspected she did not mean "reason" in the same way that the Dalai Lama meant it. Or maybe she did.

Though I was heartbroken, I took it rather well, so well that my friends inferred I didn't really love her. The truth was I understood it on a higher level. She came into my life the very moment I was about to sit down and write, a solitary work best accomplished buoyed by the love and support of a good woman. She left my life the very day that work was completed. "The Buddha sent her to me for protection," I mused. "I guess he took her away when I was done."

In actuality, she had become my Thây, the newest teacher in the Buddhism 101 course that began with Carl Taylor back at the Zen Hospice Project in San Francisco. He taught me the lesson of impermanence, if you recall, but I must have thought I could get by on the Buddhist Cliff's Notes, for here it came again. By now I was just wise enough to know that it would come again. And again. The Buddha said nothing lasts forever. He meant *nothing*.

More than Thich Nhat Hahn and Dr. Ariyaratne and Sulak Sivaraksa combined, Anh Thuy instructed me in the most personal application of socially engaged Buddhism. I attribute my ability to let her go—rather than run the obsessive tapes that accompanied past breakups—to my worldwide Buddhism faculty, her now among them. Anh Thuy, I place a lotus at your feet.

This acceptance of reality—of the way things are, not pushing away the so-called bad, not pulling toward me or clinging to the so-called good—this is how I have changed, though if you had known me before I undertook this journey, I would appear no different now. Except for a couple of pounds and shorter hair, my "before" and "after" shots would be indistinguishable. I have the same voice, mannerisms, skewed sense of humor; the same vulnerable lower back; and many of the same personal issues. In fact, I am right back where I started from: living on the island I thought I had left for good two years ago, still in debt, still without a girlfriend, still falling on and off the meditation cushion.

What has changed is my relationship to it all, but mostly my relationship with myself. Breathing in . . . breathing out . . . gives me a split second of distance from my thoughts. In that moment I can separate body from mind, sensation from reaction to sensation. There—in that momentary refuge from "myself," between the in breath and the out breath—I find salvation from ego, attachment, craving, clinging, desire and all the rest.

Something else I have noticed: I have traded in my earlier mantras for a new set. Before it was:

"You can do anything you set your mind to, man."

"Core-trunk stabilization."

"You don't have a pot to piss in."

Now the wisdom that guides me is more esoteric, unless you have been following closely in my footsteps as I followed closely in the Buddha's:

"Between now and now there is only now."

—GROVER GAUNTT III

"A dog can only be a dog."

—HOITSU SUZUKI

"The reality is . . ."
> —HIS HOLINESS THE DALAI LAMA

"What is good? What is bad?"
> —EIDO SHIMANO

"What is the difference between perception and perspective?"
> —VINSOR KANAKARATNE

"Do you want to move from existing to living?"
> —JON KABAT-ZINN VIA HELEN MA

"Impermanence, impermanence, impermanence . . ."
> —SATYA NARAYAN GOENKA

Have I found truth, meaning and happiness? Yes. And no.

Yes, I have found *my* truth, *my* meaning, *my* happiness, not yours. No, because I know they, too, will change by the time you get to the end of this sentence. And so will yours.

"I have nothing to report, my friends," wrote Ryokan, an 18th-century Japanese hermit poet. "If you want to find the meaning, stop chasing after so many things." I agree. So in one regard, my search has ended. In another, it will continue—until my last moment. I hope to be, as Bob Dylan told Martin Scorsese in *No Direction Home,* "constantly in a state of becoming."

For that latter reason, my incessant and admittedly annoying interrogation—of the way things are, of the way I am, of the relationship between the two—will not end, either. It is a sign that I have become a good student of Buddhism that I feel most of my questions have gone unanswered. And that, as a demonstration of my commitment to this path, I have more questions, including the one that has become my current koan:

"Why are there no questions in the now?"

Sitting beside Carl at San Francisco's Laguna Honda Hospital, I had come to the realization that "in the present, there are no questions; there is just being." But why? The question came to me just after I finished writing the *Geographic* story. My friend Arlan Wise and I were celebrating its successful completion, sitting in front of a typically magnificent Martha's Vineyard landscape. Often, so caught up in my own head, I drive by similar scenes here and take no note of them. But through my new door of perception, the ordinary took on extraordinary significance. We were perfectly content, with nowhere to go, nothing to do, no one to be. Questions come from dissatisfaction, from doubt and uncertainty, from thinking there is more to the picture than what you see in front of you. But to be fully in the moment, in such an altered state of satisfaction, is quite enough. Even the journalist, "stripped of his questions," can let go of his identity. Until that moment passes. As it did that day.

Of this I am certain: As Buddhism has changed and evolved, with the times and with each culture, it will continue to change and evolve. It is not static; it, too, is impermanent. The worldwide movement that I tracked, of engaged Buddhism, will also change with the needs and demands of the time and the place. I look forward to reporting on its new iteration from the moon soon.

Meanwhile, back in San Francisco, someone else has taken up the hospice bed once occupied by Carl Taylor. And beside that person is another Buddhist volunteer, just sitting.

Basic Buddhist Vocabulary

❧

Most words associated with Buddhism appear in two different spellings: one in Pali, the language spoken by the Buddha; the other in Sanskrit, the Indian language used to transcribe the texts. Below, the first spelling is in Pali.

Amitabha The Buddha of the Western "Pure Land." Also known as Amida.

anapana sati The practice of paying attention to the in and out breath.

anicca *(or* annitya) Change; the impermanence of all things, including man.

arhat A monk who has achieved nirvana.

Avalokiteshvara The Indian name for the bodhisattva of compassion.

bardo In Tibetan Buddhism, the period between death and rebirth.

bhikshu (or bhikku) Monk.

bhikshuni Nun.

bodhi Enlightenment or awakening.

bodhisattva An enlightened being who remains in this existence to help others; a saint.

Brahma One of the three major deities of Hinduism, along with Visnu (Vishnu) and Siva (Shiva). Adopted as one of the protective deities of Buddhism, he convinced the Buddha to teach.

Brahmin (or Brahman)   The priestly highest caste of Hindus, the keepers of the Vedas, Hindu texts.

Buddha   The awakened or the enlightened one.

Butsu   Japanese for the Buddha.

Ch'an   Chinese for Zen Buddhism.

dependent origination   The interconnection of all things, like cause and effect; one thing leads to another.

devas   Gods.

dhamma (or dharma)   The teachings of the Buddha, his Truths, or Buddhist philosophy of wisdom.

dhyana (also ch'an or zen)   Meditation.

dukkha *(or* **duhkha***)*   Often understood as suffering, including dissatisfaction with life and the world.

Eightfold Path   Right view, right aspiration, right speech, right action, right livelihood, right effort, right mindfulness, right concentration.

Hinayana   Southern Buddhism ("small, inferior or lesser vehicle or journey"); the practice of those who adhere only to the earliest discourses as the word of the Buddha.

Hotai (or Pu-tai)   The Laughing Buddha, the Chinese wandering monk, an incarnation of Maitreya.

Jodo/Jodo Shin   Japanese terms for "Pure Land."

kamma (or karma)   Intentional or willed act. Every physical or spiritual deed has its long-range consequences as determined by the agent's intention.

Kannon   Japanese name for Avalokiteshwara, the Buddha of Compassion.

koan   A very brief story demonstrating the paradoxical nature of dualistic thinking, in the form of an unaswerable question. Used as a path of enlightenment in Zen meditation.

Kuan Yin   Chinese name for Avalokiteshwara, the Buddha of Compassion.

lama Tibetan tantric master, now often used to refer to any respected monk.

Lotus Sutra Short name for the Sutra of the Lotus Flower of the Wonderful Law, or *Saddharma-pundarik-sutra* in Sanskrit. It is one of the most important sutras of Mahayana Buddhism, stating that all sentient beings can attain Buddhahood.

Mahayana Northern Buddhism ("large or greater vehicle or journey"). Identified with China, Korea, Vietnam, Tibet and Japan.

Maitreya Literally means "friendly and benevolent." The Buddha of the Future, who will be the next Buddha in our world.

maitri Caring, loving-kindness.

mandala Complex, circular, symmetrical image used as a power circle and object of contemplation in the rituals of Tantric Buddhism.

mantra A sacred phrase or syllable repeated during meditation.

mudra Symbolic hand positions.

nagas Great serpents (or dragons, or water creatures). The king of the Nagas protected the Buddha from a storm.

nibbana *(nirvana)* Literally, "blown out." Liberation, enlightenment, release from the endless loop of reincarnation.

Pali The language preserved by the Theravada school and, by extension, the language in which those texts are composed.

Pitaka Basket, referring to the Tripitaka or scriptures.

prētas Hungry ghosts; a state of insatiable desire, frustration and dissatisfaction.

puja Hindu ceremony in which offerings and other acts of devotion are performed.

Pu-tai (or Hotai) The Laughing Buddha, a Chinese monk, said to be an incarnation of Maitreya.

Pure Land Chinese/Japanese sect, emphasizing worship of Amitabha Buddha.

Sangha   The community of monks and nuns.

Sanskrit   An early language of northern India, modified and used as a religious language by some Buddhists.

satori   Zen term for enlightenment.

Shakyamuni   Sage of the Sakyas, a name for the Buddha.

Shakyas   A noble clan that ruled an area of southern Nepal.

Siddhartha   "He who has reached his goal."

satī *(or* **smrti***)*   Mindfulness, meditation.

Son   Korean for Zen Buddhism.

stupa   A burial mound enshrining relics of a holy person, such as the Buddha, or objects associated with his life. Over the centuries this has developed into the tall, spired monuments familiar in temples in Thailand, Sri Lanka and Burma, and into the pagodas of China, Korea and Japan.

sutta (or sutra)   Sacred texts; sayings attributed to the Buddha.

Tathagata   "Thus gone," a name for the Buddha.

thangka   A traditional Tibetan painting of holy beings.

Theravada   "Way of the elders," the surviving form of Southern Buddhism, currently the dominant form of Buddhism in Thailand, Sri Lanka and Burma.

Tipitaka (or Tripitaka)   The Three Baskets, the collection of the earliest Buddhist scriptures, divided into Vinaya Pitaka, Sutra Pitaka and Abhidharma Pitaka.

Vajrayana (also called Tantrayana, or Thunderbolt Vehicle)   A school of esoteric Tibetan Buddhism that emphasizes not only meditation but also the use of symbolic rites, gestures, postures, breathing, incantation.

vipassana   Insight, mindfulness; a type of meditation.

White Lotus School   Sect focusing on the Lotus Sutra. Also known as T'ien T'ai or Tendai.

zäzen   Sitting meditation in Zen Buddhism.

Zen   A group of Buddhist sects (Rinzai, Soto), originating in Japan, that focus on meditation and intuition rather than scripture as a means to enlightenment. See also *Ch'an, Son,* and *Dhyana.*

zendō   Zen Buddhism meditation hall.

Resources

This compendium of resources, many mentioned in *Buddha or Bust,* will aid those interested in finding more about, participating in or making donations to worldwide contemporary Buddhist activities and the socially engaged Buddhist movement. (As usual, all Web site addresses are prefixed by http://www.)

Engaged Buddhism Organizations

Buddhist Peace Fellowship
BPF.org
PO Box 3470
Berkeley, CA 94703
(510) 655-6169

Center for Contemplative Mind in Society
(established by Mirabai Bush and others)
ContemplativeMind.org
199 Main St., Suite 3
Northampton, MA 01060
(413) 582-0071

Community of Mindful Living
(established by Thich Nhat Hanh)
Mindfulnessbell.org (also see PlumVillage.org or IamHome.org)
745 Cagua S.E.
Albuquerque, NM 87108
Northern California contact: (510) 595-5574

International Campaign for Tibet (ICT)
SaveTibet.org
1825 Jefferson Place NW
Washington, DC 20036
(202) 785-1515

ICT Europe:
Keizersgracht 302
1016EX Amsterdam
The Netherlands
31 (0)20 3308265

International Network of Engaged Buddhists
(established by Sulak Sivaraksa)
Sulak-Sivaraksa.org
666 Charoen Nakorn Road
Klong San
Bangkok 10600, Thailand
(011) 662-438-9332

Sarvodaya Shramadana Movement
(established by A. T. Ariyaratne)
Sarvodaya.org or SarvodayaUSA.org
World Headquarters:
No. 98, Rawatawatta Road
Moratuwa, Sri Lanka
(011) 94 11 264-7159/94 11 555-0756/94 11 265-5255

U.S. Office:
Sarvodaya USA
744 Williamson St.
Madison, WI 53703
(608) 442-5945

Zen Hospice Project
ZenHospice.org
273 Page St.
San Francisco, CA 94102
(415) 863-2910

Zen Peacemakers
(established by Bernie Glassman)
ZenPeacemakers.org
177 Ripley Road
Montague, MA 01351
(413) 367-2048

Informational Web Sites

AccesstoInsight.org

A collection of translations of ancient Theravada Buddhist texts including *The Dhammapada,* a short anthology of verses that offers a simple introduction to the Buddha's teachings.

Adherents.com

A store of more than 40,000 statistical and religious geographical citations for more than 4,200 religions, churches, denominations, religious bodies, faith groups, tribes, cultures and movements.

BuddhistChannel.TV

This dedicated Buddhist news service provides daily updates and in-depth coverage on topics ranging from world events to archaeology to Buddhist teachings.

BuddhaNet.net

A mega-site offering lectures on Buddhist theory and belief, meditation instruction, e-books, directories of retreat centers and hospices and photo documentaries.

DharmaNet.org

Produced by DharmaNet International, based in Petaluma, California, this site also contains links and information about ongoing news and activities of many Buddhist groups.

PrisonDharmaNetwork.org

An international nonprofit, nonsectarian support network for Buddhist prisoners, volunteers and prison staff, including a newsletter, resource guides and a printing press.

Magazines

Inquiring Mind
(a semiannual publication for practitioners of *vipassana*)
InquiringMind.com
PO Box 9999
Berkeley, CA 94709

Mindfulness Bell
(published three times a year by the Community of Mindful Living; see
under "Engaged Buddhist Organizations")
MindfulnessBell.org
Subscription in U.S. and International: David Percival,
dperciva@unm.edu
Subscription in U.K.: David Tester, mindfulness_bell@yahoo.com.uk

Shambhala Sun *and* BuddhaDharma
(both published four times a year)
ShambhalaSun.com
BuddhaDharma.com
660 Hollis Street, Suite 603
Halifax, Nova Scotia B3J 1V7
Canada

U.S. Subscription Office:
PO Box 3377
Champlain, NY 12919-9868
USA
(902) 422-8404
Toll free: (877) 786-1950, ext. 10

Tricycle: The Buddhist Review
(a quarterly magazine published by the Tricycle Foundation)
Tricycle.com
92 Vandam Street
New York, NY 10013
(212) 645-1143 or (800) 873-9871

Retreats

Daibosatsu.org
The Rinzai Zen centers—Shobo-ji in New York City and at Kongo-ji in the Catskill Mountains—founded by Eido Shimano Roshi.

Deer Park Monastery
2499 Melru Lane
Escondido, CA 92026
(760) 291-1003

Dhamma.org
Maintained by the Vipassana Research Institute, this site lists international retreats in the tradition of Sayagyi U Ba Khin, as taught by S. N. Goenka and his assistant teachers.

EverydayZen.org
The Everyday Zen Foundation (established by Norman Fischer) organizes traditional Zen practice (talks, retreats, personal relationship), Jewish and Christian meditation sessions, death and dying seminars, mentoring programs for young people, and poetry and literature workshops.

48 Charlotte's Way
Muir Beach, CA 94965

Gratefulness.org
A Network for Grateful Living (aka ANG*L), founded by Brother David Steindl-Rast, a Vienna-born Benedictine monk who has practiced Zen for more than 30 years and has fostered a dialogue between Eastern and Western spiritual paths.

Iriz.hanazono.ac.jp/zen_centers/country_list_e.html
Handy list of Zen centers in the world.

Maple Forest Monastery
P.O. Box 354
South Woodstock, VT 05071
(802) 457-9442

PacificZen.org
The Pacific Zen Institute (established by John Tarrant) uses koan and other Zen practices.

P.O. Box 2972
Santa Rosa, CA 95405-0972

Thich Nhat Hanh's retreat centers:
Plum Village
Le Pey
24240 Thenac
France
(33) 5-53-58-48-58

Artists and Writers

DirectPictures.com
Direct Pictures, founded by John Bush, produces *The Yatra Trilogy,* films about Buddhist practice and sites in Tibet, Bali, Laos, Thailand, Burma, Cambodia and Java.

EthicalTraveler.org
A grassroots alliance, established by Jeff Greenwald, uniting adventurers, tourists, travel agencies and outfitters united to use their economic power to strengthen human rights and protect the environment.

PatravadiTheatre.com
The site of Thai theater director Patravadi Mejudhon.

Umong.com
The Web site of Thai artist Kamin Lertchaiprasert.

WesNisker.com
The site of Wes Nisker, Buddhist stand-up comedian, coeditor of *Inquiring Mind* and author of several books on Buddhism.

Tours

Auschwitz-muzeum.oswiecim.pl/
Official site of the Auschwitz-Birkenau Memorial and Museum in
Oświęcim, Poland.

BuddhaPath.com
Shantum Seth, of New Delhi, a teacher in the tradition of Thich Nhat
Hanh, leads well-organized tours—In the Footsteps of the Buddha—
to the sacred sites the Buddha recommended followers visit in India.
It's one of the best ways to understand the life of the Buddha.

University

Naropa.edu
The Web site of Naropa University, located in Boulder, Colorado.
The university is based on Buddhist principles that integrate contem-
plative education into its curriculum.

Bibliography

Books

Aitken, Molly Emma, ed. *Meeting the Buddha: On Pilgrimage in India*. New York: Riverhead, 1995.

Aitken, Robert, and David Steindl-Rast. *The Ground We Share: Everyday Practice, Buddhist and Christian*. Boston: Shambhala, 1996.

Allen, Charles. *The Buddha and the Sahibs: The Men Who Discovered India's Lost Religion*. London: John Murray, 2002.

Ambedkar, Dr. B. R. *The Buddha and his Dhamma*. Nagpur, India: Buddha Bhoomi Publication, 1997.

Ariyaratne, A. T. *Bhava Thana: An Autobiography*. Ratmalana, Sri Lanka: Sarvodaya Vishva Lekha, 2001.

Armstrong, Karen. *Buddha*. New York: Penguin, 2001.

Arnold, Sir Edwin. *The Light of Asia: The Life Teaching of Gautama, Prince of India and Founder of Buddhism*. Middlesex, U.K.: Tiger Books International, 1998.

Bader, David M. *Zen Judaism: For You, a Little Enlightenment*. New York: Harmony, 2002.

Bernstein, Richard. *Ultimate Journey: Retracing the Path of an Ancient Buddhist Monk Who Crossed Asia in Search of Enlightenment*. New York: Vintage, 2001.

Boorstein, Sylvia. *That's Funny, You Don't Look Buddhist: On Being a Faithful Jew and a Passionate Buddhist*. New York: HarperCollins, 1997.

Buswell, Robert E., Jr., ed. *Encyclopedia of Buddhism*. Woodbridge, Conn.: Macmillan Reference, 2004.

Byles, Marie Beuzeville. *Footprints of Gautama the Buddha*. Wheaton, Ill.: Quest Book, 1957.

Central Asian Art from the West Berlin State Museums: Along the Ancient Silk Routes. New York: Metropolitan Museum of Art, 1982.

Ch'en, Kenneth K. S. *Buddhism: The Light of Asia.* Hauppauge, N.Y.: Barron's Educational Series, 1968.

Clarke, Dr. Peter B., ed. *The World's Religions.* Pleasantville, N.Y.: Reader's Digest, 1993.

Coleman, James William. *The New Buddhism: The Western Transformation of an Ancient Tradition.* New York: Oxford University Press, 2001.

Coomaraswamy, Ananda K. *Buddha and the Gospel of Buddhism.* New York: Harper & Row, 1964.

Dalai Lama of Tibet. *My Land and My People: The Original Autobiography of His Holiness the Dalai Lama of Tibet.* New York: Warner, 1997.

de Bary, William Theodore, ed. *The Buddhist Tradition in India, China and Japan.* New York: Random House, 1972.

De Smedt, Marc. *In the Footsteps of the Buddha.* Paris: Francis Lincoln, 2000.

Dhar, P. L., *Effects of Vipassana Meditation on Quality of Life, Subjective Well-Being, and Criminal Propensity Among Inmates of Tihar Jail.* Maharashtra, India: Vipassana Research Institute, 2002.

————. *Psychological Effects of Vipassana on Tihar Jail Inmates.* Maharashtra, India: Vipassana Research Institute, 1995.

Ekachai, Sanitsuda. *Seeds of Hope: Local Initiatives in Thailand.* Bangkok: Post Publishing, 1994.

Ekman, Paul. *Emotions Revealed.* New York: Times Books, 2003.

Fields, Rick. *How the Swans Came to the Lake: A Narrative History of Buddhism in America.* Boston: Shambhala, 1981.

Fischer, Norman. *Taking Our Place: The Buddhist Path to Truly Growing Up.* New York: HarperCollins, 2003.

Fisher, Robert E. *Buddhist Art and Architecture.* New York: Thames & Hudson, 1993.

Fujii, Nichidatsu. *My Nonviolence: An Autobiography of a Japanese Buddhist.* Tokyo: Japan Buddha Sangha Press, 1975.

Goldstein, Joseph. *One Dharma: The Emerging Western Buddhism.* New York: HarperCollins, 2002.

The Great Stupa of Dharmakaya Which Liberates Upon Seeing. Boulder, Colo.: Vajradhatu Stupa Project, 2000.

Gyatso, Tenzin, His Holiness the Dalai Lama. *The Buddhism of Tibet*. Ithaca, N.Y.: Snow Lion, 1987.

Hanh, Thich Nhat. *I Have Arrived, I Am Home: Celebrating Twenty Years of Plum Village Life*. Berkeley, Calif.: Parallax, 2003.

———. *Living Buddha, Living Christ*. New York: Riverhead, 1995.

———. *Old Path, White Clouds: Walking in the Footsteps of the Buddha*. Berkeley, Calif.: Parallax, 1991.

———. *Peace Is Every Step: The Path of Mindfulness in Everyday Life*. New York: Bantam, 1991.

Hattori, Sho-On. *A Raft from the Other Shore: Honen and the Way of Pure Land Buddhism*. Tokyo: Jodo Shu, 2000.

Hesse, Herman. *The Journey to the East*. New York: Picador, 1956.

———. *Siddhartha*. New York: New Directions, 1951.

Holy Places of the Buddha. Crystal Mirror Series, Vol. 9. Berkeley, Calif.: Dharma Publishing, 1994.

Hongwanji. *Jodo Shinshu: A Guide*. Kyoto: Hongwanji International Center, 2002.

Human Rights Watch/Asia. *China: State Control of Religion*. New York: Human Rights Watch, 1997.

Kerouac, Jack. *The Dharma Bums*. New York: Penguin, 1976.

———. *On the Road*. New York: Penguin Books, 1976.

Kohn, Sherab Chodzin. *The Awakened One: A Life of the Buddha*. Boston: Shambhala, 1994.

Kornfield, Jack. *Buddha's Little Instruction Book*. New York: Bantam, 1994.

Kwong, Jakusho. *No Beginning, No End: The Intimate Heart of Zen*. New York: Harmony, 2003.

Landlaw, Jonathan, and Stephan Bodian. *Buddhism for Dummies*. New York: Wiley, 2003.

Larkin, Geri. *The Still Point Dhammapada*. New York: HarperCollins, 2003.

Leidy, Denise Patry, and Robert A. F. Thurman. *Mandala: The Architecture of Enlightenment*. New York: Asia Society Galleries; Boston, Shambala: Tibet House, 1997.

The Mahatma Beyond Gandhi. Mumbai, India: Sarvodaya International Trust, Maharashtra Chapter, 2001.

Merton, Thomas. *Thoughts on the East*. New York: New Directions, 1995.

Nanamoli, Bhikkhu. *The Life of the Buddha*. Kandy, Sri Lanka: Buddhist Publication Society, 1972.

Narasu, P. Lakshmi. *The Essence of Buddhism*. Nagpur, India: Buddha Bhoomi Prakashan, 2002.

Nisker, Wes. *The Big Bang, the Buddha, and the Baby Boom: The Spiritual Experiments of My Generation*. New York: HarperCollins, 2003.

————. *Essential Crazy Wisdom*. Berkeley, Calif.: Ten Speed, 2001.

Okakura, Kakuzo. *The Book of Tea*. Boston: Shambhala, 2001.

Parrinder, Geoffrey, ed. *World Religions: From Ancient History to Present*. New York: Facts on File, 1984.

Prebish, Charles S., and Kenneth K. Tanaka, eds. *The Faces of Buddhism in America*. Berkeley: University of California Press, 1998.

Queen, Christopher, ed. *Engaged Buddhism in the West*. Somerville, Mass.: Wisdom, 2000.

Rahula, Walpola. *What the Buddha Taught*. London: Gordon Fraser Gallery, 1959.

Sangharakshita. *Who Is the Buddha?* Birmingham, U.K.: Windhorse, 1994.

Schiller, David. *The Little Zen Companion*. New York: Workman, 1994.

Seth, Leila. *On Balance: An Autobiography*. New Delhi: Penguin Books India, 2003.

Shaku, Soyen. *Zen for Americans*. New York: Dorset, 1987.

Sivaraksa, Sulak. *Loyalty Demands Dissent: Autobiography of an Engaged Buddhist*. Bangkok: Thai Inter-Religious Commission for Development, 1998.

————. *Seeds of Peace: A Buddhist Vision for Renewing Society*. Berkeley, Calif.: Parallax, 1992.

Strong, John S. *The Buddha: A Short Biography*. Oxford, U.K.: Oneworld, 2001.

————. *Relics of the Buddha*. Princeton, N.J.: Princeton University Press, 2004.

The Stupa: Sacred Symbol of Enlightenment. Crystal Mirror Series, vol. 12. Berkeley, Calif.: Dharma Publishing, 1997.

Suzuki, D. T. *An Introduction to Zen Buddhism*. New York: Grove, 1964.

Suzuki, Shunryu. *Not Always So*. New York: HarperCollins, 2002.

————. *Zen Mind, Beginner's Mind: Informal Talks on Zen Meditation and Practice*. New York: John Weatherhill, 1970.

Tarrant, John. *Bring Me the Rhinoceros and Other Zen Koans to Bring You Joy*. New York: Harmony Books, 2004.

Thera, Ven. Nyanaponika. *Abhidhamma Studies*. Somerville, Mass.: Wisdom, 1998.

Thomas, Edward J. *The Life of Buddha as Legend and History*. New Dehli: Munshiram Manoharlal, 2003.

Thurman, Robert. *Inner Revolution: Life, Liberty, and the Pursuit of Real Happiness*. New York: Riverhead, 1998.

Tiyavanich, Kamala. *The Buddha in the Jungle*. Seattle: University of Washington Press, 2003.

————. *Forest Recollections: Wandering Monks in Twentieth-Century Thailand*. Honolulu: University of Hawaii Press, 1997.

Trungpa, Chögyam. *Cutting Through Spiritual Materialism*. Boston: Shambhala, 2002.

Tsao Hseuh-Chin and Kao Ngo. *A Dream of Red Mansions,* vols 1–3. Peking: Foreign Languages Press, 1978.

Twelfth Tai Situ Rinpoche. *The Eye of the Eye*. Himachal Pradesh, India: Sherab Ling Institute, 2000.

University Museum and Art Gallery. *In the Footsteps of the Buddha: An Iconic Journey from India to China*. Hong Kong: University of Hong Kong, 1998.

Veda, Yoshifumi, and Dennis Hirota. *Shinran: An Introduction to His Thought*. Kyoto: Hongwanji International Center, 1989.

Wallace, B. Alan. *Buddhism with an Attitude: The Tibetan Seven-Point Mind-Training*. Ithaca, N.Y.: Snow Lion, 2003.

Watson, Burton. *The Lotus Sutra*. New York: Columbia University Press, 1993.

Watts, Alan W. *The Spirit of Zen*. London: John Murray, 1955.

Zelliot, Eleanor. *Dr. Babasaheb Ambedkar and the Untouchable Movement*. New Dehli: Blumoon, 2005.

Zürcher, E. *The Buddhist Conquest of China: The Spread and Adaptation of Buddhism in Early Medieval China*. Rev. ed. Leiden: E. J. Brill, 1972.

Magazines

Becker, Jasper. "China's Growing Pains." *National Geographic* (March 2004): 68–95.

Simons, Lewis M. "Tibetans: Moving Forward, Holding On." *National Geographic* (April 2002): 2–38.

"Special Report: China's Century." *Newsweek* (May 9, 2005): 28–47.

Journal Articles

Huntington, John C. "Sowing the Seeds of the Lotus: A Journey to the Great Pilgrimage Sites of Buddhism." Parts 1–5. *Orientations,* November 1985–September 1986.

Tomatsu, Rev. Yoshiharu. "The Secularization of Japanese Buddhism: The Priest as Profane Practitioner of the Sacred." Buddhist Peace Fellowship, org. April 2004.

———. "Transforming Ritual: Transforming Japanese Funeral Buddhism." Jodo Shu Research Institute organization, April 2004.

Wuthnow, Robert, and Wendy Cadge. "Buddhists in the United States: The Scope of Influence." *Journal for the Scientific Study of Religion* (2004).

Pamphlet

Tibet: The Facts. Dharamsala, India: Department of Information and Internal Relations, Central Tibetan Administration.

Monograph

Ishii, Yoneo. *Sangha, State, and Society: Thai Buddhism in History.* Monographs of the Center for Southeast Asian Studies, Kyoto University. Honolulu: University of Hawaii Press, 1986.

Index